Saucing the Fish

Shirley King

Illustrated by
RODICA PRATO

Simon and Schuster
NEW YORK

*This book is dedicated
to my daughter Amy and my mother
with continuing love and affection.*

Copyright © 1986 by Shirley King

*All rights reserved
including the right of reproduction
in whole or in part in any form
Published by Simon and Schuster
A Division of Simon & Schuster, Inc.
Simon & Schuster Building
Rockefeller Center
1230 Avenue of the Americas
New York, New York 10020*

SIMON AND SCHUSTER *and colophon are registered trademarks of Simon & Schuster, Inc.*

*Designed by Levavi & Levavi
Manufactured in the United States of America*

10   9   8   7   6   5   4   3   2   1

Library of Congress Cataloging-in-Publication Data
King, Shirley.
  Saucing the fish.

  Bibliography: p.
  Includes index.
  1. Cookery (Fish) I. Title.
TX747.K53   1986   641.6'92   85-30451
ISBN: 0-671-54076-9

Acknowledgments

My thanks are to all the chefs, cooks, friends, and restaurant owners I have worked with over the years, for their inspiration, guidance, and camaraderie. For this book especially I thank Tom Wilkinson, owner of Wilkinson's Seafood Café in New York City, where I worked for two years as head chef. Thirty of the recipes here were on the menus during those years and some twenty-five were served as specials, particularly the imported fish dishes.

My thanks also to the fish suppliers Rozzo, Harborside, Yama Seafoods, and Flying Foods for their generally excellent fish; Oskar of Bakersfield Market for produce; and Glie Farms for fresh herbs.

Special thanks to Richard Lord, of the Fulton Fish Market Information Services; Bruce Stutz, writer and editor, New York; Peter Redmayne, editor of *Seafood Leader* magazine; Jon Rowley, president of Fish Works!; Curt Stimpson, president of The Crystal Nordic Fresh Fish Company in Seattle; Nancy Fennel, Oregon Dungeness Crab Commission; and the people at New England Fisheries Development Foundation, Boston, for all the information and invaluable help they provided me in my quest to gain as much knowledge as possible about American seafood.

It has been wonderful to be able to talk to chefs and chef/owners in the United States, however briefly: Felipe Rojas-Lombardi, of The Ballroom Restaurant, New York; Ken Frank, of La Toque in Los Angeles; John Sedlar, of St. Estephe in Manhattan

Beach, California; Michael Hutchings of Michael's Waterside Inn, Santa Barbara, California; Paul Prudhomme of K-Paul's, New Orleans; and Odette Bery, of Another Season, Boston.

My thanks to all the writers and reviewers who wrote so favorably about Wilkinson's Seafood Café when I was there. I hope they continue to do so. Thanks in particular to Marian Burros, of *The New York Times,* who enjoyed the lightness of my food; Seymour Britchky, author of *The Restaurants of New York;* and Jay Jacobs, of *Gourmet* magazine.

Thanks to my friend Roberta Miller, literary agent at United Media, who first believed in the book and sold it successfully.

I am most grateful to Carole Lalli, my editor at Simon & Schuster, who has a very understanding nature, and who is ever encouraging and clever at solving problems. I am glad that she is a friend as well.

Lastly, thanks to the friends and neighbors who sampled my experiments and the testing of numerous recipes. One night all shrimp dishes, another night squid, another time mussels, conch, crab, and so on in all forms. I appreciated their comments and criticisms.

SHIRLEY KING

Contents

Introduction

I became a professional cook fifteen years ago. I began with Lord Weinstock's family in London and later I cooked for office lunches and big parties all over England. I spent eleven years catering in London, in English country houses, and in the south of France. Then I was with a lunchtime health food restaurant in Molton Brown's Hairdressing Salon for fifteen months. In 1979, my book *Dining with Marcel Proust* was published by Thames and Hudson. When the catering business became thin because of financial depression in England, I looked to restaurants. A stint at the Vineyard Restaurant in Northampton, England, was followed by a summer doing the dinner menu at The Café in East Hampton, Long Island, then on to L'Escargot in Soho, London, where I worked mostly as fish chef. In the summer of 1982 I became chef at a new restaurant in East Hampton, The House on Toilsome, which was a great success. I decided not to return to England.

When Tom Wilkinson of Wilkinson's Seafood Café offered me the position of chef, I took it with alacrity. We received two stars from Marian Burros, restaurant reviewer for *The New York Times*, and two stars from Seymour Britchky in his restaurant newsletter. During my two years with Wilkinson's, I gained an intimate knowledge of fish available in the United States.

I grew up on both sides of the Atlantic, although most of my education was in England. I think the important influences on my interest in food and cooking were my American mother, who initiated me to good taste in food; my years as an art student living with an artist (whom I eventually married), when we would compete with other artists and their wives to produce the best dishes with food we could barely afford; and my travels through Greece, Italy, France, Portugal, Morocco, and the United States. Traveling about the United States doing research for this book has been wonderfully illuminating and great fun.

The first of these influences, my mother from Richmond, Indiana, is a wonderful cook. Even during the war years in England, when I was growing up, she managed to make appetizing dishes with the food on hand. She tended and nurtured a kitchen garden in our country cottage home thirty-five miles from London, vying with my father (who was a great gardener with an amazing love of flowers) as to how large her kitchen patch would be. She was one of the first to grow sweet corn in England, and what a struggle it was to begin with, as American seeds did not grow well in the infrequent English summer sunshine. New potatoes, young carrots, beets, peas, cucumbers, marrows, black and red currants, rhubarb, and strawberries were garnered by the family and cooked by Mother. We had fruit trees which bore Victoria, yellow, and purple plums, apples, greengages, and quince. We had a glut of green and string beans every year and plenty of asparagus in season. We canned the yellow plums in a cannery in a small nearby village for winter consumption and salted down the green beans. Mother's beehive produced wonderful honey, benefiting from my father's fascinating variety of flowers. I remember taking my turn extruding the honey from the combs (centrifugally) and chewing the wax afterward to savor the remaining honey still clinging to it.

My father used to take us children on outings along a nearby stream to collect moorhen eggs, even in the dead of winter. Moorhens lay two or three times a year and so we did not think we were diminishing their population. We had to collect the eggs from nests that were usually perched on willow branches that had grown out just above the water of the stream, and many a time we fell in the icy water!

When we were overrun by wild rabbits, my father, who loved to shoot, shot them from the dining room window at six in the morning as they were nibbling on our lawns. My mother fried them in the manner of Southern fried chicken.

On Christmas Eves in London, where my father was a general practitioner, we received hampers filled with game or birds and other good things. My mother never knew what to order in advance for Christmas, for the hampers were always a surprise. What with the pheasants and wild ducks that my father shot and the hamper gifts, I learned to pluck birds easily.

My fishing experience includes catching the occasional perch from a country stream with a bent pin and a tiny wodge of moistened bread. We fished mackerel off the Welsh coast and ate them with alacrity and joy. Years later, on visits to Scotland, I caught salmon and brown trout in Loch Ness from a wooden skiff owned by a Scottish gillie. He became a great friend during ever-changing days on that picturesque piece of water, drinking Scotch whiskey to while away the time before the fish came into the boat to be stunned by his truncheon. I sold a fish or two to local hotels, ate some, and even proudly took one down to London on the overnight train in a specially made woven salmon basket called a creel. And so I developed a taste not only in the usual foods abundant in England, but also in luxury items like lobster and pheasant and in simple fresh vegetables and fruit.

Although I have had no formal instruction from a cooking school, I've nonetheless picked up considerable knowledge about regional cooking during my travels. Close inspection of many a local open-air or super market; discussions with numerous people on food and cooking methods; working experience in all sorts of kitchens; and a continuing interest in reading current literature on cooking—those are the basis of my education as a chef. And the learning never ends! I love to experiment with new products as they come on the market, and I have learned an enormous amount through endless delightful evenings spent sampling the creations of other chefs.

About This Book

The recipes in this book have been designed to use the seafood most commonly available in the United States. Many of the recipes are newly created; some are variations on traditional, regional American recipes, while others have a European flair. No matter what their origin, I hope they will inspire a new interest in fish cookery.

Most of the recipes are easily accomplished and not time-consuming. About a fourth of these recipes have been on restaurant menus, and they range from elegant to simple. In either case the food is not fussy; I make the whole production as easy as possible.

You will find that the sauces suggested to enhance the fish usually take longer to prepare than the fish. The bases for the sauces are vegetable and herb, liquor, butter, cream, oil, and egg. Many of them are free of butter, cream, egg, and oil and are based on reductions of stock and vegetable purées.

I usually try not to overwhelm a humble fish with a luxury seafood stuffing, but I do think the recipe for lobster wrapped in (humble!) cabbage leaves is a good combination. I don't like to mix fruit with fish, except the occasional orange and lemon segment, though I do use plenty of lemon juice. I find that sweet red peppers, ginger, fennel, Pernod or Ricard, and star anise enhance the flavor of fish, but I can't say the same for mushrooms or cheese (with one exception—my recipe for Sturgeon with Duxelles on page 224). I always use unsalted butter, which has fewer milk solids and less water in it than salted butter and is therefore preferable when making beurre blanc and clarified butter. I always use coarse, Kosher salt because it is pure, with no iodine and chemicals added to aid pouring.

I do not include recipes for jambalaya, bouillabaisse, cioppino, chowder, or paella. They are good dishes but have been written up many times in other books.

There are dishes for any occasion: appetizers, hors d'oeuvre, first courses, soups (some meals in themselves), salads (for buffets), soufflés and pies (for a first course or a lunch), pasta and risotto dishes (again, meals in themselves), and main courses. For some main courses I have suggested accompanying vegetables, these being important to the presentation of the dish and the overall combination of tastes. I think that the presentation of the dish is of ultimate importance both in restaurants and at home.

Of the many species of fish for sale in fish stores and markets, some can be grouped together by type for cooking purposes and methods, though of course they will have different tastes. I have given alternative choices in many recipes. You may be taken with a cooking method or sauce that will equally well suit an available fish I have not mentioned, or the fish of your choice. So swap and change as you will.

The commercial availability of different species of fish is changing every day, beyond seasonal fluctuations. Some species may become endangered due to overfishing, pollution, or changes in habitat. Others are dangerous to eat because of contamination from municipal and industrial wastes. If you catch fish or collect clams or mussels, check with your local health department or fish and wildlife conservation departments. Local advisories often issue information concerning local species.

On a more hopeful note, it seems we are finding more and more fine species of fish that are edible and marketable. Fish such as pollock, monkfish, skate, dogfish, shark, and wolffish are not yet fully appreciated. Squid, tilefish, and grouper are growing more popular, although they are often sold by fish stores under an alias: for instance, I have found tilefish called white snapper or golden snapper. Rockfish on the West Coast is often (incorrectly) called red snapper. Dogfish, wolffish, and monkfish might have to take on new names in order to increase their appeal, but in my opinion this is ridiculous and unnecessary. Don't be afraid to get away from your old favorites and to try some of the new species on the market.

There are many fish in the seas, rivers, and lakes of this country. In addition, much fish farming is being accomplished today: we are farming catfish, trout, crawfish, oysters, striped bass, salmon, clams, mussels, and baby abalone, just to start the list. The Norwegians farm salmon, and because it is handled extremely well, it reaches your fish store in pristine condition.

People are eating more fish than ever before for its usually pleasing, light taste and more importantly for health reasons. The high amount of water in fish (60 to 80 percent) and relatively small percentage of fat (composed of unsaturated or polyunsaturated fatty acids) produce a food low in cholesterol and calories, and high in protein, vitamins, and minerals. The fatty acids in the fish oil actually can lower the cholesterol in your blood and reduce heart disease.

Fish is good for you and delicious to eat; you can get up after a meal of fish and feel svelte, yet satisfied! There is an enormous variety and so many ways to prepare it. Fish is increasingly featured on restaurant menus, and this gives me great pleasure as I nearly always choose fish dishes to eat. Even though I handle it day in and day out, I never tire of fish.

I only hope that there will be more sources of fish in the future and that ordinary supermarkets will expand their fish displays and provide a higher-quality product. (I know it is possible because I have seen wonderful displays of fresh fish and great variety in some supermarkets.)

About Seafood

Choosing Seafood

Look, feel, and smell. These are the essential things to do when buying fish.

Whole fish, even if they are to be filleted, should look bright and shiny. The scales should be firm and intact, with no signs of the fish having been bruised. If the fish has already been scaled or the particular fish has no scales, feel the firmness of the flesh. It should be elastic to the touch. Most fish should be covered with a thin transparent slime that indicates freshness.

The eyes should have clear (not opaque) color. The gills should be red, and the fins and tails should be in good order with no signs of dryness reflecting freezer burn or a long time out of the water.

Sniff the fish—if it has a pleasant sea odor, this indicates freshness. Give the fish a miss if it has an unpleasant, strong fishy odor.

Filleted fish should feel firm; each fillet should be cleancut without raggedy edges and with no water oozing out, one sign that it has been frozen badly. In Seattle, for example, FANCY printed on a store tag means that the fish has been frozen and defrosted (which is not too bad if properly done) and should be cooked and eaten as soon as possible. Red marks on the flesh indicate that the fish has been badly handled and bruised, and that bacteria are starting to grow. Fillets should also have a pleasant sea odor.

If you do not intend to cook a whole fish the day you buy or catch it, it should be gutted, rinsed, then iced down, preferably with flaked ice, and kept at 32 degrees or cooler. Place the fish belly down in the ice. The ice will prevent the flesh from drying out and slow the growth of bacteria. It is best to let the ice drain into another container as it melts, so the fish does not soak in water. Fillets should also be kept on ice, but the flesh should be separated from the ice with parchment paper or plastic wrap.

Fish to be cooked the same day it is bought or caught should be rinsed, patted dry, wrapped in parchment paper or plastic wrap, and refrigerated at 40 degrees or cooler.

Live shellfish such as lobster, freshwater crawfish, and crabs should show definite signs of life. When lifted up from the water the lobster and crawfish tails should curl under and the legs and claws of all three should move actively.

Live clams, mussels, and oysters should have closed shells. If some shells are gaping open and do not close when tapped, they must be discarded. If the animals die in your possession, it is safe to eat or cook them, but do so quickly. Also discard any with broken shells. Soft-shell clams (steamers) and geoduck clams come with slightly gaping shells; touching the neck or siphon for a reaction will ascertain if they are still alive.

Live lobster, crawfish, crabs, mussels, and periwinkles should be cooked as soon as possible, but can be stored in the refrigerator in a colander placed over a bowl of ice, so that they are kept moist and can breathe. Clams and oysters can be stored in a similar manner.

Your fishmonger should be willing to give you any necessary advice and information on the freshness of the fish, best buys, and so forth.

Freezing and Frozen Fish

It is very exciting to know that much on-the-boat freezing is being done with very strict controls to preserve fish at optimum quality. Apart from the standard fish and shellfish (such as cod, squid, prawns, and shrimp) that have been well frozen for years, I have seen the most wonderful frozen king and silver salmon on display at Jon Rowley's stand in Seafare '85, Los Angeles. Rowley, who used to fish Alaskan waters, is now president of Fish Works!

The fish on Jon's stand were labeled (just like dresses) with the name Triad. Bruce and Kathy Gore, owners of the boat *Triad*, like a few others fishing the Alaskan waters in the Pacific Northwest, are producing custom fish with "designer" labels.

I have not tasted the frozen salmon, but Julia Child has confirmed that in some cases they taste better than a not-so-freshly-caught salmon. That's true of all fish. The salmon are handled with great care on board after being stunned on the head while still in the water so they do not bruise themselves on the deck. They are flash (blast) frozen at minus 40 degrees and then dipped in a mixture of seawater and corn sugar to create an elastic coating so the fats will not turn rancid, nor will the flesh dehydrate. Storage is at minus 20 degrees. Such loving care obviously produces wonderful results, and although you are charged more for this product, it is worth it.

As long as the fish have been frozen by the best methods, you will enjoy them as much as fresh fish. To guarantee satisfaction, look to make sure that the seafood has retained good color, is not dried out, and that there are no ice crystals inside the package.

Guide to Fish

Preface

The more I get involved with fish, the more I encounter diverse opinions about the flavor, texture, and taste of fish. Some like a fine-textured fish and others prefer a coarser texture. Some relish it dense, like swordfish; others opt for fish that flakes easily. Some enjoy their oysters with a saline flavor, others like them sweet. Smoked fish is difficult to assess just by looking at it and should be tasted before you buy it; people have very different criteria here, too. Some like it oily; others don't. Some like it sweet; others prefer a distinctive strong taste. *Chaqu'un à son gout,* I say, but it is difficult for me to make a dispassionate assessment of the quality of particular fish in the following listing.

Do you have memories of the most delicious steaks you have eaten in your life? Probably you remember only a few and you can most likely recall details of the occasion, whom you were with, and where! Well, I can remember one or two steaks and innumerable fish dishes that were memorable to me, but I have my own likes and dislikes and I recognize they may not be yours.

I have endeavored to give useful information about the nature of seafood, where it is usually harvested, some details on how to prepare it, and different cooking methods.

The information should enlarge your knowledge of fish and make it easier to substitute one species for another in particular recipes. (In any case, you will often find substitutes listed in the recipes themselves.) Keep in mind that there is much tasty seafood available, and in most cases you need only decide the cooking method and accompanying sauce and you're in business.

I have tried to give enough information so that you can go confidently into a fish market. Because some fish are marketed under several names, perhaps to gain favor in the market, try to learn the real names of the species from the following list and from the fishmonger. When fish belong to a family, I have listed them together under the family name.

Lastly, when reading this guide, know that there are many other fish in the sea that, while not generally marketed as of this writing, are eminently suitable for the table. In Europe, conger eel harvested from the Atlantic is sold everywhere and, with its firm texture, is good broiled or used in soups, stews, or casseroles. Also from the Atlantic come sea robins *(grondins)*, which in flavor and texture are not unlike red mullet *(rouget)* from the Mediterranean. They are good in fish stews and casseroles and can be broiled or fried whole or in fillets. The flesh is firm, white, and fine textured.

Skate, herring, shark, gaff-topsail catfish, dogfish, jacks, mullets, and wolffish are some of the other fish that are not generally marketed, and one ought to take advantage of them when they are available.

Abalone

Large abalone, found on the Pacific coast, are becoming scarce, partly because sea otters (who know a good thing when they taste it) are so fond of them. There is a possibility that the otters will be put on the endangered species list, and then it might be goodbye altogether to the large abalone, even though abalone is not the otters' only food. There are other contributing factors to explain the scarcity of abalone: they have been overharvested, and the seaweeds upon which they live are dwindling. Red and green abalone come from the Pacific. Abalone have a delicious sweet flavor and are worth seeking out. Smaller abalone, called ormer, are available off the Atlantic coast in Europe.

Abalone flesh is naturally tough and must be gently tenderized before cooking or eating raw. Abalone is usually sliced, tenderized, then lightly coated with flour and egg and sautéed. The tenderized slices can also be eaten raw, as for sushi or sashimi. For instructions on how to extract the flesh and prepare abalone see the recipe on page 251.

There is a recipe for baby abalone on page 98. These abalone are farmed by John McMullen at Ab Lab in Port Hueneme, California. They are about 1½ inches in length after approximately eighteen months of growth, are easy to shuck, and do not need tenderizing. John can produce about 2500 baby abalone per month, and, although expensive, they deserve to be marketed in a big way soon. Four or five baby abalone make a fine appetizer, although they are so good I could easily eat a main course of them.

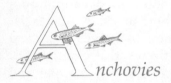

Anchovies

Anchovies are harvested from the Pacific, north Atlantic, and Mediterranean. Sometimes available fresh from Long Island and the Pacific, they are good to eat simply grilled. Most anchovies are salted and canned, with or without oil, as flat or rolled-up (sometimes stuffed) fillets, and when the salt is washed off they have excellent flavor. They are also made into a paste that is used to flavor sauces. (Patum Peperium, Gentleman's Relish, made in England, is a special spread made with anchovies, butter, spices, and herbs that I like to spread thin on toast for breakfast.) Preserved anchovies, with their salty, distinctive flavor, are not to everyone's taste; a little goes a long way. When making a pissaladière (anchovy and cheese pie), as on page 160, the anchovy fillets can be halved down the middle to cut down on the amount needed.

The Bass Family

Black sea bass has a fine firm texture and is sold whole or in fillets. Black sea bass can be baked, poached, deep-fried, broiled, or steamed. The fish can also be cut into steaks and sauced, or added to stews or soups. Harvested from the Atlantic, black sea bass weighs between one and a half and five pounds. It is a fairly inexpensive bass to buy.

Chilean sea bass has been imported for a couple of years, especially in Los Angeles and other cities up the Pacific coast. It has a fine reputation for having a firm white fillet with fairly high oil content.

Striped bass is caught from the Gulf of Mexico to the Gulf of St. Lawrence, but in Maryland and points farther south it is called rockfish. Introduced to the West Coast in the late 1800s, striped bass exists from South California to Washington. However, it can't be sold commercially—although a recreational fishery exists for striped bass.

Because of recent regulations brought about by declining populations in some places and contamination by PCBs in others, striped bass fishing has been prohibited in some areas. Constant checks are being made, however, and things will change. But until pollution is cleared up and stocks return, red snapper and imported bass—such as *branzino* from Italy, also called *loup de mer* in France—are good alternatives. This splendid fish is prized for its distinctive taste, texture, and looks.

One of the most popular dishes at Wilkinson's Seafood Café was striped bass with sake and black bean sauce. We poached filleted striped bass and served it skin side up, producing a beautiful effect with the other accompaniments. Red snapper is now served with sake and black bean sauce.

Whole striped bass broiled in the oven is also a spectacular culinary delight. Filleted, cut in steaks, or whole, striped bass can also be poached, baked, or used in stews or soups.

Grouper has firmly textured, excellent meat. Filleted or cut into steaks, it can be baked, broiled, grilled, or used in soups and stews. The skin is thick and should be removed before cooking. Grouper is fished throughout the warm waters of the world and grows to 500 pounds. Related to the bass family, it is sometimes erroneously called sea bass. Some species of grouper are yellow-fin, Nassau, black, red, rock hind, gag, scamp, Warsaw grouper, jewfish, and California sea bass. They can be cooked interchangeably with other bass.

White sea bass from the Pacific is a different species and is listed under Drums, Spots, and Croakers on page 34.

lowfish

Blowfish, also called northern puffer and swellfish, is sometimes marketed as chicken of the sea and sea squab. Though once readily available along the New Jersey and Long Island shores, it has become scarce in markets. Unlike the skin of some species of puffers from other waters, that of the blowfish is not toxic. These ugly creatures are terrifying to behold when caught because they puff up, and they are difficult to kill with their prickly skins. To kill them, cut off the head; then, handling them with heavy gloves, peel back the skin with pliers to reveal a sweet morsel of flesh much resembling a chicken leg. Depending on their size, three or four tails suffice for one serving. Lightly coated with seasoned flour, they are easily sautéed, fried, or grilled over charcoal.

luefish

Since bluefish is caught in profusion off eastern Long Island, where I have spent many a summer, I am keen on this fish when it is extremely fresh. Luckily for me, I am often the recipient of blues caught off Montauk by friends. They can be broiled or baked. Small bluefish can be wrapped whole in foil and grilled over a charcoal fire. Seasoning can be strong—add rosemary, black pepper, and lemon juice to enhance the taste. To make a bluefish salad (page 167), bake them whole and pick the flesh away from the skin and bones. This fish smokes well.

Small bluefish are called snappers, and when they get larger they are called choppers, for they are voracious eaters.

uffalofish

This fish is popular in the southern states, and is fished from the Mississippi and the Great Lakes. The buffalofish has firm, sweet white flesh that can be cooked in a variety of ways.

utterfish

Butterfish is harvested in the Atlantic. This small fish with a high fat content is sold fresh and smoked. The gray flesh turns white when cooked. It can be broiled, baked, or fried. Sablefish fillets are sold under the name of butterfish.

arp

Carp, first bred in China, has also become popular eating in Central Europe. I have seen these overgrown goldfish growing in manmade ponds on the grounds of the great houses of France and England. Carp has a firm, rich, dark flesh much like meat. With its distinctive taste, however, I find a little goes a long way. I include a small amount in the recipe for gefilte fish on page 242. It is best to cut off the darker part of the flesh before cooking; it can be baked whole or stuffed, or broiled or steamed in fillets.

Catfish

Catfish has a firm white texture and is delicious cooked any style. It is often coated with cornmeal and deep-fried whole. A large amount of channel catfish are farmed in Mississippi, much of it frozen in fillets. Other catfish is fished in the Great Lakes and rivers of the United States. There are many species, but channel catfish is the best known. The tough skin is always removed before cooking. Saltwater gaff-topsail catfish is good eating too.

Caviar

Caviar is one of the most highly prized foods in the world, and rightfully so, for it is a real delicacy. Genuine caviar is the roe of sturgeon. The beluga is the largest sturgeon, weighing up to 2500 pounds. It produces roe that ranges in color from black to gray. The osetra (or osietr) sturgeon is smaller and usually produces a slightly smaller roe whose color is brownish black. Sevruga sturgeon produces a roe that ranges from black to slightly gray. Sevruga is my favorite.

The highest quality caviar is known as malosal, which means it has been cured with the minimum amount of salt. It must be kept refrigerated at 26 to 32 degrees to maintain its quality. At lower temperatures caviar will freeze but this is to be avoided as the little eggs burst, lose quality, and eventually spoil.

Other roes are *called* caviar. Golden whitefish "caviar" is the roe of whitefish, naturally golden in color. This caviar must be kept frozen (unlike the other caviars) until an hour or so before eating. It is very tasty, far less expensive than sturgeon caviar, and worthy in its own right.

American caviar is made with the roe of paddlefish from the Mississippi and sturgeon from other parts of America. They produce a roe which is generally blackish gray.

Lumpfish caviar is the roe of lumpfish, harvested primarily in Icelandic waters. The roe is dyed to obtain a black or red color. It is inexpensive but useful for garnishes and canapés. It is certainly more salty than the rest of the caviars.

It is hard to explain the delicacy of the true caviar, made from sturgeon roe. It should not be too salty; the roe should be firm, so the individual eggs can burst with flavor in your mouth; and the taste should be sweet and slightly fishy. The quality can differ according to the quality of the roe and its curing as well as the temperature it has been kept at. It is best to buy it from a reliable source, ideally with an opportunity to sample a little before purchase.

Clams

Hard-shell clams collected from the northwestern Atlantic are named according to size. The smallest are littlenecks, then cherrystones and chowder clams. Littlenecks are usually served raw on the half shell, cherrystones may be stuffed and baked, and chowder clams—known as quahogs—are of course used for chowder. Surf clams, which are massive, have a large commercial market (Howard Johnson restaurants use them cut into strips for fried clams). Clams harvested from the Pacific are Manila and Pacific littlenecks, and butter clams. The shells of these clams should be fully closed when purchased or should close when tapped.

To shuck clams, first scrub them under running water. Take the shell in your left hand (if you are right-handed), with the hinged and higher part of the clam near your thumb. Use a clam knife or thin paring knife wedged between the shells to open it, sliding the knife just inside the shell, so you do not cut into the clam flesh, and severing the muscles on each side of the hinge. Do this over a small bowl to catch the juice. Put the juice through a fine sieve before using. When open, scrape the clam from the top shell into the bottom shell, releasing the clam by scraping underneath it. If serving on the half-shell, discard the top shell and add some of the strained juice to the clam. If you are going to cook clams, as in chowder or a sauce, put them in a hot oven or steam them open using very little water.

Soft-shell clams, usually called steamers, are mostly harvested from the northwestern Atlantic, though sometimes also from the Pacific. Despite the name their shells are not so much soft as brittle. These clams have partially opened shells because the siphon or neck does not fully retract into the shell. Before cooking, rinse the soft-shell clams in water, rub them with a plastic scouring pad, and let them soak in fresh lightly salted water for an hour to purge them of sand. Steamed open in a little dry white wine and served with the strained broth and a small bowl of melted butter to dip them in, they are excellent fare. They also can be shucked and eaten raw. I give a recipe for deep-fried soft-shells, one of my favorite New England lunches, on page 77.

Razor clams are available from both the Atlantic and the Pacific and can be prepared in the same way as soft-shell clams.

The geoduck clam, a huge relative of the soft-shell clam weighing at least two and a half pounds, is harvested in the Pacific Northwest and near Alaska. It has a very long siphon or neck that protrudes from the shell to a great length, giving the creature a somewhat lewd aspect. In Seattle at the Pike Street Market they are displayed in such a way that they create great interest. The super-long phallic siphons attached to the overweight shells lie draped on seaweed in large wooden barrels.

The taste of the geoduck—pronounced *gooey duck*—is similar to that of the soft-shell clam, but much richer and more intense. A little goes a long way. Loosen the clam from its shell with a thin knife and put the whole thing in warm water for five minutes. The siphon skin will lighten in color and then can be peeled or cut off. Scrape off the dark part of the strip and discard the belly. The flesh is similar to abalone in that it is naturally tough, but it can be easily tenderized by pounding gently with a smooth mallet. It can be eaten raw, as in sushi or sashimi; sautéed quickly, as in the recipe on page 109; or deep-fried. Chopped and added raw to a chowder base, it makes a wonderful-tasting soup.

The Cod Family

Cod fishing is a very important industry in the northwestern Atlantic, particularly in New England and farther north. **Atlantic cod** is a reasonably priced fish marketed in great quantities. Cod has a lean white flesh with a flaky texture and lends itself to many cooking methods, such as baking, broiling, poaching, and deep-frying (coated in a batter); it can also be used in stews, casseroles, and soups. It is advisable to embellish and baste cod with a sauce to keep it from drying out.

In addition to steaks and fillets, cod cheeks are sometimes available and they are delicious. The head and bones make a rich stock (see the recipe for Bourride on page 146). Smoked cod roe can be used to make taramasalata, as on page 123.

In the eastern states, schrod and scrod refer to cod or haddock weighing under two and a half pounds.

Pacific cod, also called true cod, is very similar to the Atlantic cod and can be treated as such.

Tomcod, available in both the Atlantic and the Pacific, is a relatively small member of the cod family. It is harvested from the coastal areas of the northwestern Atlantic in November, when the fish go inshore to spawn.

Salt cod is salted and dried codfish, and needs to be soaked to rehydrate it. It is called *bacalhau* in Portugal, *baccala* in Italy, *morue* in France, and *bacalao* in Spain and the West Indies. **Stockfish** is cod that is dried but unsalted, and just needs to be soaked to rehydrate it. Both have a distinctive flavor that many (including me) like. See the recipe for Salt Cod Beignets on page 78.

Cusk is important in the Maine fishing industry and is gradually finding a bigger market. The flesh is similar to cod and can be treated as such.

Haddock is similar to cod and considered better-tasting by some. Usually haddock commands a higher price than cod. It is sold filleted with the skin on.

Some haddock is smoked, either on the bone or filleted, and is often known as finnan haddie, after the village of Findon, Scotland, where very good smoked haddock is produced. The taste is addictive (see recipes for Smoked Haddock Tartlets, Smoked Haddock Phyllo Triangles, and Smoked Haddock Soufflé on pages 76, 116, and 131). The flavor of smoked haddock on the bone is definitely superior to that of the smoked fillets, but the former is not always available. Smoked cod is sometimes sold as finnan haddie.

Atlantic pollock, called coley and saithe in England, is harvested in the north Atlantic. It has a slightly darker flesh but is otherwise similar to cod. Broiled, baked, fried, used in stews and soups, I find it an excellent fish. It is hard to find in many fish markets, but is fast gaining recognition. Some are reluctant to market this fish under the name pollock because it is hardly glamorous. Boston bluefish is one name given to it.

A large amount of **walleye pollock** is harvested in the Bering

Sea and Gulf of Alaska. Much of it is frozen at sea in fillets and then reprocessed. Fresh fillets are also available. Pollock is used to produce surimi, which, with the addition of flavorings, is made to resemble crab, scallops, shrimp, and lobster.

White hake, which is usually sold filleted, is sometimes called haddock or cod, when their supply is short. Other names for hake are red, ling, and squirrel hake.

Whiting grows to three pounds. Being very cheap, it is useful in making a light fish stock. However, it is also fine eating when poached, fried, baked, or used in stews or soups. The Atlantic whiting is also called silver hake. Pacific whiting is also very good.

onch

Conch are found in the Atlantic from Florida to Long Island. Their beautiful shells contain a good-tasting meat, not unlike abalone in texture. Similarly, the flesh must be sliced and pounded or cooked to tenderize it. Some frozen, precooked conch meat is available.

The pointed end of the shell coils up, rather like a corkscrew, into the top of the crown. It is at the end of this coil that the flesh is attached to the shell with a muscle, and it is necessary to detach this muscle to extract the flesh. With the claw of a hammer make a hole in the shell about one inch down from the top of the crown, as near as possible to the place where the coil ends. Insert a sharp, pointed knife and scrape the muscle free. Put the tip of the knife under the operculum (the hard covering) at the opening of the shell and pull the flesh out. You can also smash the shell with a mallet. Cut off the operculum and the long tough pointed appendage from the conch. If you are going to cook the conch whole, as for the recipes in this book, leave the intestines in, and don't bother to skin the conch; both can be removed after they are cooked (boiled in lightly salted water for about one and a half hours). Alternatively, you can make a slit in the flesh where the intestines are and remove them and peel the tough skin off the conch before pounding or cooking.

If you want to eat the conch raw, slice it thin and pound it gently with a smooth mallet until it is tender but not torn up, much as you would do with abalone or geoduck clam.

 rabs

Crabs have a delicious meat, and they are possibly my favorite shellfish. On nights off I like to head for the nearest crab house. A few steamed jumbo blue crabs served on a paper tablecloth, a lot of napkins, a small wooden mallet, and plenty of time to pick out the sweet white meat are more than satisfying. In England, where the fishmongers boil the crabs, I would pick up a large crab and devour both the brown and white meat therein. Dungeness crabs also have fine meat and like the others do not need any sauce or accompaniment. Snow and king crab legs have a sweet and tender texture. Soft-shell crabs (also blue) are another favorite with me. But stone crabs probably have the best flavor of all, tasting very much like lobster.

There are many species along the North American and Canadian shores. They include the blue, stone, red, rock, and snow on the East Coast, and the Dungeness, snow, and king on the West Coast. Snow crabs have smooth legs. King crabs have knobby legs. Stone crabs come from Florida and the Gulf of Mexico, while golden crabs come from just the Gulf of Mexico.

The terms lump and backfin denote the two pieces of meat taken from the back fins of the crab. Special describes the flaked meat from the body and claws of the crab. Crab meat is always cooked, sometimes pasteurized, before eating and should always be refrigerated; it needs to be picked over to remove any cartilage, but is otherwise easy to use. Needless to say, it is also expensive. (The legs of the snow and king crabs and the claws of the stone crab, which hold most of the edible meat, are cooked and usually frozen.)

Apart from steaming whole crabs, there are other exciting ways to prepare crab. It is often used in gumbo (page 144), and it makes a good salad or appetizer. I prefer to kill a crab by steaming it. The recipes in this book usually specify lump or back fin crab meat, except for those recipes for Dungeness crab, which is steamed, and the soft-shell crabs (see below), which do have to be killed before cooking.

To eat steamed crabs, first remove the tail (or apron), then break off the claws to eat later. Next pull off the top shell of the crab. Brush off the feathery gills and break the body in two. You can use a knife to cut the two halves into quarters or simply break them again with your hands. You will need a small pick or fork to take out the lump meat and fat. A small wooden mallet or nutcracker will help you to crack the claws without crushing the meat inside. Do the same with the large legs. Smaller legs can be cracked with your teeth and the meat sucked out.

In the trade, **soft-shell crabs,** which are blue crabs that have shed their hard shells and are in the process of hardening new ones, are graded according to size. Mediums are 3½ to 4 inches wide, Hotels are 4 to 4½ inches wide, Primes are 4½ to 5 inches wide, and Jumbos or Whales are 5 to 6 inches wide—so you can serve 4, 3, or 2 per person accordingly. Their season is from mid-April to September, and I think they must be bought live, although they are available frozen.

To prepare the live soft-shell crabs for cooking it is necessary to cut off their faces, then remove the tails, and lastly lift up the side spines and remove the feathery gills inside. All this can be accomplished with kitchen scissors or shears. I'm squeamish about doing this. I've tried, but I simply can't hold on to the crab when it wiggles. I love eating them, and handling them after they have been prepared is no problem. It is perfectly admissible to ask to have the soft-shell crabs prepared at the fish store for you.

rawfish or Crayfish

These freshwater creatures resembling tiny lobsters are called crayfish up North and crawfish or crawdads in the South. In Florida, crayfish is also the name for spiny lobster. I choose to call them crawfish because that is what they are called in Louisiana, where 85 percent of the world's supply is harvested from the swamps, bayous, and rice fields. I have had them flown up to me along with some soft-shell crawfish, which are simply marvelous when deep-fried. Crawfish are also harvested in Oregon, California, and Washington; in fact, crawfish grow in streams and rivers all over the country but are not marketed to any extent. I wish they were more readily available.

Usually a crawfish weighs between an ounce and two ounces. Five pounds of crawfish produces about 1 pound of tail meat. Although the meat and delicious fat in the head and tail are the main edible parts of the crawfish, the claws hold delicious meat as well. Crawfish tail meat is available already shelled.

Crawfish can be eaten simply steamed, hot or cold, in the shell. You will need a finger bowl, plenty of napkins, a bowl to throw the shells in, and some perseverance, but they are worth the trouble. Usually the claw shells are tender enough to be broken with your teeth to suck out the meat. They are often sautéed, steamed, and used whole in the shell as a garnish or, shelled, in a salad, or used in a casserole or crawfish cakes. In this book, there are recipes for a bisque and a pie. Paul Prudhomme deep-fries them for an appetizer and calls them Cajun popcorn!

To rid the crawfish of mud or sand, put them in a bowl or colander and run cold water over them until it runs clear. Remove the crawfish from the water with a slotted spoon or skimmer and discard any dead ones.

To shell and devein tail meat from a cooked crawfish, first break the tail away from the head, and with it will come the delicious orange-yellow fat. Then peel the shell off and, when you get near the tail fins, take the middle fin in your fingers, give it a twist and a pull, and the vein should come out in one piece. If this does not work, make a groove in the top of the tail meat and remove the vein. Once you get used to this procedure you can peel and devein the tails faster than you would think.

 rums, Spots, and Croakers

Drums and croakers are so called for the drumming noises they make in the water with their air bladders. The spot gets its name from a black spot it carries behind its shoulders.

Red drum, or channel bass, commonly called **redfish,** is very popular in the Gulf and south Atlantic states. Blackened redfish is a famous recipe of Paul Prudhomme's, and different versions of it are served in restaurants across the country. Try it—it's wonderful. Redfish can be fried, broiled, grilled, baked, and smoked.

Sheepshead is a delicious freshwater fish. Caught in the lakes and rivers of America, it is popular in the Midwest and adaptable to any cooking method.

Speckled or **spotted trout** is prized in the South and has a firmer flesh than the weakfish (sea trout). It is very popular in New Orleans, and Paul Prudhomme's recipe for Speckled Trout with Pecan Sauce is famous. See my version of this recipe on page 232.

Weakfish, also called sea trout or gray sea trout, is good eating. Despite the name weakfish, referring to its delicate mouth, which can be broken by a hook, the flesh has a fine texture and is sweet and lean. It tends to spoil quickly and so should be eaten fresh. I served many fillets of this fish when cooking for an East Hampton restaurant, and although some skeptics started out thinking weakfish had soft flesh, they were soon won over. It is good broiled, grilled, and baked. It lives in warm water and is fished from Florida up to Massachusetts (in the summer).

White sea bass is a drum often marketed as sea bass. A large fish from California, usually weighing more than ten pounds, its flesh is not unlike striped bass or grouper and may be treated as such. Other members of this family include the northern and southern kingfish. These are small panfish and have no relationship to the king mackerel, which is sometimes also called kingfish.

Eel (American)

Most freshwater eel is catadromous; that is, it is born in the sea and swims to fresh water to grow. The eel's oily flesh is perfect for smoking. Fresh, it can be fried, baked, used in stews and soups, or made into jellied eel.

latfish

The best-known flatfish are **flounder, fluke,** and **sole.** However, there is no true sole in American waters. Although the only true sole is the Dover sole, from north European waters, many flounder are called sole on both the Atlantic and Pacific coasts in the United States. The fish are flat bodied and swim horizontally. Both eyes are on the top, dark side of the fish. They can be broiled or fried whole, or filleted. The flesh is mild-tasting and has a fine texture. They are usually sold skinned as double fillets (that is, one fillet from each side of the fish). The scales of flatfish are so small as to be negligible, but still should be scraped off before cooking.

Gray sole (witch flounder) is the most favored sole on the Atlantic coast. Sand dabs, also called American or Canadian plaice, have a large market in the Northeast. There are also yellowtail flounder, blackback flounder (winter flounder), and lemon sole (which is a blackback flounder weighing more than three and a half pounds). Fluke is a summer flounder. These are all northwestern Atlantic fish.

On the Pacific Coast there are petrale sole, rex sole, Californian "Dover" sole, "English" sole (called lemon sole), butter sole, and sand dabs. The petrale, "Dover," and "English" sole weigh between one and five pounds; rex, butter, and sand dabs are smaller. There are also yellowfin, curlfin, and starry flounder.

Dover sole from Europe has firm white flesh that lends itself when filleted to a multitude of recipes. The sole's shape is elliptical and deep bodied, whereas flounder is more rounded in shape with a flatter body. I prefer to cook the fish whole; it is easy to lift the flesh off the backbone after cooking, and because it is cooked on the bone, the flesh is juicy and moist (see the recipe on page 218). In fact, the backbone when dry is so simply constructed that you could use it to comb your hair.

Halibut has a sparkling white flesh that is dense. The fish is usually large, weighing up to 750 pounds. It is caught in the northwestern Atlantic and in the northeastern Pacific. In California there is a different, smaller species called the California halibut, which grows up to fifty pounds. It is usually steaked or filleted. I prefer to fillet it. It can be broiled, baked, or poached. It is delicious served plain or with a number of glazes or sauces.

Turbot and **brill** are magnificent fish with exquisite flavor. Imported from Europe, turbot, turbotin (a small turbot), and brill are well worth seeking out. For a dinner party I have poached whole turbot in dry white wine. I like to broil the smaller turbotin whole with paprika and oil (see page 235 for a recipe). Brill is very similar to turbot but smaller.

 *erring and Family*

Alewife, caught from Newfoundland to North Carolina, is an anadromous fish. Born in fresh water, it goes out to sea to grow, and returns to rivers or lakes to spawn. Alewife is an important species in the Great Lakes, where it has been locked into fresh water. The roe is delicious.

Herring is harvested on both sides of the north Atlantic and along the north Pacific coast, but is not often available fresh in retail markets. It has a fine soft flesh, high in fat, and is delicious broiled. Also try it breaded or sprinkled with a little oatmeal and fried in a little fat. In the United States nearly all the catch is either cured and preserved, smoked (after which it is known as kipper), pickled and bottled (known as rollmops, matjes, and schmaltz), salted, or canned. The young herring caught off Maine are canned as sardines. I wish more fresh herring were available, for although I like pickled herring, I miss the fresh ones I used to eat in England.

Sardines, in the United States, are actually young herring. They are available fresh on the Maine coast. True sardines, however, are imported from Europe. Their distinctive and rich flavor makes them ideal for grilling, the way they are most often served in Portugal, Spain, and the Mediterranean. Simple tin grills are brought to the beach and elsewhere outdoors, and rows of little sardines are grilled and eaten with local bread. It is a pity that few Americans know the joy of eating a grilled sardine (see page 214 for a recipe).

Shad, like alewife, is anadromous, in that it is born in fresh water, goes out to sea to grow, and returns to the rivers to spawn. Caught in the spawning season, the shad is much prized for its soft rich flesh and roe. The season begins in January in Florida and goes on through early June, when shad is harvested from rivers as far north as Connecticut.

There are those who eat shad and/or its roe whenever they go to a fish restaurant during this season. Shad is very bony—a man filleting shad in the Fulton Fish Market told me each fish has 365 bones—and it takes great skill to fillet these fish. Shad roe must be handled very carefully to prevent the roe from breaking out of their sac. The shad fillets and roe are good broiled or baked, and the roe also can be poached. Shad from the Delaware River in Pennsylvania is sometimes pickled.

Whitebait is any small fish, including silversides and sand lances. The tiny fish are good lightly coated with flour and deep-fried whole. They are found in the summer as they run into estuaries, but are primarily used as bait, which is a shame.

acks

The most highly prized jack in U.S. waters is the pompano. This beautiful-looking fish has a silver skin with blue-green-gray and yellow hues. The flesh is firm and sweet and is best baked, broiled, or sautéed. I like it filleted and served skin side up, partially wrapped with a grape leaf (see recipe on page 202).

Other jacks are permit, jack crevalle, blue runner, amberjack, look down, moonfish, and rainbow runner—all from the Gulf of Mexico and the tropical waters of the Atlantic. Jack crevalle is also found off the Pacific Coast of North America, as is yellowtail. Yellowtail, also available frozen from Japan, is used in sashimi.

ingcod

Lingcod, from the West Coast, is not related to cod but to the greenling family. It grows to fifty pounds. When cooked the flesh is white and has a firm texture. It can be cooked as cod: coat the fillets lightly with a batter and fry, or broil, or bake a tail end as in the recipe on page 196.

Lobster

The **American lobster,** harvested in the northwestern Atlantic, is of very high quality, extremely popular, and relatively expensive. Next to stone crab meat, this is my favorite seafood. It is great fun choosing a lively lobster from a holding tank and taking it home to be simply boiled or steamed. This is an easy and rich meal to serve. However, there are many other ways to enjoy lobster, such as sautéed or broiled or in a stew, bisque, or salad.

Lobsters are priced according to size and are usually sold weighing from one to five pounds. Years ago, I bought a fifteen-pound lobster on Long Island. I asked the fishmonger to kill it for me and then I broiled it on a charcoal fire. It was delicious; though some consider the larger lobsters to have tough meat, they can be wonderful eating if cooked carefully.

Small, one-pound lobsters have delicate and succulent flesh, but I think a two-pound lobster has a stronger flavor and better texture. Larger lobsters can be shared, and one- to one-and-a-half-pound lobsters are suitable for individual servings. Always look for a lively lobster, with claws that reach into the air and a tail that curls under when the lobster is picked up.

Sometimes it is necessary to extract raw meat from the lobster, and this entails killing it before cooking. You may kill the lobster by putting it in boiling water for one minute without cooking the meat through. Afterward the meat can be easily extracted. (This is the most painless way to kill a lobster—for the lobster and perhaps for you.) Or you may ask the fish store to do this and rush home to use it. Or (if you are extremely brave) place the lobster on its back on a board and, wearing oven gloves if desired, plunge a heavy pointed knife into the place where the tail joins the body, severing the tail. The lobster will die instantly, but wait a few minutes until the creature stops moving. Then split the body with a knife. With kitchen scissors cut the underside of the tail shell down the middle and lift out the flesh in one piece. Remove the vein running down the back. Collect the coral (a dark, green substance), if there is any, and the pale green tomalley and put them in a bowl. Take off the claws and crack them with lobster crackers or nutcrackers and take out the meat intact.

Remove the meat from the body where the legs are attached. Remove the gritty stomach sac from behind the eyes.

The first method is the best when you want to extract raw meat; the meat is easily removed because the preliminary heating of the shell makes the flesh separate slighty from it.

Spiny or **rock lobster** is harvested from the warm waters off the Carolina coast down through the southern Gulf of Mexico and the Caribbean Sea. Other spiny or rock lobsters are imported (frozen) from the cold waters of South Africa, Australia, and New Zealand. These lobsters are distinguished from the American lobster by their reddish brown color, mottled with yellow, orange, green, and blue. They lack large claws and it is the tail meat we enjoy. They are often called crayfish—but should not be confused with the smaller freshwater crustacean.

The Mackerel Family

Atlantic mackerel abounds on both sides of the north Atlantic. It is an oily fish, with a rich meat that spoils quickly. I have caught mackerel off the coast of Wales and it is delicious to eat. However, in the United States, it is not marketed in any great quantity in fresh form, nor is it very popular eating (or so I have found in New York restaurants). It can be broiled or baked split and butterflied open. It is possible to make a gravad of mackerel, using only very fresh mackerel (see the recipe on page 118 for Gravad Lax of Baby Coho Salmon).

Smoked mackerel is very tasty and I use it in the recipe for Smoked Mackerel Phyllo Triangles on page 74. When I worked for a charcuterie in London I used to make pounds and pounds of smoked mackerel pâté.

King mackerel, also known as kingfish, is harvested from the Gulf of Mexico and from the Carolinas to Florida. Spanish mackerel comes from the Gulf of Mexico. A few years ago I enjoyed catching these fish one hot day in the Gulf of Mexico off Sarasota, Florida.

onkfish

Also known as anglerfish, goosefish, bellyfish, and *lotte* (in French), this fish is caught off the northern shores of the Atlantic. The whole fish weighs up to fifty pounds, but the tail meat is all that is sold. Like that of the blowfish, the flesh surrounds a thick central spine that makes it easy to fillet or cut into a steak; sometimes the tail is roasted whole. The flesh is firm and sweet, and to some the texture and taste resemble those of lobster. Monkfish is suitable for stews and soups because it tends not to flake, and it can be sautéed, fried, broiled, or poached. The French dish *gigot de lotte* resembles a leg of lamb in shape and is sometimes basted with lamb stock! Monkfish cheeks are occasionally available and are delicious morsels. Tiny monkfish tails can be cooked like blowfish.

It is necessary to remove the skin and membrane before filleting and cooking, because both are unsightly and the membrane shrinks and turns black as it cooks, distorting the fish's appearance. To prepare a monkfish tail, first cut off the dorsal fin, then pull off the skin with your hands. Using a long thin knife, insert it under the membrane and curve the knife down and around the flesh. Be brutal, even if it means that you have to cut into the flesh at some points, in order to remove every trace of membrane. To produce fillets, cut the flesh away from the spine.

ullet

Striped and **silver mullet** are harvested from the western Atlantic and the Gulf of Mexico, but mostly in Florida waters. They are also harvested south of central California in the Pacific.

Red mullet, known as *rouget* in France, *triglia* in Italy, and *salmoneta* in Spain, are imported from the Mediterranean.

Mullet can be filleted or left whole, baked, broiled, or fried. The flesh is mild and nutty. The roe is excellent.

ussels

Blue mussels are becoming more and more popular in the United States. The price is right and they are low in calories. The best are harvested between fall and spring, before they spawn. They are sold live or frozen on the half shell, and the meats are canned and bottled. The simplest way to serve them is to steam them open with a little dry white wine, some herbs, and chopped vegetables. Serve them cold in salads, hot in soups or ragouts, baked on the half shell, or make them into a bisque or risotto (pages 150 and 181).

For some it is daunting to contemplate how many mussels you will have to clean, purge, and debeard to satisfy your guests, even though mussels are quickly cooked. However, most mussels come to the market fairly clean of mud and sand and the cultivated mussels, which are grown on ropes suspended from floats or rafts, are particularly clean. These cultivated mussels cost more than the wild ones (which are also cleaned), but they are worth it for they are labor-saving and tend to have thinner shells and plump meat—but come without pearls!

Having cleaned bushels of mussels in my life, I have devised a simple way to do the job. Put the mussels in a large container with cold running water and move them around vigorously with your hands, so that they scrape together and they rub off the mud and sand from the shells. Discard any mussels with shells that are gaping open and any with broken shells. Pour the old water away and cover with fresh, lightly salted water. Sprinkle three tablespoons of flour on top of the water and set aside for an hour or so, so they plump up and clear themselves of sand. At the end of this time scrub them only if necessary, and pull or cut off the beards. They are now ready to steam. Steam them in a covered saucepan only until they open, and if you are going to use the mussels out of their shells, shuck them as soon as they are cool enough to handle. This prevents them from shriveling up. Also check to see if any beards are still attached to the flesh and remove.

The color of **green-lipped mussels,** so called because of their beautiful shells, graduates from light brown at one end to bright green at the tip, and they are striated with thin black stripes.

They are imported from New Zealand and are spectacular in both looks and taste. There is nothing quite like them; they are exquisite. Although expensive and not generally available, they are worth looking for, and I think they are best cooked the simplest way—steamed so you can savor their fine unique flavor. They are sold live as well as frozen (cooked on the half shell).

ctopus

Octopus is harvested from the Pacific and on the Atlantic coast from the Carolinas to Florida. This harmless cephalopod holds terror for some, but properly cooked it is delicious to eat. The flesh, which includes the tentacles and the head, is tough and must be beaten with a smooth mallet or boiled for one to two hours, according to size, to tenderize it. I have seen the fishermen in Greece beat them on rocks. Octopus is also available precooked or frozen. After beating or boiling, octopus can be cut into pieces, simply grilled, and served as an appetizer—in Greece it is served as *meze* with drinks. Octopus can also be used in stews and soups, or it can be fried, sautéed, or broiled.

To prepare the octopus for cooking, first turn the head inside out, clean out the inside under running water, and then turn it back again. Cut off the part where the eyes are located and discard. Boil until tender, one to two hours. When cool enough to handle, carefully pull off the purplish membranes from the head and underside of the tentacles.

range Roughy

Orange roughy, which has been marketed only since 1979 and was not even discovered until 1975, is fished in the Tasman Sea in the South Pacific in New Zealand waters. It has a firm white flesh and is sold in fillets. The fish is frozen at sea, thawed on shore, and then filleted and refrozen. The market for this fish has grown enormously, as has the price, in recent years. It is exported to the United States, Australia, and Europe in large quantities. This excellent if somewhat bland fish can be cooked in all the usual ways and you would never know that it has been frozen twice because it has such a good texture.

 *ysters*

There are oyster lovers everywhere. In America the supply seems to be keeping up with consumption; in both the Atlantic and Pacific, some oyster beds have dwindled while others are now flourishing. During the gold rush in California the demand exceeded the supply, but since then the Japanese oyster, also called the Pacific oyster, has been introduced to help keep pace with demand, and it does well. The Olympia oyster *(Ostrea lurida)* is also making a comeback.

It is difficult to assess which oysters are the tastiest; people have different favorites. The quality, taste, and name of the oysters differ according to the region they come from. The American or Eastern oyster *(Crassostrea virginica)* is harvested from the Gulf of Mexico to the northern Atlantic. The best-known Eastern oysters come from Virginia shores, Long Island and Cape Cod, variously called Blue Point, Chincoteague, Apalachicola, Kent Island, Wellfleet, and Cotuit. Golden mantel, petite kumomoto, Willapa Bay, and quilcene *(Crassostrea gigas)* are some of the best-tasting on the West Coast. Belon oysters *(Ostrea edulis)*, indigenous to France, are now farmed in Maine, California, and Washington.

Oysters are available live in the shell, and shucked, fresh or frozen. They also come canned, smoked, dried, and in soups. Their unique flavor is best savored when eaten raw on the half shell, with a bit of lemon juice. However, I have included recipes for warmed oysters with different mild sauces and an Oyster and Clam Soufflé (see recipes on pages 96, 97, and 134).

Oysters stay alive for nearly a week out of water. Store them in the refrigerator in a colander set over ice. Be sure the shells are closed. If some shells are gaping open and do not close when tapped, they must be discarded. Before shucking, scrub the outside shell with a stiff plastic brush under running water.

To shuck oysters, hold them with a heavy folded cloth or wear a garden glove, in case the pointed knife you will be using should slip. Push the tip of a sturdy oyster knife into the hinge at the pointed end of the oyster. Twist and release the top shell, sliding your knife under the shell to free the muscle. Also slip your knife under the oyster to release it from the lower muscle. Retain as much juice as possible in the bottom shell and pick out any pieces of broken shell before serving.

If you need oysters out of their shells for a soup or soufflé, you can break the thin end of the shell, slide your knife around to open the shell, and release the oyster. Be sure to discard any pieces of broken shell.

Perch

Perch is a freshwater fish. The best known, walleye, sauger and yellow perch, are small fish that are best pan-fried. They are fished from the Great Lakes as well as from other lakes and rivers in the United States and Canada.

Periwinkles

Periwinkles, called winkles in England, are small sea snails that are quite delicious when cooked. They are harvested along the entire coast of the United States, and are found on pilings and rocks. They are pretty little things easily prepared for eating.

Wash the periwinkles in plenty of cold running water, moving them around in the water with your hands to get rid of any sand or mud. When the water runs clear, put them in a saucepan of cold water. Bring the periwinkles to the boil. Boil for three minutes and then drain. Remove the operculum (the tiny foot) with the point of a small sharp knife. Serve them with little lobster forks, toothpicks, or paper clips to extract the meat. Dip them in melted butter flavored with lemon juice, or use them in the recipe on page 97.

ike

Northern pike is a fine fish with which to make quenelles because of its snowy white flesh—non-oily and mild-tasting. It is used to make the gefilte fish on page 242.

Pike are voracious eaters and the scourge of small rivers. In England, the local fishermen are very proud to catch a pike, as it is wily and difficult to fish and nabbing one gives the other fish in the river a chance to live.

orgy

Porgies, known as sea bream in Great Britain and *dorade* in France, are small fish from the warm waters of the Atlantic. The flesh is lean and fairly coarse; and pan-dressed, it can be fried, broiled, or baked. Served stuffed or with a rough tomato sauce, porgies improve in flavor. They are bony and the small sharp bones should be picked out of fillets; whole fish can be slashed before cooking.

ockfish

There are more than sixty species of Sebastes rockfish on the Pacific coast of North America. Ocean perch (also known as redfish, or rosefish) is caught in the north Atlantic, from Maine to Norway. Rockfish from the Pacific is often misnamed snapper, but fishmarkets can be fined for this. Rockfish is an extremely colorful fish. When it is called "black" or "red" it is truly named; "canary" denotes a bright orange-red color. Rockfish has strong spiny dorsal fins and its opercle (gill covers) are like armor.

Other popular species are the Alaskan black, blue, widow, yellow eye, vermillion, boccacio, and chili pepper. Rockfish can be cooked many ways.

Sablefish

Sablefish or black cod (unrelated to the cod family) is usually served in its smoked form. The flesh, soft and oily with a fine texture, is eminently suitable for smoking. It is fished in the Pacific from northern California to Alaska. It commonly grows to twenty-five pounds, and specimens over a hundred pounds have been caught. When filleted, it is known as butterfish.

It is not easy for me to recommend cooking sablefish in its fresh form, because I don't like its taste or texture. However, there are those who enjoy it. It can be steaked, or filleted to be fried, broiled, or baked. It can be roasted whole or in a chunk weighing several pounds.

Salmon

Both the Pacific and Atlantic are blessed with salmon. This king of the sea is fabulous both to cook and to eat. The distinctive pink to red flesh is moist and tender. There is also a white-fleshed king salmon. With its fairly high oil content, salmon can be broiled, grilled, steamed, poached, and baked. Additionally, salmon is smoked, or pickled and made into gravad lax (marinated with sugar and salt). It is sold filleted, whole, and steaked. I like to serve thin escalopes of salmon, cutting them one-eighth inch thick and broiling them on a plate, and at other times cutting a serving-size escalope to cook in one piece (see recipes on pages 208–209).

Farm-raised Atlantic salmon is imported mainly from Norway and some from Scotland and Ireland. In the Pacific, the king or Chinook salmon commands the highest price, with silver or coho coming next. Pink, sockeye or blueback, and chum or dog salmon are available fresh and frozen, but they are mostly found canned. About 95 percent of the salmon produced in the United States comes from Alaska, with the rest from Washington, Oregon, and California.

Imported Atlantic salmon arrives in pristine condition, because harvesters have very strict controls on handling the fish.

Scallops

Sea scallops are mollusks that thrive in deep Atlantic waters. The round muscle that fastens the two shells together is the sweet rich scallop we eat. In Europe the roe or coral attached to most scallops is eaten as well; it is a delicious and colorful addition to scallop dishes. France, Holland, the Isle of Man and New Zealand are exporting scallops with roe to the United States. I'm hoping that American fishermen will start to include the roe or coral with their catch soon. Scallops may be broiled, sautéed, poached, baked in the shell, or deep-fried.

Bay scallops are smaller scallops with a delicate sweet flavor. Long Islanders look forward to the scallop season, which begins each year on September 15. Bay scallops can be eaten raw if very fresh, and they taste as sweet as candy. Otherwise, they need very brief cooking, quick sautéing over high heat or baking—overcooked, they lose their juice and toughen. Cook both sea and bay scallops only until they lose their translucency.

Calico scallops are a southern "bay" scallop harvested off Florida. They are steam-shucked at processing plants, and this probably is the reason they simply do not have the sweet quality of the bay and sea scallops from northern waters. However, they are cheap and abundant and have their fans.

Sea Urchins

Sea urchins are spherical shells covered like porcupines with spines. The animal inside contains a delicious roe during the spawning season. Found clinging to rocks, they eat kelp and can pose a hazard to swimmers. Once when swimming in a rough Italian sea, I was nearly unable to reach shore when confronted by rocks encrusted with sea urchins.

Green sea urchins are harvested along the Maine coast, while red, green, and purple sea urchins come from California waters. They are popular in France, where they are prepared by cutting into the shell around the mouth, which is discarded, exposing the orange and yellow roe and viscera. There is a large market for this delicacy in Japan, where it is called *uni* and usually featured as part of a sushi selection. I find the raw roe delicious when eaten out of the shell, but I also like to make an urchin soufflé, soup, and sauce (see recipes on pages 136, 152, and 301) because I like their slightly sweet and unctuous flavor when cooked.

Fortunately in New York, Los Angeles, and San Francisco, one can obtain little trays containing a half pound of roe from Japanese fish stores, thus avoiding the bother of extracting the roe from the urchin in any quantity. However, should the need arise, here is how to extract sea urchin roe. Wear a heavy gardening glove or cover your hand with a heavy cloth so the spines of the sea urchin do not stick into you. Insert kitchen scissors into the mouth of the creature, make a cut about one inch away from the mouth, curving the scissors around and continuing to cut until you have a lid you will discard. With a teaspoon scoop out the orange or yellow roe, avoiding the brown viscera. Depending on the size of the sea urchins (and they can be quite large in California), you will need between ten and twenty to obtain a half pound of roe.

The Shark Family

Those who know and appreciate shark meat are fortunate. The flesh is firm and mild-tasting, not unlike swordfish. The mako shark is becoming very popular (in the summer) on the Atlantic coast and the dusky shark, fished off New Jersey, also has good meat. In the Pacific, thresher, soupfin, and leopard sharks are widely enjoyed. Shark is best filleted, steaked, or cubed, then grilled, broiled, or used in stews and soups. See the recipe on page 228. Swordfish may be used interchangeably with shark.

The **dogfish** is much maligned in America. This small shark is delicious eating and has been appreciated in Europe for a long time. In England it used to be called rock salmon, but that practice has been stopped. Dogfish is also known as huss or tope. In France it is known as *roussette* or *petite roussette*. It is very good fried in fillets or used in stews or soups. Smoked dogfish is available in the United States and it is excellent. I hope that fresh dogfish will be more readily available in the markets soon.

Shrimp

The tender, delicately flavored, and colorful shrimp is a widely popular shellfish. It is available fresh, head on or off; frozen, cooked or raw, shell-on or peeled; and canned, cooked and peeled. Sometimes fish stores will cook, shell, and devein them for your convenience.

Shrimp are marketed in many different sizes. Shrimp range in size from four hundred (cooked and peeled) to a pound, just right for the potted shrimp on page 92, to eight to the pound (frozen, shell on). I use sixteen to twenty shrimp per pound in most of the recipes here, but occasionally I use small shrimp, fifty or more to a pound. Fish stores usually grade and sell them as jumbo, large, medium, and small. Since most shrimp available in a market have been frozen and defrosted, be sure to patronize a reputable store that has kept the shrimp on ice. Give them a sniff to make sure they do not smell of ammonia—a sure sign of spoilage. Defrost frozen shrimp overnight in the refrigerator or cover with cold water for several hours.

Northern shrimp are harvested off Maine across to Norway. Brown, white, and pink shrimp are harvested from South Carolina to Texas and Louisiana in the Gulf of Mexico. They are sold fresh with heads on, as opposed to the normally available frozen shrimp, which have their heads removed.

Many of the northern shrimp are sold already cooked, peeled, and frozen, but some are available fresh in the spring. Warmwater shrimp come from all over Central and South America and the Far East. Mexico is the largest exporter to the United States, Ecuador the second. Brazil, India and Panama also export large quantities.

The versatile shrimp can be poached, steamed, broiled, grilled, sautéed, deep-fried, and used in soups, stews, and terrines. Served with sauces that enhance their fine taste, they are always a treat. It is essential that shrimp be cooked only until they lose their translucency. You can test doneness by cutting off a piece from the head end. When overcooked, shrimp toughen and diminish in flavor.

One of the finest and simplest ways to serve shrimp is to steam a pound or two of tiny whole head-on shrimp and serve them cold with lemon wedges, plenty of napkins, finger bowls, and a bowl for discarded heads and shells—don't forget to suck the heads when they are broken away from the tail for the delicious bit of fat inside. This was an easy enough treat to manage in England, but it is difficult to find the tiny whole shrimp in New York, except when the shrimp come down to us from the Maine Coast in the winter and spring. Another very special shrimp is the spot prawn or shrimp, harvested in the northeastern Pacific, which has a very special flavor and sweetness, but is not yet widely available. Those living near the coasts of Maine, California, Oregon, and the Gulf of Mexico are lucky.

The question often arises as to whether it is necessary to shell and devein the shrimp tails before eating. I think that the tiny headless shrimp need not be shelled and deveined if they are to be grilled, for the shells impart a special flavor to the shrimp and the veins are negligible. In larger shrimp, the veins, though edible, are unsightly and often removed for aesthetic reasons. Shrimp cooked in their shells are delicious but a bit messy to eat. Moreover, the problem of shelling at table must be resolved! Try to suit the method of preparation to the occasion.

When shelling and deveining, it is usually best to leave on the shell at the tip of the tail; the shrimp can then be handled with the tip and will look more attractive. To devein shrimp, first peel off the shell, then take a knife and make a small incision down the back of the shrimp. Remove the vein and discard. To butterfly shrimp, shell and devein the shrimp, leaving on the tip of the tail shell. Make a cut down the back nearly all the way through the shrimp and spread it open.

Skates and Rays

Skates and rays, underappreciated in the United States, are rarely available in retail markets. Only the triangular-shaped wings of the skates and rays are eaten. Once they are skinned, the white flesh, formed in long thin strands, is visible atop a thin transparent membrane, or "bone." When the skates and rays are very small, the membrane is tender enough to be eaten.

In Europe, where skate with brown butter *(raie au beurre noir)* is popular, the fish is easily obtainable. However, this is not the only way to cook skates and rays. They can be fried or poached and can also be used in salads or pies (see the recipes on pages 162 and 217). Skates and rays are fished in both the Atlantic and the Pacific. When available in fish markets, their names are used interchangeably.

melt

Smelt are anadromous and are caught in seawater when returning to spawn. They are silvery green, nearly transparent, and measure seven to eight inches long. When fresh and in season—they have different seasons in different parts of the country—they are popular food. They fry well and can be filleted like sardines. See the recipe on page 218.

moked Fish

Many fish and shellfish are delicious when smoked. Generally the more oily fish smoke the best. Some fish and shellfish that are smoked are salmon, trout, mackerel, bluefish, haddock or cod (finnan haddie), tuna, sturgeon, sablefish (black cod), whitefish, chub (a small whitefish), eel, blackfish (wrasse), dogfish, halibut, butterfish, mullet, mussels, shrimp, scallops, oysters, squid, and octopus.

Before smoking, the fish is treated with a dry salt cure (salt, saltpeter, brown sugar—and sometimes rum, as with Scotch salmon), or with a salt brine solution (salt, saltpeter, sugar, black pepper, and bay leaf). Hot-smoking is accomplished in a short time and can be done in homemade smokehouses or even in a covered outdoor grill. The fish will keep only a few days by this method. Cold-smoking is a more lengthy process: fish is smoked for a longer time at a far lower temperature. Cold-smoked fish will keep for a long period and is sometimes frozen, although freezing is not suitable for all fish. Whitefish, chub, and mackerel should not be frozen, as they lose quality. Generally, the short curing and longer smoking methods produce the best smoked fish.

Smoked fish should appear bright and glossy with a firm texture. Salt crystals on the surface may mean that the brine was too salty and the fish therefore has become unpalatable. Everyone has his own criteria for good smoked fish and opinions differ considerably. If possible, ask the fish store or market to let you have a little taste before buying any smoked fish.

nappers

Possibly the best-known snapper is the red snapper, one of the finest fish obtained on the Gulf Coast and East Coast. Most believe that it has the best flavor of all the many snappers. However, there are those who prefer the yellowtail snapper from the Atlantic. The mild, sweet, firm flesh lends itself to many cooking methods, such as broiling and baking, and it can be added to stews and chowders. The light red skin should be left on for color. From the warm waters of the Atlantic and the Caribbean come the yellowtail snapper, mutton snapper, vermillion snapper (also called bee liner), mangrove snapper (or gray snapper), silk snapper, and more than twenty other varieties.

quid

Squid (or calamari), once used mainly as fishing bait, is now gaining popularity as a fine food. It is found in great abundance along the north Atlantic coast, particularly near New Jersey, and in the north Pacific, especially off Monterey. Commercially sold squid ranges in size from three to twelve inches long, and is retailed cleaned and uncleaned. Larger squid is good for stuffing, and smaller ones are suitable for frying or a quickly made stew. Squid will toughen if cooked too long, so the faster you cook it the better. However, squid regains its tenderness if cooked even longer. It is done as soon as it loses its translucency. As mentioned in my recipe for calamari fritti (fried squid) on page 108, I used to eat tiny whole squid in Greece. Any squid longer than the first joint of your thumb was considered not worth frying. However, small squid three or four inches long cut into one-eighth-inch slices retain their tenderness if properly cooked.

To clean squid, gently pull the head and tentacles from the body. Then remove the viscera and plastic-like quill from the inside of the body. Set aside the ink sacs from inside the mantle to use in the recipe for black risotto on page 179. Wash the interior. Cut the tentacles from the head. Remove the small round beak from the base of the tentacles and trim the two longer tentacles. Now remove the fine membrane that covers the body. If you like them, cook the tentacles along with the squid body, or use them for stock (see page 108).

Sturgeon and Paddlefish

The anadromous sturgeon is a grand old fish of river and sea that can grow to enormous size. Although sturgeon is not often marketed because of its scarcity, the present situation may change because sturgeon is being farmed today. I know that Dafne and Mat Engstrom, of California Sunshine Foods in San Francisco, are beginning to farm it in Oregon. This will undoubtedly produce more sturgeon, so that we can partake of both the fish and the caviar, which is so precious.

Sturgeon meat is extremely firm and high in fat. It is perhaps best known in its smoked form, but fresh sturgeon can be grilled, broiled, or baked in cubes, steaks, or escalopes (see recipes on pages 224 and 225). The spinal cord, or notocord, can be removed from the tail end by twisting it and pulling.

Paddlefish can be treated in the same manner as sturgeon.

 *unfish*

There are several species of freshwater sunfish—black and white crappies, and bluegill, green, warmouth, and pumpkinseed sunfish. This usually small fish can be pan-dressed, fried, deep-fried, broiled, or baked. The flesh is lean and delicate. Large and small mouth bass are members of the sunfish family and should not be confused with black sea bass. They have a lean and fine-textured flesh, and I am told they are fun to catch through the ice.

 *wordfish*

Swordfish is extremely popular for its dense, firm white meat when cooked. Swordfish is huge and fished worldwide. Swordfish obtainable in the United States is mainly from the northwestern Atlantic and the Pacific; but it is also available from Chile, Spain, and other areas. East coast swordfish, because of the way it is handled, is considered superior. But its supply is dwindling. I think swordfish is best steaked or cubed, then grilled or broiled (see recipes on pages 226–229).

 *ilefish*

Fished from the Gulf of Mexico up to Massachusetts, tilefish has a firm texture and tasty white meat. Tilefish is spectacular to look at, with yellow spots along the body. It can be cut into steaks or filleted, and then fried, broiled, grilled, poached, baked, and

used in stews and soups. In some shops, tilefish is often misla-
beled snapper and bass.

rout

There are many species of freshwater trout. Rainbow trout, which
is farmed mainly in Idaho, is popular. Many are boned out, making it easy to fry or broil them. Lake and brook trout can be
cooked in similar fashion. See recipes on pages 229–231.

una

Many people know tuna as a canned product, but there are a
growing number who appreciate fresh tuna and it is one of the
finest fish to be had. There are many species available from tem-
perate waters worldwide, such as albacore, yellowfin, bluefin,
skipjack, blackfin, bigeye, and bonito. Blackfin is fished from the
western Atlantic, and southern bluefin comes from the Southern
Hemisphere. Now that many canneries have had to close in the
United States because of competition from imported canned tuna,
more fresh tuna has become available to the consumer. Albacore,
often frozen at sea, is an excellent product.

Tuna flesh is dense and fairly high in oil content. The flesh
when raw is usually dark but turns light or white when cooked.
Its thick skin must be cut off before cooking. Tuna is easily overcooked and great care should be taken to remove it from the heat
as soon as it is cooked through and before it dries out. See recipes
for albacore on page 234 and Broiled Tuna with Onion and Black
Olive Confit on page 233. Raw tuna is delicious as part of a sushi
or sashimi dish.

hitefish

It is important that whitefish be cooked when very fresh because of the high fat content. It is suitable for smoking, and also can be used in gefilte fish, as on page 242. The flesh is white, firm, and sweet-tasting. It can be poached, broiled, grilled, or baked. Caught in cold water lakes and rivers, a considerable amount of whitefish is imported from Canada. Whitefish yields a good percentage of flesh, because the head is so small.

Cisco is the correct name for **chub,** a member of the whitefish family. Chub is usually smoked.

olffish

Wolffish is not generally marketed, although it has a sweet firm flesh. Caught in the north Atlantic and north Pacific, it is often called ocean catfish, although this species is not a true catfish. The French call it *loup marin.* Its frightening long front teeth and crushing back teeth allow it to eat crustaceans, thereby creating a delicious meat. Usually sold in fillets, it can be sautéed, fried, and broiled.

The rasse Family

This large family of fish includes the blackfish (or tautog) and cunner from the north Atlantic; the hogfish, bluehead wrasse, and the California sheephead and señorita.

Most are distinguished by fierce, long protruding teeth, with which they eat crustaceans.

The Accomplished Seafood Cook

Fish Filleting Techniques

Flatfish (flounder, sole, halibut, turbot, brill, etc.) can be filleted to produce two or four fillets. *To produce two fillets:* make a cut across the body of the fish behind the head and the pectoral fin, down to the backbone. Make another cut across the flesh just above the tail. With the head away from you and the dark skin side up, make a long cut following the dorsal fin. Starting at the head end of the fish cut the right-hand fillet away until you reach the center of the backbone, ease your knife over it, and continue to cut off the left-hand fillet—leaving both fillets joined together. Do not cut the whole fillet completely off; leaving it on will facilitate filleting the other side of the fish. (See Note below about the roe sacs.)

Turn the fish over and repeat the procedure with the tail end away from you, this time cutting the fillet completely off both sides. Holding the fillet at the tail end with your fingertips, use a heavy knife held at a slight angle to separate the fillets from their skins. Trim off the little bones on the edge of each fillet.

To produce four fillets: with the light side of the fish up and the tail toward you, cut the flesh down the middle of the central spine, from head to tail. (There is a fine line on the skin of the fish that indicates where it is.) Then with your knife at an angle, cut the left-hand fillet away from the bones with long strokes. Do

FLATFISH

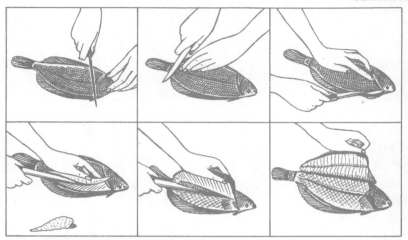

TO PRODUCE TWO FILLETS

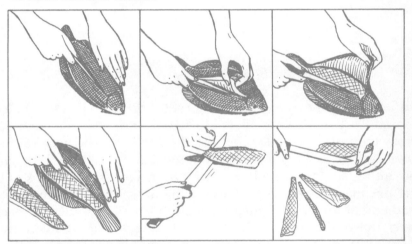

TO PRODUCE FOUR FILLETS

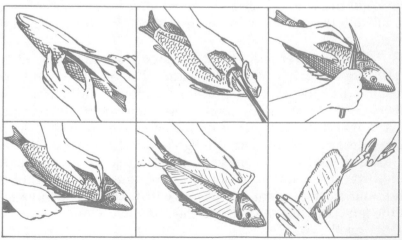

TO PRODUCE TWO FILLETS   **ROUNDFISH**

not cut the fillet completely off, as leaving it on will facilitate filleting the other side of the fish. Turn the fish head toward you and cut the fillet away from the bones as before, again not completely off.

Turn the fish over and repeat the procedure, cutting the two fillets from this side completely off. Release by cutting the two fillets on the light side. Holding the fillet at the tail end with your fingertips, use a heavy knife held at a slight angle to separate the fillets from their skins. Trim off the little bones on the edge of each fillet.

Commercially filleted fish is cut using the first method described—one piece from each side of the fish—and is usually skinned. If the fillets are of any size, remove the rough tissue down the center of both fillets, creating two fillets instead of one, or four to a fish. Place the fillets on a cutting board. Run your finger down the middle of each and you will feel a strip of rough tissue. Cut the fillet lengthwise on either side of the tissue and discard it.

Note: If you should find roe sacs in these fish during filleting, release them and put to the side. They can be cooked with the fillets or separately.

Filleting **roundfish** (bass, bluefish, cod, grouper, herring, mackerel, pollock, pompano, red snapper, rockfish, salmon, sea trout, sturgeon, tilefish, speckled trout, wolffish, etc.) produces two fillets.

If the fish has scales, use a fish scaler, table knife, or tablespoon to scale it starting at the tail end and moving toward the head. This is best done by placing the fish in a sinkful of water and scaling it underwater so that the scales do not fly all over the place. After scaling, rinse the fish and pat it dry.

Make an incision at the vent and slit the belly up to the head. Empty out the internal organs and scrape the dark secretion of blood away from the backbone. Also cut out the gills with kitchen shears and discard them if you are going to serve the fish head-on or make fish stock. Cut the fins off with kitchen shears. Rinse the inside of the fish.

With the fish lying flat on a board and its back facing you, head on your right, take a long thin sharp filleting knife and make a diagonal cut behind the head and pectoral fin until you touch the backbone. With your knife close to the backbone, cut away the fillet, starting at the head and going down to the tail, easing your knife above the protruding rib near the head and cutting down steeply on the other side of the center of the backbone. Lift up the fillet and continue to cut away from the rib cage, without cutting the fillet completely off. (Leaving the fillet on facilitates filleting the other side of the fish.)

Now turn the fish over and make an incision across the fish just above the tail, then cut as before close to the backbone until you reach the head. Make a diagonal cut behind the head and pectoral fin as before. Cut the fillet off, turn the fish over, and make the final cut to release the second fillet. Trim the fillets of any raggedy edges.

If you wish to skin the fillets, place them skin side down, hold on to the tail end with your fingertips, and using a heavy knife held at a slight angle cut the fillets away from their skins.

Use pin nose pliers or tweezers to remove the pinbones. You can feel these bones with your fingers down the center of each fillet, four or five on a two-pound fish. Pluck these bones out, pulling toward the head end of the fillet to ensure the fillet remains unbroken.

Restaurant Cooking Methods

As I wrote in my introduction, some of the recipes in this book were worked out in restaurants and contain tips and methods learned there.

Restaurants often use sizzle plates to cook fish fillets. These are shallow oval platters made of thick aluminum that come in various sizes from ten to twelve inches long and hold only one or two pieces of fish, as the fish are cooked to order. For baking or bake-poaching the oven is set at 425 degrees. When bake-poaching in the oven, the fish is covered with a lettuce leaf to keep the moisture in. We use the slightly wilted outer leaves of lettuce.

Broiling is done at highest heat with the fish about four to five inches away from the heat. Dry white wine is poured ⅛ inch deep into the sizzle pan, sometimes with the addition of a little melted clarified butter drizzled over, depending on the kind of fish. Then the fish is laid on top—skin side up when baking, skin side down (usually) when broiling. The wine prevents the fish from sticking to the pan and gives it a good taste.

In restaurants thin escalopes of salmon are broiled directly on an ovenproof serving plate that has been thinly coated with melted clarified butter; then the fish is slid onto a clean warm serving plate. This may not be practical in the home, when more than one helping must be prepared at a time.

Poaching is done using a large heavy oven pan or fish poacher, usually placed on top of two burners, containing barely simmering stock or poaching liquid. Putting the fish in a strainer, lift-out tray, or rack facilitates removal when the fish is cooked.

Various sizes of frying and sauté pans are used over medium to high heat. Deep-frying is accomplished using an electric deep-fryer with wire baskets; the heat of the oil is maintained as close as possible to 375 degrees.

Fish takes a short time to cook and is easily ruined by overcooking. Test for doneness either by pressing down with your finger or thumb (the flesh should be firm to the touch) or by inserting a knife or fork into the thickest part and twisting to see when the flesh has lost its translucency. The fish is done at this point. There is no need to turn a fish fillet during cooking; however, a whole fish should be turned when broiling in the oven or over a charcoal fire.

Abalone, scallops, lobster, shrimp, crawfish, and squid must not be overcooked or they will toughen; they are ready when the flesh is opaque. To ascertain this, cut off a small cross section to make sure flesh is cooked all the way through. Squid may be cooked for an appreciably longer time, until they regain their tenderness.

In restaurants fish and sauces are refrigerated until final cooking. Although cooked in aluminum, all fish and sauces are stored in stainless-steel holding trays or bains-marie. (In the home it is advisable to remove the fish from the refrigerator a little beforehand to ensure even cooking.) Sauces are heated or created to order; the cooking of vegetables and other accompaniments is timed to coincide with the completion of the cooked fish and sauce.

Home Cooking Methods

Baking or bake-poaching. Many of the recipes in this book require baking in a hot oven set at between 400 and 450 degrees. The fish cooks quickly and is usually prevented from drying out by being wrapped or covered. When bake-poaching, moisture is held in by positioning the fish skin side up or by placing a lettuce leaf over the fish (a slightly wilted outer one that is discarded after the fish is cooked). Pouring white wine to a depth of ⅛ inch keeps the fish from sticking to the oven pan, as well as adding moisture and good taste. Other times the fish is wrapped in a lettuce leaf, grape leaves, parchment paper *(en papillote)*, phyllo pastry, or aluminum foil.

Boiling. Lobster, shrimp, and crawfish are boiled in liquids, using beer or wine and herbs and spices mixed with water. This "boil" is cooked for a few minutes before the fish are added. All shellfish require little cooking time.

Braising. Braising is a combination of cooking methods. First the fish is sautéed in oil or clarified butter and then a little liquid and other ingredients are added. It takes just a bit longer for the fish and other ingredients to cook and the flavors to develop. See the recipes for Ragout of Fish and Shellfish, and Monkfish and Fennel Tagine, on pages 278 and 200.

Broiling. Broiling tends to dry out fish; keeping the broiler at high heat, however, helps seal in the juices. Basting, marinating, and brushing with clarified butter or oil also help produce a flavorful moist fish. Be sure to preheat the broiler to ensure maximum heat. In my recipes I usually recommend pouring white wine to a depth of ⅛ inch into the broiler pan before adding the fish.

Broiling–Grilling on open fire. This popular cooking method, especially when done over charcoal mixed with a small amount of wood chips, vines, or stalks (previously soaked in water), such as cherry, hickory, corncob and sugar maple, mesquite, grape vines, or dried fennel stalks, is a fine way to cook firm-fleshed fish. When cooking a whole fish or fillets of a flaky fish, it is important to have an oiled two-sided hinged grill with handle to lay over the fire. The fire must be very hot and on its way out, and the fish drained of any marinade to prevent flare-ups and consequent burning.

Deep Frying. Although this is one of the commonest ways to prepare fish I do not always think it most satisfactory. However, many deep-fried dishes are delicious. A light coating of seasoned flour or batter keeps the fish from drying out. The quality and temperature of the oil are of utmost importance. I use Crisco vegetable oil with good results. When the oil has cooled, strain it through a double thickness of cheesecloth and store it in the same bottle. Throw it away when it grows dark or has been used two or three times. Peanut and safflower oil are equally good.

To control the temperature of the oil it is advisable to have an electric fryer or a fat and oil thermometer. Best deep-frying temperatures are between 350 and 375 degrees; it is important that the oil remains at a steady temperature when frying batches of fish.

Frying and sautéing. It is generally best to shallow-fry with clarified butter and/or oil. The fish is usually lightly coated with seasoned flour and/or cornflour. First sear the fish over medium to medium-high heat, then lower the heat to finish cooking.

Poaching. Very good results are obtained by poaching fish at a low simmer. There is a recipe for Poaching Liquid on page 304. The main component of the liquid is water, with wine and chopped vegetables added. Poaching can be done in a fish poacher with a lift-out tray, a large saucepan with shallow sides, or an oven pan with four-inch sides. For the last two, use a metal strainer with a flat bottom to cook the fish in.

Steaming. Steaming is done over water and/or wine and is a satisfactory though somewhat dull method of cooking fish. The fish retains its flavor perfectly, and it can be enlivened with seasonings and herbs. It is inadvisable to steam an oily fish, such as herring, sardines, or mackerel. Use a plate laid on a metal steamer placed in a saucepan of water; on a fold-out steamer over water in a saucepan; or inside a bamboo steamer over water in a wok. All of these need lids and the water should be kept at a medium boil.

Steam mussels and soft-shell (steamer) clams in a covered container with a little water and/or wine; the shellfish are ready when they open and have released their liquid.

Batterie de Cuisine

Although I do not expect that everyone will have all the utensils I use in my tiny New York City kitchen, I do recommend that you have most of the following list.

STOVETOP POTS, PANS AND CASSEROLES

1 large (18-quart) lobster pot with 2 looped handles and lid
1 large (8-quart) pot with 2 looped handles and lid
2 medium (2-quart) saucepans with handles and lids
1 metal steamer with lid to fit over 2-quart saucepan
1½-quart double boiler, or 1-quart bowl that will fit over medium saucepan
2 10-inch frying or sauté pans
1 8-inch frying or sauté pan
1 large heavy wok, 14 inches across the top
1 round casserole, 12 inches across the top, 2½ inches deep, preferably cast-iron and enamel-coated

OVEN AND BROILER PANS

1 baking pan, 15 × 11 inches, 3 to 4 inches deep
2 baking sheets, 16 × 11 inches, with ½-inch sides
broiler pan and rack
fish poacher (optional)

MOLDS AND PIE PANS

2 terrine molds with slanted sides, one 3 × 8½ inches and
    another 4½ × 9½ inches (bottom measurements)
1 10-inch metal pie pan with fluted edges
1 10-inch Pyrex pie plate
8 china (porcelain) ¾-cup ramekins, 3 inches in diameter and
    1½ inches high
8 oval metal timbale molds, 3¼ × 2 inches and 1½ inches
    high
2 muffin or tart pans, each containing 12 2½-inch-diameter
    molds
6 sea scallop shells available from fish stores, cooking utensil
    stores, or novelty stores
1 10-cup soufflé dish, preferably a Cousances (made in France
    of cast iron and covered with enamel) rather than the usual
    porcelain

BOWLS

assorted bowls, 1-quart to 4-quart capacity
mortar and pestle

STRAINERS

colander
1 metal strainer
1 fine tea strainer or 6-inch-diameter fine metal strainer
1 flat-bottom strainer for poaching
2 chinois (china caps), one coarse, with holes, and another
    fine, with fine mesh
sterile cheesecloth

MEASURING ITEMS

2 glass measuring pitchers, one 1-quart and another 2-cup
1 set of metal measuring cups for dry measuring

1 set of measuring spoons
1 fat and oil thermometer
1 Taylor Bi-Therm Pocket Dial Thermometer for internal heat
    measuring or 1 meat thermometer
1 weighing scale up to 10 pounds

SMALL APPLIANCES

1 blender
1 electric coffee grinder for grinding spices
1 food processor
meat grinder
pepper grinder
salad spin dryer

KNIVES

1 filleting knife, 6 to 8 inches long
1 chef's knife, 8 inches long
2 or 3 paring knives, 3½ to 4 inches long
1 meat cleaver
1 oyster shucking knife
1 clam shucking knife

MISCELLANEOUS

1 slotted spoon
1 large metal spoon
2 wooden spoons
1 soup ladle
2 wire whisks, large and small
1 large wooden fork
2 rubber spatulas
1 wide flat metal spatula for lifting and turning
2 garlic presses, 1 with very fine holes
1 stainless-steel smooth mallet
1 claw hammer
1 olive or cherry pitter (optional)
1 vegetable peeler or swivel-bladed vegetable scraper
1 fish scaler
1 stiff hand brush
1 lobster or nut cracker
1 pair small pin nose pliers
1 pair kitchen scissors

1 pair kitchen shears
1 nutmeg grater
1 ginger grater (optional)
1 grater with small holes for lemon or orange zest and cheese
1 can opener
1 juicer
1 pair snapper tongs
1 plain round pastry cutter, 4 inches in diameter
2 fluted round pastry cutters, one 4 inches and another 3½
   inches in diameter
2 pastry brushes, 1 inch and 1½ inches wide

Herbs, Spices, Condiments, and Other Supplies

Apart from the basics, like flour, butter, oil, vinegars, salt, and pepper, there are a number of items you will need to make these recipes.

When fresh herbs are not available, dried herbs are very useful although different in taste. Often dried herbs are stronger in flavor than fresh, and I advise you to taste the difference before using and to use lesser or greater amounts than I have specified, accordingly. Dried herbs gain in flavor as they cook, especially in liquids. I have indicated when fresh herbs are necessary to the recipe.

DRIED HERBS

basil
bay leaves
celery seeds
dill weed
marjoram
oregano
rosemary
tarragon
thyme

SPICES

When possible, I like to grind my own spices in an electric coffee grinder. This way they have fresher flavor and can be ground as fine or coarse as you desire. Black and white pepper, mace, coriander seeds, mustard seeds, and dried chili peppers (to make cayenne) all grind well. Coriander can be ground in a mortar and pestle and nutmeg should be ground with a nutmeg grinder or fine grater.

cayenne (ground dried chili peppers)
coriander seeds
curry powder
green peppercorns
mace
dry mustard
nutmeg
saffron threads
star anise
sweet paprika
white peppercorns

OTHER ITEMS

preserved (dry) black beans (available in Chinese grocery stores)
cornflour (available in health food stores)
coarse yellow cornmeal
Dijon mustard
frying oil (Crisco preferred)
olive oil
virgin olive oil
sesame oil
soy sauce
Tabasco
tomato paste
raspberry vinegar
red and white wine vinegars
Worcestershire sauce

WINE AND SPIRITS MOST OFTEN USED

cognac
Pernod or Ricard
dry white wine (inexpensive)
red wine
dry Vermouth (can be substituted for dry white wine; use a smaller quantity)

Hors d'Oeuvres

Cold Shrimp with Rouille

Broiled Butterflied Shrimp with Bacon,
Scallions, and Soy Sauce

Fried Goujonettes of Sole with Sauce Gribiche

Smoked Mackerel Phyllo Triangles

Smoked Haddock (Finnan Haddie) Tartlets

Deep-Fried Soft-Shell Clams

Salt Cod Beignets (Puffs)

Crab Critters

Conch Fritters

Anchovy and Cheese Straws

Cold Shrimp with Rouille

This dish is good served at a cocktail party or buffet. Large peeled and cooked shrimp draped en masse from a large glass bowl filled with ice—the look and taste are magnificent. Rouille makes a delicious dip for the shrimp.
SERVES 20

> about 6 pounds large shrimp (12 to 15 per pound), shell on
> 3 cans (4½ cups) light (not dark) beer
> 5 cloves garlic, very finely chopped
> 3 pinches cayenne

ROUILLE (2 CUPS)
> 2 cups thick Mayonnaise (page 286)
> 5 cloves garlic
> ¼ cup tomato paste
> 1 teaspoon saffron, steeped in ¼ cup dry white wine for 1 hour
> 10 drops Tabasco
> pinch cayenne

Peel and devein shrimp, leaving on the tails. In a large saucepan, bring the beer, garlic, cayenne, and enough water to cover the shrimp to a boil. Boil for 7 minutes, then add the shrimp. Boil until just cooked through, about 3 minutes. To make sure the shrimp are done, remove one and cut off the head end. The flesh should have lost its translucency and become opaque all the way through.

Now make the rouille. One by one, drop the garlic cloves into a food processor or blender, with the motor running, through the feed tube and process until very finely chopped. Add the remaining ingredients and process until thoroughly mixed.

To serve, fill a large glass bowl with ice cubes or crushed ice. Drape the shrimp over the edge, tails downward. Serve the rouille in a small bowl in the center of the shrimp or on the side.

Broiled Butterflied Shrimp with Bacon, Scallions, and Soy Sauce

These shrimp are a great favorite at large fancy cocktail parties. Be sure to provide receptacles for discarded tail shells. This avoids the situation at a garden party I catered in London, where the guests threw the tail shells onto the flowerbeds, much to the disgust and chagrin of the host. He requested one of my waiters to pick them out of the flowerbeds. The waiter replied, "What? And get my fingernails dirty?" My clients were lovely people but they had borrowed the house and garden from a very finicky man. And there lies more to this story! . . .

This recipe can be multiplied.

SERVES 4

1 pound medium to large shrimp (16 to 20 per pound), shell on
8 ounces sliced bacon, finely chopped
soy sauce to taste
superfine sugar to taste
freshly ground black pepper to taste
3 scallions, trimmed of their roots and some green leaves, finely
   chopped

Shell and devein the shrimp, leaving on the tails.

Butterfly the shrimp by cutting them nearly all the way through from the top. Spread the shrimp open and lay on a lightly oiled broiler pan. Sprinkle them with bacon bits, soy sauce, a little sugar, pepper, and scallions.

Preheat the broiler and broil the shrimp for 4 to 5 minutes, 3 inches from the broiler flame, until they are cooked through and the bacon is crisp.

Fried Goujonettes of Sole with Sauce Gribiche

Fillets of sole cut on the diagonal into thin strips, then lightly coated with seasoned flour and deep-fried, are called goujonettes —from the French word *goujon*, a tiny fish known in English as a gudgeon.

These are great to serve at a cocktail party, dipped into sauce gribiche, which is similar to a mayonnaise but highly flavored.

Goujonettes may also be served as an hors d'oeuvre or a main course.
SERVES 10 AS HORS D'OEUVRE OR APPETIZER; 5 OR 6 AS A MAIN COURSE

2¾ *pounds skinned fillets of gray sole or other sole or flounder (try to buy wide ones)*
1 *quart oil (Crisco preferred)*
2 *cups all-purpose flour*
1 *tablespoon salt*
1 *tablespoon freshly ground black pepper*
2 *pinches cayenne*
1 *recipe Sauce Gribiche (page 300)*

Feel for the tiny bones down the middle of each fillet. Cut closely down each side of these bones, removing and discarding them; you will end up with 4 fillets from each fish. Cut the fillets on a strong diagonal into strips ½ inch wide and 4 to 5 inches long.

Heat the oil in an electric deep-fryer, wok, or saucepan to 375 degrees.

Mix the flour, salt, pepper, and cayenne together in a medium bowl.

Preheat the oven to 200 degrees.

The goujonettes should be fried in batches. First put a handful of sole in the flour to coat well, then put in a sieve held above the bowl and shake off excess flour. Drop goujonettes into the hot oil and fry just over 1 minute. Remove and cut one goujonette in half; if it is opaque all the way through, it is cooked. Remove the others with a slotted spoon, drain on paper towels or a cloth, and keep in the warm oven while you fry the rest. Be sure the oil is at 375 degrees before adding the next batch.

Serve with sauce gribiche on the side.

Smoked Mackerel Phyllo Triangles

These crisp packets of phyllo pastry are delicious served hot. They are two-bite size and ideal with drinks or wine.

The paper-thin pastry, made by Greek bakeries, is used to make the popular dessert baklava as well as apple and cheese strudel.

Phyllo dough is sold rolled up in pound packages and is usually frozen. The frozen pastry has to defrost overnight in the refrigerator before you can use it. If defrosted at room temperature, the inside sheets tend to stick to each other.

These triangles can be prepared beforehand and reheated at serving time, or they can be frozen, cooked or uncooked, in plastic bags.

MAKES ABOUT 85 TRIANGLES

> 1¾ pounds smoked mackerel fillets
> 7½ ounces farmer's cheese (no salt added) or ricotta cheese
> juice of 2 lemons
> ¼ cup Mayonnaise (page 286)
> 1 teaspoon sweet paprika
> 1¼ pounds unsalted butter
> 2 pounds phyllo pastry leaves, each about 15 x 12 inches

Skin the mackerel and put the flesh in a bowl, removing the small bones from the center and sides of each fillet. Flake the fish with a fork, removing any bones you might have missed. Add the farmer's cheese or ricotta, lemon juice, mayonnaise, and paprika. Mix well with the fork.

Melt the butter in a saucepan over low heat. Remove the phyllo from package and unroll the leaves on a clean surface. Carefully place a sheet of phyllo with the longer side facing you on another clean surface. Keep the rest of the pastry covered with a slightly damp cloth. Lightly brush the pastry all over with melted butter, using a wide pastry brush. Lay another sheet on top and brush with butter; repeat until you have 4 layers.

With a sharp thin knife, cut the pastry into strips about 2½ inches wide and 12 inches long. You should have six strips. Place a teaspoon of the filling at the bottom of each strip. Fold one corner of the pastry over the filling, creating a triangle. Now fold the filled triangle up, alternating the folds from left to right keeping the triangular shape (like folding a flag).

Repeat with the other phyllo leaves and filling. Place the triangles, not too close together, on buttered baking sheets. Refrigerate the triangles for 15 minutes as you fill the baking sheets and before baking. If you do not have enough baking sheets to hold all the triangles at one time, stack the triangles in the refrigerator.

Preheat the oven to 375 degrees. Brush the tops of the triangles with more melted butter and bake until golden brown and crisp, 18 to 20 minutes. Serve hot.

Smoked Haddock (Finnan Haddie) Tartlets

These hot tartlets are a great favorite at cocktail parties. They are somewhat time-consuming to make, but the reward is great and they will disappear fast.

I think haddock smoked on the bone has better flavor than the boned smoked haddock. Smoked haddock on the bone is sometimes available at Macy's.

You will need two baking pans with 12 tartlet (muffin) molds 2½ inches in diameter each and a 4-inch round pastry cutter.

This recipe can be multiplied.

MAKES 24 TARTLETS

> 2¼ pounds smoked haddock (finnan haddie) on the bone, or 1½
>   pounds boneless smoked haddock
> 1½ cups milk, plus more as necessary
> 4 tablespoons (½ stick) unsalted butter
> 3 tablespoons all-purpose flour
> ¼ teaspoon freshly ground black pepper
> pinch cayenne
> 2 tablespoons finely grated Parmesan cheese
> 1 large egg
> 2 bottom-shell recipes Pastry (page 306).
> sweet paprika to taste

Preheat the oven to 375 degrees. Lay the haddock in a baking pan and pour the milk over. Bake for 20 minutes. Remove haddock to a plate and strain off the milk into a measuring pitcher. Add or pour off milk so that it measures 1½ cups.

When the haddock is cool enough to handle, pick off all the flesh from the bones and skin. Flake the flesh with a fork and discard any bones you may have missed.

Melt the butter in a saucepan over medium heat. Stir in the flour with a wire whisk and cook 30 seconds. Add the reserved milk and slowly whisk until the mixture thickens. Cook over low heat for another 2 minutes, stirring occasionally.

Put this mixture in a bowl, and add the flaked haddock, pepper, cayenne, and Parmesan. Lightly beat the egg and add to the mixture. Set aside.

On a lightly floured board, roll out the pastry ³⁄₁₆ inch thick and cut rounds with a 4-inch-diameter pastry cutter. Press the rounds into the molds and prick with a fork. Refrigerate for 15 minutes.

Adjust oven to 350 degrees. Bake the tartlets until they begin to brown, about 20 minutes. If the pastry has puffed up, press it back into shape while still warm.

When the tartlets are ready, fill with the smoked haddock mixture, sprinkle with a dash of paprika, and bake for another 15 minutes, until lightly browned.

These tartlets can be reheated, or frozen when they have cooled.

Deep-Fried Soft-Shell Clams

These delicious morsels, whose bellies burst with flavor in the mouth, are served in little roadside stands and large restaurants up and down the East Coast. The owners or chefs obtain the clams already shucked. To partake of these at home, you will have to learn how to shuck them, if you do not already know.
SERVES 6

36 (2¼ pounds) medium to large soft-shell clams (steamers)
¾ cup all-purpose flour
¼ cup cornflour (available in health food stores)
1 teaspoon salt
freshly ground white pepper to taste
2 teaspoons sweet paprika
2 large eggs, separated
1 cup light (not dark) beer
1 quart plus 1 tablespoon oil (Crisco preferred)
6 lemon wedges

Preparing unshucked soft-shell clams is a relatively simple operation. First, put them in a container and cover with cold water. Then rinse under running water, rubbing them with a plastic scouring pad. Soak in fresh lightly salted water for an hour, changing the water several times, so they rid themselves of sand.

Meanwhile, put the flour, cornflour, salt, pepper, and paprika in a medium bowl and stir well. Make a well in the mixture and into it put the egg yolks, beer, and 1 tablespoon oil. Gradually whisk the wet ingredients into the dry. Let stand for 1 hour.

To shuck the clams, insert a clam knife or sharp knife between the shells near both sides of the hinge and pry open. Loosen the clam from the shell, and remove it in one piece. Cut off the neck from each clam. Now you will see the belly with a ring of flesh around it. (This flesh is called the strip, and it sometimes is the only thing that is fried. However, I like the bellies better.) Put the clams in a bowl of cold water when they are shucked to further rid them of sand. Before frying them, dry them on three layers of paper towels with another piece of paper towel on top.

Preheat the oven to 200 degrees.

Heat the oil in an electric fryer, wok, or saucepan to 375 degrees. If you do not own a deep-frying thermometer, throw in a 1-inch cube of bread. If it sizzles and browns in 1 minute, the oil should be hot enough.

Beat the egg whites until stiff and fold into the batter. Coat the clams, one at a time, with the batter, letting the excess batter drip off before putting in the oil. Fry about 12 clams at a time until brown, about 1 minute on each side. Remove the fried clams and keep them warm in the oven while you fry the rest. Serve them as soon as possible with the lemon wedges.

Salt Cod Beignets (Puffs)

Not everyone likes salt cod, which is not necessarily salty but does have a strong and distinct flavor. It is especially popular in Portugal, Italy, France, Spain, and the West Indies. Be daring and unusual and serve these little beignets at your next party. You'll be surprised how many people will love the taste.

The beignets puff up in the hot oil and it is best to eat them hot. However, I have been known to serve them at room temperature when I wanted to come to my own party with all the food prepared beforehand.

MAKES ABOUT 50 BEIGNETS

1 pound salt cod
4 medium red skin potatoes (about ¾ pound), rinsed but not peeled
¾ cup milk, scalded and kept warm
5 cloves garlic, boiled in water until tender, 20 to 30 minutes
freshly ground white pepper to taste

¼ *cup olive oil*
3 *large eggs*
1 *quart oil (Crisco preferred)*

Cut the salt cod into pieces about 5 inches wide, put in a container, and soak overnight or in frequent changes of cold water for 4 hours.

Pour off the rinsing water. Put the fish in a medium saucepan, cover with cold water, and bring to a boil over medium heat. Lower the heat and simmer for 30 minutes, until the fish is tender. Drain.

Meanwhile, steam or boil the potatoes until tender, about 25 minutes.

When the fish is cool enough to handle, flake into a medium bowl, removing any skin or bones.

Peel the potatoes and rub through the fine mesh of a food mill into a saucepan. Stir in the milk, beating with a wooden spoon until you have a light and fluffy purée.

Purée the garlic cloves in a food processor or blender; add the flaked fish, potato purée, and pepper. Process this mixture for 30 seconds. With the motor running, add the olive oil in a steady stream through the feed tube. Then add 1 egg at a time, beating well after each addition.

Heat the oil in an electric deep-fryer, wok, or saucepan to 375 degrees. If you do not own a thermometer, throw in a 1-inch cube of bread and if it browns in 30 seconds you are ready to fry. Preheat the oven to 200 degrees.

Using a teaspoon, put 8 spoonfuls of the batter at a time into the hot oil. Turn the beignets as they puff up and become golden brown. Drain on paper towels and keep warm in the oven until all are cooked. Ideally they should be eaten right away, when still puffed up.

Crab Critters

These little fritters, which look like tiny crabs with legs sticking out, are a delight to serve at a cocktail party or as an appetizer.
MAKES ABOUT 35 TEASPOON-SIZE FRITTERS; SERVES 6 AS AN APPE-
TIZER

> 1 pound lump or back-fin crab meat, picked over and cartilage
>   removed
> 1 cup all-purpose flour
> 1½ teaspoons baking powder
> 1 large egg
> ½ cup milk
> 1 clove garlic, finely minced
> 3 tablespoons finely chopped fresh parsley
> ¼ cup fresh lemon juice
> 2 tablespoons Worcestershire sauce
> 8 drops Tabasco
> ½ teaspoon salt
> ¼ teaspoon freshly ground black pepper
> pinch cayenne
> 1 quart oil (Crisco preferred)
> 8 lime wedges

Sift the flour and baking powder into a medium bowl. Beat the egg with the milk and gradually whisk the egg mixture into the flour.

Add the crab meat, garlic, parsley, lemon juice, Worcestershire sauce, Tabasco, salt, pepper, and cayenne to the egg mixture and mix together. Let stand 10 minutes.

Meanwhile, heat the oil in an electric deep-fryer, wok, or sauce-pan to 375 degrees (or until a 1-inch cube of bread browns in 30 seconds' time). Preheat the oven to 200 degrees.

Drop 6 to 8 teaspoonfuls of the crab mixture into the oil and fry for a minute or 2, turning them over as they brown. When nicely browned, remove with a slotted spoon to a baking dish lined with 2 layers of paper towels. Keep warm in the oven while you fry the remaining critters. Remember that the oil must return to 375 degrees before frying the next batch. Serve hot with lime wedges.

Conch Fritters

Conch fritters are a great favorite in the Bahamas and Florida, particularly Key West. I present this recipe in the hope that the rest of the country can find precooked conch, which makes the recipe easier.

This produces a lot of fritters and is eminently suitable for a cocktail party. You can make them in advance and warm them in the oven before serving or serve them at room temperature. The recipe can be cut down to make fewer fritters.

MAKES ABOUT 60 TEASPOON-SIZE FRITTERS

2½ pounds conch, preferably precooked
1 cup all-purpose flour
2 teaspoons baking powder
1 large egg
1 cup milk
1 medium onion, finely chopped (¾ cup)
2 cloves garlic, finely minced
1 green bell pepper, stems, seeds, and ribs removed, finely chopped
1½ fresh, bottled, or canned jalapeño peppers, stems and seeds
  removed, finely chopped (1 tablespoon)
3 tablespoons finely chopped fresh parsley
1 teaspoon dried thyme
2 teaspoons salt
¼ teaspoon freshly ground black pepper
2 teaspoons sweet paprika
½ teaspoon red pepper flakes, ground in mortar with pestle
pinch cayenne
10 drops Tabasco
1 quart oil (Crisco preferred)
10 lime wedges

If the conch has not already been cooked, rinse and put in a saucepan of lightly salted water. Bring to the boil, reduce the heat, and cook until tender, 1½ hours. Drain and let cool.

Clean and trim the conch of tough skin as directed on page 31. Put the flesh through the fine cutting plate of a meat grinder.

Sift the flour and baking powder into a large bowl. Beat the egg with the milk and gradually whisk the mixture into the flour.

Add the ground conch meat and all the remaining ingredients, except, of course, the oil and lime. Mix thoroughly and let stand 10 minutes.

Meanwhile heat the oil in an electric deep-fryer, wok, or saucepan to 375 degrees. Preheat the oven to 200 degrees.

Put 6 to 8 teaspoonfuls of the conch mixture into the oil and fry for a minute or 2, turning them over as they brown. When they are nicely browned, remove with a slotted spoon to a baking dish lined with 2 layers of paper towels. Keep warm in the oven while you continue frying the rest. Remember that the oil must return to 375 degrees before frying the next batch.

Serve hot conch fritters with lime wedges.

Anchovy and Cheese Straws

If you like a sharp-tasting cheese straw, use Gruyère. Cheddar cheese produces a milder-tasting straw.
MAKES ABOUT 100 LITTLE STRAWS

4 ounces canned flat-filleted anchovies, drained
1¾ cups all-purpose flour
1 tablespoon dry mustard, or 2 tablespoons whole-grain mustard
2 pinches cayenne
1½ sticks (6 ounces) very cold unsalted butter, cut into 16 pieces
6 ounces Gruyère or sharp Cheddar cheese, finely grated
1 large egg, beaten with 3 tablespoons cold water

Mash or chop the anchovy fillets. Sift the flour with the dry mustard, if using, and cayenne into the bowl of a food processor. Add the butter and whole-grain mustard, if using. Process until the mixture resembles fine bread crumbs, 5 seconds. Add the anchovies and cheese and process for 3 seconds. With the motor running, add the egg and water through the feed tube and process until the dough gathers into a rough ball. Lift the dough out of the food processor and knead on a floured surface until smooth. Flatten the dough into a disk. Cover with plastic wrap and refrigerate for 1 hour.

Preheat the oven to 400 degrees.

Remove the dough from the refrigerator and let soften for a few minutes. Cut the dough into 4 pieces and shape each with your hands into a square or rectangle. Lightly flour a clean surface and roll out the dough ¼ inch thick. Cut into sticks ⅜ inch wide and 3 inches long.

Using a metal spatula, place the sticks slightly apart on ungreased baking sheets. Bake until golden brown, 8 to 12 minutes. Cool the cheese sticks on a cake rack. Stored in an airtight container, they will keep well for a week. They can also be frozen.

Note: If you would like to make larger twists, roll the dough a little thicker, cut the strips wider and longer, and twist before placing on the baking sheet.

Appetizers or First Courses

Artichokes Stuffed with Shrimp

Broiled Marinated Shrimp with Sweet Red Pepper Glaze

Shrimp with Remoulade Sauce—New Orleans Style

Potted Shrimp

Shrimp and Scallop Terrine with Lemon
and Dill Beurre Blanc

Scallop Gratin

Warmed Oysters with Orange Butter

Warmed Oysters with Crème Fraîche and Capers,
Garnished with Periwinkles

*Baby Abalone with Enoki Mushrooms
and Dill Beurre Blanc*

Clams on the Half Shell with Shallot and Wine Sauce

Broiled Clams with Sweet Red Pepper and Oregano

Clams Steamed in Foil

Sautéed Clams with Chive-Butter Toast

Lobster Flan with Avgolemono Sauce

Salmon Terrine with Watercress Sauce

Marinated Squid

*Calamari Fritti (Fried Squid) with Tomato and
Tarragon Sauce*

Sautéed Geoduck Clam

Hot Crab Timbales with Sorrel Cream Sauce

Cold Crab Timbales with Remoulade Sauce

Baked Crab with Gremolata

Mussels in Puff Pastry Cases with Saffron Cream Sauce

Baked Mussels with Garlic and Tomato Butter

Smoked Haddock (Finnan Haddie) Phyllo Triangles

*Roulade of Sole with Vermouth Cream Sauce and
Julienned Vegetables*

Gravad Lax of Coho Salmon with Mustard Dill Sauce

Smoked Trout and Horseradish with Avocado

Spinach Roulade with Smoked Trout Filling

Taramasalata

Layered Raw Fish with Pickled Ginger and Wasabi

Smoked Fish Plate with Cucumber and Ginger

Artichokes Stuffed with Shrimp

Artichokes are such fun to eat; dinner guests feel a camaraderie picking off the leaves and dipping them in melted butter or a vinaigrette, depending on whether they are served hot or cold. I give both versions here.
SERVES 6

> *¾ pound small shrimp (40 to 50 per pound), shelled*
> *6 large artichokes*
> *1 lemon, halved*
> *3 tablespoons oil*
> *6 lemon wedges*

> To SERVE HOT
> *3 sticks (12 ounces) unsalted butter*
> *2 teaspoons fresh thyme leaves, or ½ teaspoon dried thyme*
> *pinch salt*
> *freshly ground black pepper to taste*
> *4 tablespoons fresh lemon juice*

> To SERVE COLD
> *1 tablespoon Dijon mustard*
> *1½ cups olive oil*
> *2 teaspoons fresh thyme leaves, or ½ teaspoon dried thyme*
> *5 tablespoons fresh lemon juice*
> *1 tablespoon vinegar*
> *¾ teaspoon salt*
> *freshly ground black pepper to taste*

Cut off the stalks of the artichokes so they can stand up on a plate. Remove the bottom circle of leaves and cut ¾ inch from the top of the artichoke. Trim the points of the outer leaves with kitchen scissors. Rinse and rub all over with lemon halves, squeezing some of the juice into the centers of the artichokes.

Bring a large saucepan of salted water to the boil. Put the artichokes in upside down and pour the oil over them. Squeeze the remaining juice from the lemon halves over them and add the halves to the water. Bring to the boil. Very large artichokes take 40 to 45 minutes to cook, smaller ones take about 25 minutes. To test for doneness, pull off a leaf from the bottom of the artichoke and taste to see if flesh is tender. Drain the artichokes upside down for a few minutes. When cool enough to handle, remove the centers by pulling out some of the small leaves and using a teaspoon to scrape out the choke.

To serve hot. Melt 1½ sticks (6 ounces) butter in a frying pan over medium heat, add the thyme, shrimp, salt, pepper, and lemon juice, and cook the shrimp for just 2 minutes, turning occasionally. Stuff artichokes with equal portions of shrimp and pour the remaining butter- and lemon-sauce over all. Meanwhile melt the rest of the butter and pour around artichokes. Serve with lemon wedges.

To serve cold. Cook the shrimp in boiling water for 1 minute, drain, and let cool. Mix the mustard, oil, thyme, lemon juice, vinegar, salt, and pepper together with a wire whisk. Stir the shrimp into the vinaigrette and stuff artichokes with equal portions of shrimp; pour the remaining sauce over all.

Serve the stuffed artichokes with the lemon wedges on dinner plates, so your guests have somewhere to put the discarded leaves, with finger bowls on the side.

Broiled Marinated Shrimp with Sweet Red Pepper Glaze

Small shrimp really do not need to be shelled. If the shrimp are grilled over charcoal, the shells impart a wonderful flavor and are quite edible. Have finger bowls ready, however, in case your guests decide to peel them. If you prefer to eat shelled shrimp, shell them but don't bother to devein them, because the vein is negligible in small shrimp.

Start this dish the day before you plan to serve it, for the shrimp must marinate for 24 hours.

SERVES 6

1½ pounds small shrimp (36 to 40 per pound), shell on
1 cup olive oil
¼ teaspoon cayenne
1 tablespoon fresh thyme leaves, or 1 teaspoon dried thyme
1 recipe Sweet Red Pepper Glaze (page 270)

Mix together the oil, cayenne, and thyme in a bowl large enough to hold the shrimp. Add shrimp and marinate, covered and refrigerated, for 24 hours.

The next day, prepare the red pepper glaze.

Prepare a charcoal fire or preheat the broiler.

Broil the drained shrimp, turning after a minute or 2, until lightly browned and cooked through.

Serve with the warm glaze.

Shrimp with Remoulade Sauce—New Orleans Style

Shrimp served cold with this highly seasoned sauce is a popular item in New Orleans restaurants.
SERVES 4

20 (about 1 pound) medium to large shrimp, shell on

REMOULADE SAUCE (1⅓ CUPS)
  1 cup Mayonnaise (page 286)
  1 tablespoon Dijon mustard
  1 teaspoon dry mustard
  1 tablespoon prepared horseradish
  1 tablespoon tomato paste
  2 tablespoons fresh lemon juice
  1 tablespoon sweet paprika
  2 pinches cayenne
  salt to taste
  freshly ground white pepper to taste
  2 tablespoons very finely chopped chives or green part of scallions

  2 cans (3 cups) light (not dark) beer
  2 cloves garlic, very finely chopped
  pinch cayenne
  peeled and seeded cucumbers, cut into matchsticks

Make the remoulade. To the mayonnaise add the remaining sauce ingredients. Stir well and add a little hot (not boiling) water if the sauce is too thick—it should have the consistency of a thin mayonnaise.

Peel and devein the shrimp, leaving on the tails. Bring the beer, garlic, and cayenne to a boil in a medium saucepan. Boil for 7 minutes, then add the shrimp. When the liquid has returned to the boil, stir and cook for another 30 seconds. Drain immediately and let cool.

To serve, place the cucumber sticks in the middle of individual plates or a serving platter and arrange the shrimp decoratively around the edge. Spread the remoulade sauce over the shrimp or spoon the sauce around the cucumber sticks in a circle.

Potted Shrimp

This dish of English origin keeps well and can be eaten all year round. I especially enjoy it at Christmas time.

Already cooked and shelled tiny shrimp are available canned or frozen, and they make the work easy. Be sure they are quality shrimp and have some taste before working with them. In my experience the canned shrimp are usually tastier than the frozen, although somewhat salty.

SERVES 6

1 pound shelled and cooked minuscule shrimp, canned or frozen (see
*   headnote)*
3 sticks (12 ounces) unsalted butter
¼ teaspoon ground mace
½ teaspoon ground nutmeg
½ teaspoon cayenne
2 teaspoons salt
1 teaspoon freshly ground white pepper
8 tablespoons Clarified butter (page 304)

Drain shrimp if using canned, and pat dry with paper towels. Defrost shrimp if using frozen by running cold water over them for 1 minute; pat dry with paper towels.

Melt the butter in a medium saucepan over medium heat. When the butter begins to foam, stir in the mace, nutmeg, cayenne, salt, and pepper. Add the shrimp and turn them in the butter with a spoon. Let the butter bubble for 30 seconds.

Divide the mixture among 6 ¾-cup ramekins, or pour into a 5-cup serving dish with 2-inch-high sides. When the shrimp and butter mixture has cooled a little, put in the refrigerator to chill for 3 hours.

Melt the clarified butter and pour over the top, cover with plastic wrap, and refrigerate another hour.

Serve at room temperature with thinly sliced toasted brown bread.

Shrimp and Scallop Terrine with Lemon and Dill Beurre Blanc

This terrine is a favorite appetizer. It makes an elegant first course for a party of ten and is very easy to make.

See Note if you wish to prepare the terrine in advance.

SERVES 10

> 1 pound bay or sea scallops
> 1 pound shrimp, shelled and deveined
> 6 ounces skinned salmon fillet, bones removed with pin nose pliers
> 4 large egg whites
> 1¾ cups heavy cream
> pinch salt
> 1 bunch fresh dill weed
> 1¾ cups Beurre Blanc (page 289)
> 2 tablespoons fresh lemon juice

Preheat the oven to 350 degrees. Butter a terrine mold 9½ by 4 inches at the top and 3 inches deep. Also have ready a baking pan large enough to fit the terrine to act as a bain-marie.

If using sea scallops, cut the little muscle off the side of each. Process the scallops in a food processor or blender until almost smooth, about 1 minute. With motor running add 2 egg whites through the feed tube and process 15 seconds longer. Then pour in 1 cup heavy cream and process until you are sure mixture is smooth and airy, about 30 seconds. Transfer the scallop mixture to a medium bowl.

Process the shrimp in a food processor or blender for just 15 seconds. You want this mixture to be chunky. With the motor running add salt, the other 2 egg whites, and the remaining ¾ cup cream through the feed tube; process only briefly, as there is no need for this mixture to be smooth. The flecks of shrimp should stand out in the finished terrine.

Fold the shrimp mixture into the scallop mixture with a rubber spatula. Set aside.

Slice the salmon lengthwise ¼ inch thick.

Put half the shrimp and scallop mixture into the buttered mold. Cover with snippets of dill weed. Lay the salmon slices on top. Cover with the other half of the shrimp and scallop mixture and smooth the top with a spatula. Cut a piece of parchment paper to cover the top of the terrine and grease it with butter. Lay the paper on top of the terrine mixture. Cut a length of aluminum foil large enough to overlap the mold by 2 inches all around and butter the center of it. Lay it, buttered side down, over the parchment paper and fold the edges under to seal. Place the terrine mold in a baking pan and pour in hot water halfway up the sides of the terrine mold.

Bake until a meat thermometer inserted reads 140 degrees or the terrine feels firm and it has started to come away from the edges—45 minutes to 1 hour.

When the terrine is cooked, let it rest for half an hour and then unmold onto a plate.

For the sauce, make the beurre blanc and set aside in a warm place, uncovered. Pick small fronds of dill weed off the bunch to make ¾ cup. Set aside. In a frying pan reduce the lemon juice until nearly evaporated. Remove from the heat immediately, add the beurre blanc, and swirl around the pan to incorporate the lemon juice. Cover individual plates or one large serving platter with this sauce. Sprinkle the dill decoratively on the sauce, then slice the terrine and lay the slices on top of the sauce, allowing one per plate if using individual plates.

Note: If you choose to make the terrine in advance, wrap it in plastic wrap when it has cooled and refrigerate. You will need a little dry white wine and some lettuce leaves. Make the beurre blanc shortly before serving the terrine. Preheat the oven to 450 degrees. Pour white wine into a large baking pan to a depth of ⅛ inch. Slice the terrine, lay the slices on the wine, and cover with slightly wilted lettuce leaves (I use the outer leaves of a head of lettuce, which are often wasted) to keep in the moisture. Warm the terrine through in the preheated oven for 10 minutes. Remove the lettuce leaves, and with a wide metal spatula place the slices of terrine on the lemon and dill beurre blanc.

Scallop Gratin

This dish is very easily prepared, pretty to look at, and quickly cooked. A prerequisite: you must have 6 sea-scallop shells, which can be found in fish stores, cooking utensil stores, or novelty stores.

If you can locate scallops with their roe (coral), buy them. The dish looks and tastes even better with the pink-orange roe. You may substitute monkfish for the scallops if desired.

SERVES 6

> 1½ pounds sea scallops (preferably with their roe), or bay scallops, cleaned
> 1 stick (4 ounces) unsalted butter, melted
> 1 cup Fresh Bread Crumbs (page 308)
> 3 cloves garlic, finely chopped
> 4 tablespoons finely chopped fresh parsley
> juice of ½ lemon
> salt to taste
> freshly ground white pepper to taste

Preheat the oven to 400 degrees.

Brush a tablespoon of melted butter into each scallop shell. Sprinkle half the bread crumbs evenly among the shells.

If using sea scallops, cut off the small muscles on the side. Cut sea scallops (or, if using, monkfish) into ½-inch cubes. Put in a bowl with the rest of the melted butter, garlic, parsley, lemon juice, salt, and pepper. Mix together and divide among the scallop shells. Sprinkle with the remaining bread crumbs, place shells on a baking sheet, and bake for 10 minutes. Serve immediately.

Warmed Oysters with Orange Butter

This dish is very popular with restaurant customers. It is unusual, easy to prepare and will delight your guests in no time at all.
SERVES 4

> 24 oysters
> 1 bunch watercress, stemmed and finely chopped
> 12 to 16 chicory leaves, washed, dried, and trimmed about 3½ inches
>   long
> 1½ cups fresh orange juice
> 1½ cups Beurre Blanc (page 289)
> 8 orange segments (Cut off all peel and pith from an orange. Use a
>   sharp thin knife to cut down against the inside of the membrane of
>   each segment. Then cut against the membrane on the left side of
>   each segment and, without removing the knife, turn the blade up
>   against the membrane on the right side, releasing it.)

Shuck the oysters (see page 44) and leave on the half shell, reserving the juice for another purpose. Place a teaspoon of chopped watercress at one end of each oyster. Arrange a few chicory leaves fanned out from the center on individual serving plates.

Preheat the oven to 400 degrees.

Ten minutes before putting the oysters in the oven, begin reducing the orange juice in a medium frying pan over medium high heat until ¼ cup remains. The juice should be thick and syrupy. (This should be timed to coincide with warming through the oysters.)

Put the oysters in a shallow baking pan or on a baking sheet and heat in the oven for 3 to 4 minutes, until they are warm and slightly puffed up.

Add the beurre blanc to the reduced orange juice and stir well. Place 6 oysters on each serving plate and spoon the orange butter onto each oyster. Serve immediately, each plate garnished with 2 orange segments.

Warmed Oysters with Crème Fraîche and Capers, Garnished with Periwinkles

This tasty dish is wonderful-looking and satisfying.
SERVES 4

> 28 (about 4 ounces) periwinkles (page 45)
> 24 oysters
> 5 tablespoons drained nonpareil (small) capers
> 1½ cups crème fraîche (available in specialty stores, or make your own)
> 20 chicory leaves, rinsed, dried, and trimmed

Wash the periwinkles in cold water. Half fill a small saucepan with cold water. Add the periwinkles and bring to the boil. Boil for 3 minutes and drain. Remove the tiny thin foot from each periwinkle with the point of a small sharp knife.

Shuck the oysters and place (on the half shell) on a baking sheet.

Preheat the oven to 425 degrees.

Mix the capers with the crème fraîche and put in a small frying pan.

Place 5 chicory leaves on individual plates in a starlike fashion.

Heat the oysters in the oven for 4 minutes, until they plump up. At the same time warm the crème fraîche and capers over very low heat, only until the crème fraîche melts.

Arrange the oysters in between the chicory leaves and spoon equal amounts of crème fraîche and capers onto each oyster. Place a periwinkle between each oyster and one in the middle of each plate.

Give your guests small forks and spoons to eat this dish with. The spoons are for the oysters and their sauce, the small forks to extract the periwinkles from their shells.

Baby Abalone with Enoki Mushrooms and Dill Beurre Blanc

If you are ever near Port Hueneme, California, give John Mc-Mullen a call, for he is the man who farms baby abalone.

They are about 1½ inches in length and take eighteen months to grow to that size.

They are a great delicacy and the shells are the prettiest things you will ever see. John supplies Chef Michael Hutchings with baby abalone. Michael is chef-owner of Michael's Waterside Inn at Santa Barbara in association with the Roux Restaurants of London. Michael has handled abalone for years, and the following recipe is a version of one of his.

Michael notes that shrimp make an elegant substitute for the abalone.

SERVES 4

> *16 baby abalone*
> *¾ cup all-purpose flour*
> *salt to taste*
> *freshly ground white pepper to taste*
> *1½ cups Beurre Blanc (page 289)*
> *1 teaspoon lemon juice*
> *1 medium tomato, peeled, seeded and cut in ¼ inch dice (½ cup) and*
> *drained*
> *1 package enoki daki mushrooms (3½ ounces) chopped in half*
> *1 bunch fresh dill weed*
> *8 tablespoons Clarified Butter (page 304)*
> *4 large eggs, well beaten*
> *4 plum tomatoes, made into roses (see Note)*
> *3 to 4 ounces golden caviar*

Remove the abalone from their shells by running a small knife between meat and shell. Remove the intestines and cut off the head, located in the front area. Scrape the dark edge. Place the abalone between two moist tea towels and lightly pound to even them out.

Mix the flour, salt, and pepper in a bowl.

Stir lemon juice, diced tomato, mushrooms, and 2 tablespoons chopped dill into the beurre blanc. Set aside.

Preheat the oven to 200 degrees.

Heat the clarified butter in a large frying or sauté pan over medium high heat. Coat the abalone first with the flour mixture and then with the beaten eggs. Fry them in batches for 5 to 10 seconds on each side and drain on paper towels. Keep them warm in the oven while you finish frying the remaining abalone.

Spoon the beurre blanc onto individual plates. Place 4 cooked abalone on top and garnish with dill sprigs and tomato roses. Fill the abalone shells with a little golden caviar and arrange around the abalone.

Note: Holding a tomato upright, cut a wide but thin strip of peel, starting at the bottom of the tomato. Continue cutting the strip, which will become less wide as you reach the top of the tomato. Twist the peel into a roselike shape with the wider end of the peel on the outside.

Clams on the Half Shell with Shallot and Wine Sauce

This sauce provides a nice piquant contrast to the sweetness of the clams.
SERVES 4

24 *littleneck or cherrystone clams, cleaned (page 28)*

SHALLOT AND WINE SAUCE
3 cups dry white wine
8 shallots (6 ounces) finely chopped
salt to taste
½ teaspoon freshly ground black pepper
1 head of chicory, rinsed, dried, and trimmed
2 tablespoons very finely chopped parsley

Open the clams and catch the juice in a bowl and reserve. Loosen the clam from both top and bottom shells. Discard the top shell, leaving the clam in the bottom shell. Cover with plastic wrap and refrigerate.

Put the wine, shallots, and ½ cup reserved clam juice (strained through a fine chinois or strainer) in a medium frying pan. Cook over medium heat until reduced to 1 cup, about 45 minutes. Stir in a little salt and the pepper. Pour into a bowl and cool as quickly as possible in the refrigerator or over ice.

To serve, place the clams on a bed of chicory leaves and spoon a little sauce onto each clam. Sprinkle each clam with a pinch of chopped parsley.

Broiled Clams with Sweet Red Pepper and Oregano

SERVES 4

> 24 littleneck or cherrystone clams, cleaned (page 28)
> 2 sweet red peppers, stems, seeds, and ribs removed, halved
> 1 clove garlic
> 2 tablespoons fresh oregano leaves
> 2 sticks (8 ounces) unsalted butter, softened
> salt to taste
> freshly ground black pepper to taste
> juice of 1 lemon
> 20 to 24 arugula leaves

Preheat the oven to 500 degrees. Place the red peppers, skin side up, on a baking dish and roast for 20 minutes, or until the skin is slightly blackened.

Remove from the oven and, when they are cool enough to handle, remove and discard the skin and coarsely chop. Put the garlic in the food processor or blender with the oregano leaves and process until finely chopped. Add the softened butter, salt, pepper, and lemon juice and process until light and airy. Lastly add the red peppers and process only for a few seconds—you do not want to purée them. Put the sauce aside. If you want to prepare this beforehand, cover and refrigerate.

When ready to serve, remove the red pepper butter mixture from the refrigerator and let soften to spreading consistency. Shuck the clams, loosening them from their shells, discarding the top shell, and leaving the clams in the bottom shell. Pour off the clam juice and reserve for another use.

Spread a tablespoon of red pepper butter atop each clam. (This can be accomplished beforehand and refrigerated, covered with plastic wrap.)

Preheat the broiler. Put the clams in a broiler pan and broil for just 5 minutes.

Arrange arugula leaves on individual plates, with the clams on top.

Clams Steamed in Foil

This dish is fun to cook over a charcoal fire. The aroma when you open the foil is fabulous.

The clams can also be baked in an oven if you wish. See Note at the end of the recipe.

SERVES 4

32 littleneck or small cherrystone clams, cleaned (page 28)
1 medium onion, finely chopped (1 cup)
2 green bell peppers, stems, seeds, and ribs removed, finely chopped
4 cloves garlic, finely chopped
4 tablespoons fresh parsley, finely chopped
4 slices bacon, fried until crisp and crumbled
½ cup fresh lemon juice

Cut 8 pieces of heavy aluminum foil into 15-inch squares. Use 2 pieces for each portion. Place 8 clams on each double thickness of foil, then sprinkle equal amounts of chopped onion, green pepper, garlic, parsley, bacon, and lemon juice over the clams. Fold the foil over the clam loosely, to give the clam shells room to open. Fold the edges of the foil together several times to seal properly.

When the charcoal fire is ready, place the bundles on a grate above the fire and cook for 20 to 25 minutes, until the clams open. You can unfold one of the bundles and peek inside to check.

Note: The clam bundles can be baked on baking sheets in a 450-degree oven for the same length of time.

Sautéed Clams with Chive-Butter Toast

In Portugal, the restaurants serve heaps of tiny clams *(amêijoas)* briefly sautéed in garlic, a little oil, and wine until the shells open. In the United States make this dish with the smallest clams you can find.
SERVES 4

> *30 very small littleneck clams, cleaned (page 28)*
> *¼ cup finely chopped chives*
> *1 stick (4 ounces) unsalted butter, softened*
> *1 loaf semolina bread (available in Italian or specialty stores), or 1*
>   *loaf French bread*
> *¼ cup olive oil*
> *8 cloves garlic, finely minced*
> *1 cup dry white wine*

Mix together chives and butter and set aside.

Cut the bread into ½-inch-thick slices.

Heat the oil in a large frying pan or shallow casserole over medium heat. Add the garlic and clams; swirl around and turn in the oil for 1 minute. Add the wine, cover with a loose-fitting lid, and cook just until all the clams open.

In the meantime, toast the bread and spread with the chive butter.

To serve, arrange some of the toast on a warmed serving platter or on individual plates and pour the clams and juice over. Serve immediately with extra toast on the side for mopping up the juices.

Lobster Flan with Avgolemono Sauce

This amazing flan is very simple to make and so rich that only one small slice per person is needed for an appetizer.
SERVES 8

1 3-pound lobster or 3 1-pound lobsters
2 cups heavy cream
1 recipe Avgolemono Sauce (page 299)
tarragon sprigs or fennel fronds

Refer to page 261 for how to obtain raw lobster meat. Omit beer.

Simmer the heavy cream in a frying pan or sauté pan over low heat until reduced by half, to 1 cup.

Measure out a piece of foil to cover the bottom and long sides of a greased terrine mold 8½ by 3 inches and 3 inches high and line it to facilitate the removal of the flan from the mold. Don't bother to line the ends.

Preheat the oven to 350 degrees.

Put the raw lobster meat in the bowl of a food processor or blender and process until the flesh becomes a bright pinky orange and is very smooth. This takes 3 to 5 minutes. Pour in the heavy cream while the motor is running and blend well. Using a rubber spatula transfer the mixture to the terrine mold. The mixture will only come up 1½ to 2 inches.

Place the terrine mold uncovered, in a baking pan that will accommodate it and pour in hot water halfway up the sides of the mold.

Bake for 25 to 30 minutes; the flan should have come away slightly from the sides of the mold. Remove the mold from the pan and let cool for 15 minutes. Then, carefully lifting the edges of the foil, take the flan out of the mold and turn onto a warm plate.

The preparation of the flan may be done in advance. Wrap it in plastic wrap when it is cold and refrigerate. Before serving, have ready the avgolemono sauce and preheat the oven to 400 degrees. Pour dry white wine ⅛ inch deep into a baking pan and place the whole flan or 1-inch slices of the flan in the wine. Bake in the oven 5 minutes or until heated through. The flan may be served whole, from a warmed platter, or on individual plates. In either case, pour sauce to the side and garnish with tarragon sprigs or fennel fronds.

Salmon Terrine with Watercress Sauce

This is simple to make, besides being elegant and tasty. The terrine is enclosed in a vegetable aspic and served with a watercress sauce.

You will need two terrine molds, one slightly smaller than the other: one 3 by 8½ inches on the bottom, 3 inches high, and another 4½ by 9½ inches (bottom measurements), 4 inches high. SERVES 8 TO 10

1½ pounds skinned salmon fillet, small bones removed with pin nose
  pliers
2 ounces salmon roe
3 carrots, scraped and thinly sliced
3 celery stalks, trimmed and coarsely chopped
1 small onion, coarsely chopped (½ cup)
1¼ teaspoons salt
1½ cups heavy cream
1 large egg plus 2 large egg whites
freshly ground white pepper to taste
6 tablespoons chopped fresh dill weed
2 packets (5 teaspoons) unflavored gelatin
1 bunch watercress
1 recipe Watercress Sauce (page 299)

Put the carrots, celery, and onion in a medium saucepan with 5 cups of cold water and ½ teaspoon salt. Bring to a boil over medium high heat, then lower the heat and simmer for 35 minutes. Set aside.

Preheat the oven to 350 degrees.

Whip the cream until thick. Set aside. Cut the salmon into 1½-inch cubes and put into a food processor or blender. Process until creamy and smooth, about 3 minutes. With motor running add the whole egg through feed tube and process briefly, then gradually add the egg whites followed by ¾ teaspoon salt and the pepper. Transfer this mixture to a bowl and fold in the salmon roe, 3 tablespoons dill weed, and then the whipped cream. Taste for seasoning.

Butter a piece of parchment paper and use it to cover the bottom and long sides of the smaller terrine mold. Butter the ends of the mold. Spoon the salmon and cream mixture into the mold. Cut a piece of parchment paper to cover the top of the terrine and grease it with butter. Lay the paper on top of the terrine mixture. Cut a length of foil large enough to overlap the mold by 2 inches all around and butter the center of it. Lay it, buttered side down, over the parchment paper and fold the edges under to seal. Place the terrine mold in a baking pan and pour in hot water halfway up the sides of the terrine mold.

Bake until a meat thermometer inserted reads 140 degrees or the terrine feels firm and it has started to come away from the sides, 45 to 50 minutes. Let cool for 20 minutes at room temperature, then refrigerate another 20 minutes.

In the meantime, strain the vegetable stock into a bowl and add the gelatin, whisking to mix thoroughly. Heat the bowl of stock over a saucepan of gently simmering water until the gelatin has dissolved. (You can tell by stirring with a metal spoon and looking to see if any granules are left on the spoon.) Let cool a little and then add the rest of the dill.

Pour the stock into the large terrine mold to a depth of ⅝ inch and place in the freezer to gel quickly. This should take about 20 minutes. By now the terrine can be unmolded. Slip a thin knife between the edge of the terrine and the mold at each end and turn upside down onto a cutting board. Remove the parchment paper.

Invert the larger mold of gelled vegetable stock over the unmolded terrine, then reverse the procedure so the board is covering the large mold. Remove the board, then pour in more of the stock around the edges up to the top of the mold and put in the freezer until it gels. Chill the terrine in the refrigerator until serving time.

To serve, warm the outside of the terrine mold with a damp hot towel or cloth. Place a serving dish on top and then invert so the terrine comes out of the mold.

Garnish with watercress sprigs and serve with watercress sauce.

Marinated Squid

I like to serve this as a first course in my home. It reminds me of the bounteous cold tables in Italian restaurants, where one can choose hors d'oeuvres from a large variety of cold cooked foods.
SERVES 6

> *3 pounds squid (heads and tentacles included), cleaned (page 53)*
> *zest of 1 lemon, removed in thin strips with a vegetable peeler*
> *¼ cup olive oil*
> *3 cloves garlic, finely chopped*
> *10 basil leaves, rinsed if necessary and dried*
> *salt to taste*
> *freshly ground black pepper to taste*
> *6 tablespoons fresh lemon juice*
> *1 head lettuce*
> *12 small radicchio leaves (optional)*

Cut the squid tentacles away from the heads and pop out the little round beaks. Also trim the longer tentacles. Slice the squid into thin, ⅛-inch rounds.

Cut the lemon zest into very fine slices.

Heat the oil in a large frying pan over medium high heat. Add some garlic and some squid. They need plenty of room and only a minute to cook; overcooking will toughen them. Cook until they turn from a translucent to an opaque white, with a purplish tinge. Quickly transfer the squid with a slotted spoon to a serving dish. Repeat with the rest of the garlic and squid.

Add the basil, lemon zest, salt, pepper, lemon juice, and the remaining oil and garlic. Toss together.

Leave to cool, turning the squid every now and again.

Serve at room temperature, on a small bed of lettuce and radicchio leaves.

Calamari Fritti (Fried Squid)
with Tomato and Tarragon Sauce

When I was living in Greece, many years ago, we wouldn't eat squid if they were any longer than the first joints of our thumbs. These baby squid, called *kalamaraki*, are simply delicious briefly deep-fried whole. In the United States usually only the larger variety are available. My method of cutting them into very thin rings and deep-frying them results in a dish that runs a very close second to those delectable tiny squid I knew in Greece.

SERVES 8 AS AN APPETIZER; 4 AS A MAIN COURSE

> 4 pounds squid (heads and tentacles removed and reserved) cleaned
>   (page 53)
> 2½ cups Tomato Coulis (page 298), using 2-pound, 3-ounce can of
>   tomatoes
> 2 tablespoons fresh tarragon leaves, or 1 tablespoon dried tarragon
> ¾ cup heavy cream
> 1 bunch parsley, rinsed and dried
> 1 quart oil (Crisco preferred)
> 1½ cups all-purpose flour
> 1½ teaspoons salt
> ½ teaspoon freshly ground white pepper
> 1 tablespoon sweet paprika
> pinch cayenne
> 8 lemon wedges

Put the heads and tentacles in a medium saucepan and add 2 cups of cold water. Bring to a boil, lower the heat, and boil gently for 30 minutes.

Strain off the stock and reserve, discarding the heads and tentacles. Put the stock, tomato coulis, and tarragon leaves into a medium saucepan and boil gently for 30 minutes. Add the cream and continue to cook for another 15 minutes, until stock and liquids have reduced and the sauce has thickened. Set aside.

Cut the squid across the body into very thin rounds, ¼ inch wide. Separate the parsley into 3-inch-long sprigs, being sure they are completely dry.

Heat the oil in an electric deep-fryer, wok, or saucepan to 375 degrees. Preheat the oven to 200 degrees.

Mix together the flour, salt, pepper, paprika, and cayenne in a medium bowl.

The squid should be fried in batches. First put a handful of squid in the flour and coat well. Then transfer to a sieve over the bowl and shake off excess flour. Drop squid into the hot oil for barely a minute. Remove the squid rings quickly, drain on a cloth or paper towels, and keep warm in the oven while you fry the rest. Be sure the temperature of the oil has returned to 375 degrees before frying the next batch of squid. Last, fry the parsley sprigs for just a few seconds, until they turn a dark green.

Serve the squid on a warmed serving platter or individual plates with the fried parsley on top. Pour some warm sauce on the side and arrange the lemon wedges around the edge.

Sautéed Geoduck Clam

If you are not familiar with geoduck, read the instructions for preparing it. The flesh must be sliced and tenderized, but then it cooks in just a few seconds.
SERVES 6

1 geoduck clam (about 3 pounds)
4 tablespoons Clarified Butter (page 304)
2 tablespoons freshly grated ginger
1 clove garlic, finely minced
4 scallions, finely chopped
¼ teaspoon hot sesame oil
2 tablespoons fresh lime juice

Prepare the geoduck as directed on page 29. Detach the siphon from the strip and trim off the tip; then cut the siphon into 1¼-inch-thick slices. Cut the slices lengthwise but not all the way through. You will see that the siphon is hollow like a pipe. Spread the pieces open and tenderize gently with a smooth mallet. They will look a little like butterflies. Cut the strip into the same size slices and tenderize them as well.

Heat the clarified butter in a large frying, sauté pan, or wok over medium high heat. Add the pieces of geoduck and the ginger. Sauté, stirring, for 10 seconds. Turn the pieces and cook 10 seconds longer. Remove to a warm serving platter or individual plates and add the remaining ingredients to the pan. Sauté, stirring constantly, for 2 minutes; then shake the ingredients of the pan together and pour over the geoduck.

Hot Crab Timbales with Sorrel Cream Sauce

Little oval timbale molds are lined with blanched lettuce leaves and a smooth crab forcemeat mixed with chopped water chestnuts is added. They are baked in a bain marie and unmolded atop a warm creamy sorrel sauce. This makes a very pretty appetizer.

You will need eight 3-inch-long oval metal timbale or dariole molds.

SERVES 8

> 1 pound lump or back-fin crab meat, picked over and cartilage
>   removed
> 8 small leaves green-leaf lettuce
> 10 water chestnuts
> pinch salt
> 1 tablespoon sweet paprika
> 1 tablespoon Dijon mustard
> 1 large egg, plus 1 egg yolk.
> 1¼ cups heavy cream
> 2 tablespoons chopped fresh dill weed
> 1 recipe Sorrel Cream Sauce (page 296)

Blanch the lettuce leaves in boiling water for 5 seconds. Refresh in a bowl of cold water and then dry on paper towels or a cloth.

Butter the molds. Cut 2 of the water chestnuts into 4 thin slices each and place a slice in the bottom of each mold. Chop the rest of the water chestnuts into ¼-inch cubes and set aside. Line the molds with the lettuce leaves.

Preheat the oven to 350 degrees.

Put the crab meat, salt, paprika, and mustard into a food processor or blender and process until smooth, about 2 minutes. Add the egg yolk and process until blended. Add the egg and process again. With the motor running, slowly pour in 1 cup of the cream through the feed tube. Transfer the mixture to a bowl and fold in the chopped water chestnuts and dill weed. Fill the timbale molds with this mixture and smooth the tops. Place the molds on a baking pan with ½-inch edges and pour hot water to halfway up the sides. Bake for 30 minutes.

Gently reheat the sorrel cream sauce over low heat.

When the timbales are done, take them out of the oven and trim the tops so that they are flat. Pour the sorrel cream sauce onto small individual plates and unmold the timbales onto the sauce. (If the slices of water chestnut have stuck to the bottom of the molds, retrieve them and place on top of the crab timbales.) Serve right away.

Cold Crab Timbales with Remoulade Sauce

You will need eight ¾-cup ramekins, 3 inches in diameter, as molds for the crab meat.
SERVES 8

1 pound lump or back-fin crab meat, picked over and any cartilage removed
2 teaspoons unflavored gelatin
⅓ cup fresh lime juice
2 stalks celery, very finely chopped
2 tablespoons Dijon mustard
2 tablespoons chopped fresh parsley
5 drops Tabasco
1 cup Mayonnaise (page 286)
salt to taste
freshly ground white pepper to taste
8 sprigs parsley
1 recipe Remoulade Sauce (page 91)
8 slices tomato, cut in half

Dissolve the gelatin in the lime juice in a bowl over simmering water. You can tell the gelatin has dissolved by stirring with a metal spoon and looking to see if any granules are left on the spoon.

In a medium bowl, mix together the crab meat, celery, mustard, parsley, and Tabasco. In another bowl, stir the gelatin and lime juice into the mayonnaise. Add this mixture to the crab meat and season with salt and pepper. Mix well.

Place a parsley sprig at the bottom of each ramekin (see head-note). Spoon the crab meat mixture into the ramekins, cover with plastic wrap, and chill in the refrigerator for 4 hours.

To serve, unmold the crab meat from the ramekins by warming the outsides with a hot damp cloth and slipping a thin knife around the edges. Arrange the timbales on individual plates, with a generous tablespoon of remoulade sauce on the side and each garnished with 2 half slices of tomato.

Baked Crab with Gremolata

Gremolata is a lovely Italian mixture of parsley, garlic, and lemon zest that is sprinkled over osso bucco and veal marengo. Here, I have added orange zest to the mixture.

This dish can also be made with monkfish, tilefish, or bay scallops.

SERVES 8 AS AN APPETIZER

> 1 pound lump or back-fin crab meat, picked over and any cartilage
>   removed
> ¾ cup fresh finely chopped parsley
> 3 cloves garlic, finely chopped
> finely grated zest of 1 orange
> finely grated zest of 2 lemons
> pinch cayenne
> 1½ sticks (6 ounces) unsalted butter, melted
> juice of 1 lemon

Preheat the oven to 425 degrees.

Break up the crab meat in a medium bowl. In another bowl, toss the parsley, garlic, orange and lemon zests together to make the gremolata. Add the gremolata to the crab with the cayenne and melted butter.

Have ready 8 sea-scallop shells or small casserole dishes and divide the crab mixture evenly among them. Bake for 10 minutes and squeeze lemon juice onto the crab meat before serving.

Mussels in Puff Pastry Cases with Saffron Cream Sauce

SERVES 6

3 pounds mussels (cultivated preferred), cleaned (page 42)

CREAM SAUCE (2 CUPS)
1 cup dry white wine
5 shallots, finely chopped
5 cloves garlic, finely chopped
1½ cups heavy cream

1 pound Puff Pastry (page 307), or 1 pound frozen prepared puff
  pastry (Saucier makes a good one), thawed 4 hours in the
  refrigerator
1 large egg yolk, beaten with 1 tablespoon water
1 teaspoon saffron, steeped in ¼ cup dry white wine for 1 hour

To make the sauce, pour the wine into a medium saucepan and add the shallots and garlic. Bring to a boil over high heat. Lower the heat and simmer over medium heat for 7 minutes. Add the mussels and cover the pan. Raise the heat and cook until the mussels open, about 5 minutes. Strain through a fine strainer or chinois, reserving the mussel juice and the mussels separately.

Pick 36 nice plump mussels from their shells and remove any beards you find. Put them in a covered bowl and refrigerate.

Cook the heavy cream in a frying pan over low heat until reduced to 1 cup. Cook the mussel juice in a saucepan or frying pan over medium heat until reduced to ¾ cup.

Whisk the reduced mussel juice into the cream and strain through a fine sieve or chinois. Set aside.

Preheat the oven to 350 degrees.

Take 2 round fluted pastry cutters (one measuring 4 inches in diameter and the other 3½ inches in diameter) and bend them into oval shapes. The larger one should be 4¼ inches long by 3½ inches wide, and the smaller cutter should measure 3¾ inches long by 2¾ inches wide.

Roll out the pastry ¼ inch thick on a floured board. Using the larger cutter, cut 6 pastry ovals and then, using the smaller cutter, make an impression halfway through each pastry oval, leaving a ¼-inch rim. This will create a lid for the pastry case.

Beginning at the center and going outward, brush each oval lightly with beaten egg yolk; avoid getting the beaten egg yolk into the cut or on the outside, ¼-inch rim of the pastry because this will prevent the pastry from rising properly. Make 3 or 4 light crisscross cuts in the center of each pastry oval with a sharp thin knife. Place the pastry ovals 1 inch apart on a baking sheet that has been lightly brushed with water. Bake until they have risen nicely and are golden brown, about 20 minutes. Cool on a wire cake rack. When they are cool enough to handle, cut the lid away from each case with a sharp thin knife. Pull out and discard the partially cooked pastry underneath. Reserve the lids.

The sauce and the pastry cases may both be prepared beforehand.

When ready to serve, stir the saffron mixture into the cream sauce. Heat the mussels in the sauce while warming the pastry cases in a 200-degree oven. Put the pastry cases on warmed individual serving plates, spoon 3 or 4 mussels with some sauce into each case, and top each case with a lid. Serve the remaining mussels and sauce on the side.

Baked Mussels with Garlic and Tomato Butter

This is a wonderful way to use any left-over cooked mussels (as from Mussel Bisque on page 150).
SERVES 6

48 mussels (cultivated preferred) (about 4 pounds), cleaned (page 42)
5 cloves garlic
3 sticks (12 ounces) unsalted butter, softened
juice of 1 lemon
½ teaspoon salt
6 tablespoons finely chopped fresh parsley
1 medium tomato, skinned, seeded, and cut into ¼-inch cubes (page 305), drained 1 hour
2 cups dry white wine
lemon curls (Thinly slice a lemon, then make a cut from the center of each slice outward; twist slice into a curl.)
1 bunch mâche (lamb's lettuce) or arugula, rinsed and dried

Put the garlic cloves in a food processor or blender and process until very finely chopped, about 30 seconds. Add the butter and process until light and airy. Add the lemon juice and salt and process for a few seconds until thoroughly mixed. Transfer the garlic butter to a bowl and fold in the parsley and tomato. Cover with plastic wrap and set aside.

Put the mussels and wine in a large saucepan. Cover and bring to boil. Boil until all the mussels open, 5 to 8 minutes. Take the saucepan off the heat and immediately strain the broth from the mussels, reserving broth for another use.

When the mussels are cool enough to handle, pick them out of their shells, saving one half shell for each mussel. Remove the beards and place each mussel in a half shell.

Using a spreading knife, spread the garlic and tomato butter over the mussels. Place them on a baking sheet. You may cover them with plastic wrap at this point and refrigerate until ready to bake.

Preheat the oven to 450 degrees. Bake the mussels until bubbling hot, about 7 minutes.

To serve, place on a serving platter or individual plates and garnish with lemon curls and mâche or arugula.

Smoked Haddock (Finnan Haddie) Phyllo Triangles

I used to serve these phyllo triangles as a first course at dinner parties and lunches I catered in London. They could also be a light lunch.

See the Smoked Mackerel Phyllo Triangles recipe on page 74 to familiarize yourself with the pastry.

SERVES 8

> 2¼ pounds smoked haddock (finnan haddie) on the bone, or 1½
>   pounds boneless smoked haddock
> 1 pound phyllo pastry leaves (you will use 16 leaves for this recipe;
>   the rest can be refrozen for another use)
> 4¾ sticks (1 pound, 3 ounces) unsalted butter
> ¼ cup all-purpose flour
> 1¾ cups milk, plus more as necessary
> 3 tablespoons finely chopped fresh parsley
> finely grated zest of ½ lemon
> ¼ teaspoon freshly ground black pepper
> pinch cayenne
> 2 tablespoons finely grated Parmesan cheese
> 1 large egg
> 2 bunches watercress

If you are using frozen pastry, defrost the phyllo leaves overnight in the refrigerator.

Prepare the filling, using the method in the recipe for Smoked Haddock Tartlets (page 76) with 2¾ sticks (11 ounces) butter, and adding the parsley and grated lemon zest with the seasonings and Parmesan.

Melt the remaining 2 sticks (8 ounces) of butter in a saucepan over low heat. Remove the phyllo from the package and unroll the leaves onto a clean surface. Carefully place a sheet with the longer side facing you on another clean surface. Keep the rest of the pastry covered with a slightly damp cloth. Lightly brush the pastry all over with melted butter, using a wide pastry brush. Lay another sheet on top and brush with butter; repeat until you have 4 layers.

With a sharp thin knife, trim 2 inches of pastry from one of the short sides and cut down the middle so you have 2 layers of pastry leaves each 5 by 15 inches. Place ⅛ of the filling (a large cooking spoonful) at the bottom of each strip. Fold one corner of the pastry over the filling, creating a triangle. Now fold the filled triangle up, alternating the folds from left to right and keeping the triangular shape (like folding a flag).

Put the 2 triangles on a baking sheet and brush the tops with more butter. Make 8 triangles in all and refrigerate them for 30 minutes.

Preheat the oven to 375 degrees. Bake the phyllo triangles until golden brown and crisp, 35 minutes.

To serve, lay watercress sprigs on individual medium plates and place the smoked haddock phyllo triangles on top.

Roulade of Sole with Vermouth Cream Sauce and Julienned Vegetables

This is a delightful and pretty first course that can of course be served as a light lunch. Thin fillets of sole or flounder are rolled up and placed on top of julienned vegetables with a vermouth and cream sauce to glaze them.
SERVES 8

> 8 skinned fillets of gray sole or flounder (6 to 8 ounces each)
> 1 cup dry vermouth
> 2 cups heavy cream
> salt to taste
> freshly ground white pepper to taste
> 8 stalks celery, trimmed and washed
> 2 medium carrots, scraped
> 4 leeks, trimmed of their roots and tough green leaves, halved
>   lengthwise, and rinsed
> 1 tablespoon unsalted butter
> 2 tablespoons finely chopped fresh parsley

In a small frying or sauté pan, simmer the vermouth until reduced to ½ cup, about 15 minutes. Whisk the cream, salt, and pepper into the vermouth and simmer until reduced to 1½ cups, about 15 minutes.

In the meantime, cut the celery, carrots, and leeks into very fine julienne strips about 2½ inches long. Try to cut them as thin as hay or straw. Steam the celery and carrots in a sieve or vegetable steamer above boiling water for 10 minutes. Then add the leeks and continue to cook for another 5 minutes. Toss the hot vegetables with the butter, season lightly with salt and pepper, and place in a shallow oven dish that can be brought to the table.

Preheat the oven to 400 degrees. Remove the row of rough tissue down the middle of each fillet (see page 59). Roll the fillets up, starting at the narrow end, and arrange on top of the vegetables. Spoon two thirds (1 cup) of the thickened cream sauce over the rolled fillets and bake for 20 minutes. Simmer the rest of the cream while the fillets bake, so that a tablespoonful of the very thick cream sauce can be used to glaze each rolled fish fillet just before serving.

Sprinkle with chopped parsley and serve.

Gravad Lax of Coho Salmon with Mustard Dill Sauce

This is a Swedish method of curing salmon. The fish is not heat-cooked but cured with salt and sugar, which is rubbed into the flesh. The fish is wrapped in foil and weighted for two days. Usually this method is used on full-size salmon, but I like to use boned baby coho salmon.

SERVES 6

> 2 baby coho salmon, boned (each about 8 ounces)
> 2 tablespoons coarse salt
> 2 tablespoons sugar

1 teaspoon freshly ground black pepper or ground juniper berries
1 bunch fresh dill weed

MUSTARD DILL SAUCE
  2 large egg yolks
  2 tablespoons Dijon mustard
  ¾ cup olive oil
  ¼ cup Fish Stock (page 305)
  juice of 1 lemon
  salt to taste

6 square slices pumpernickel bread, buttered

Cut the heads, tails, and fins from the salmon with kitchen scissors. Mix the salt, sugar, and black pepper or juniper berries together.

Spread the salmon flat, flesh side up, sprinkle the salt and sugar mixture all over the flesh, and rub it in lightly. Lay a dill sprig on each fillet and close the fish up. Wrap them in aluminum foil and put on a plate. Cover them with a baking sheet and place 3- to 5-pound weights on top. Refrigerate for at least 2 days. They will keep well for 4 days.

On the day you wish to eat the gravad lax, make the sauce, using the same method as for Mayonnaise on page 286. First beat in the oil, then the fish stock, and then the lemon juice. Season with salt. The sauce should be thin. Finely chop enough dill to measure ½ cup, and fold it into the sauce.

Unwrap the gravad lax. With a large sharp knife, peel the skin off, starting at the tail end, sliding the knife between flesh and skin on the diagonal. Place 1 fillet on each serving plate. Spoon some sauce on the side and garnish with a dill sprig. Cut the buttered pumpernickel bread into triangles. Place 4 triangles on each plate or serve bread separately.

Smoked Trout and Horseradish with Avocado

This pretty and tasty appetizer can be made in no time at all.
Prepare the smoked trout mixture beforehand and slice the avo-
cados at the last moment.
SERVES 10

> 5 smoked trout (each about 8 ounces)
> 3 tablespoons prepared horseradish
> juice of 4 lemons
> 8 ounces sour cream
> ¾ cup olive oil
> salt to taste
> freshly ground white pepper to taste
> 3 avocados
> 12 lemon wedges

Remove the heads and skin from the trout and discard. Pull the
flesh carefully away from the bones and put the flesh in a bowl.
Flake the fish with a fork, removing any small feathery bones you
might have missed. Add the horseradish, juice of 3 lemons, and
sour cream and mix well.

Prepare a light dressing for the avocados by mixing together
the oil, the remaining lemon juice, salt, and pepper in a small
bowl. Peel the avocados, slice them onto a serving dish or onto
individual plates, and pour over the dressing. Place portions of
the smoked trout mixture alongside the avocados and serve with
the lemon wedges.

Spinach Roulade with Smoked Trout Filling

This is a flourless soufflé rolled up to enclose a smoked trout filling. It resembles a jelly roll in appearance and can be made beforehand and reheated at serving time (see Note at the end of the recipe).

SERVES 8 AS AN APPETIZER; 4 AS A MAIN COURSE

1 smoked trout (about 8 ounces)
1½ cups Beurre Blanc (page 289)
¾ cup sour cream
pinch cayenne
3 tablespoons unsalted butter, melted
2½ pounds fresh spinach, stemmed, rinsed twice, and dried (14 cups
*   fairly tightly packed)*
salt to taste
freshly ground white pepper to taste
½ teaspoon ground nutmeg
5 large eggs, separated
2 tablespoons grated Parmesan cheese
8 sprigs tarragon

If you are planning to serve the roulade immediately, prepare the beurre blanc first; otherwise begin making the beurre blanc 30 minutes before serving the roulade.

Take the head and skin off the trout and discard them. Pull the flesh carefully from the bones. Put the flesh in a medium bowl and flake it well with a fork, looking for any bones you might have missed. Add the sour cream and cayenne. Beat this mixture well with a fork and put it in a small saucepan.

Preheat the oven to 425 degrees. Have ready a jelly roll pan 13¼ by 9½ inches and ¾ inch deep. Cut a sheet of parchment paper or aluminum foil large enough to line the bottom and sides of the pan by 1½ inches. Make creases in the foil or paper so it fits nicely in the pan. Brush with 1 tablespoon melted butter.

Using only the little bit of water left on the spinach leaves to steam them with, put the spinach in a large frying pan (it will be very full). Cook over medium heat for 2 to 3 minutes, turning occasionally, until it has all wilted. Drain the spinach in a sieve, pushing as much water as possible from it with a large spoon.

Chop coarsely on a cutting board, then when it is cool enough to handle, squeeze more water from it by the handful and put into a food processor or blender. Add salt, pepper, nutmeg, 5 egg yolks, and 2 tablespoons melted butter. Process for 2 minutes, scraping down the sides once. Transfer to a medium bowl.

Beat the egg whites only until they hold soft peaks and still look grainy. If they become too stiff and dry they will lose some of their airiness when mixed with the spinach base.

Stir a tablespoon or 2 of the whites into the spinach base and carefully fold in the rest, using a rubber spatula and turning the bowl occasionally to incorporate the whites evenly. Turn the mixture into the lined baking pan. Spread out evenly and sprinkle with Parmesan. Bake for 12 minutes.

In the meantime, cook the smoked trout mixture over low heat until just warmed through.

When the soufflé is done, remove from the oven and let cool for 5 minutes on a wire cake rack. Then invert it onto another piece of parchment paper or foil with the Parmesan side face down. Lift off the original parchment paper or foil and discard. Spread the soufflé with the smoked trout mixture. Roll the soufflé up starting at one of the shorter (9½-inch) edges, and then roll the paper or foil around the roulade. Let rest for 5 minutes. Remove the paper or foil and cut the roulade into 8 slices. If serving as an appetizer, place one slice on each individual plate with a little beurre blanc on the side and garnish with tarragon. If serving as a main course slide the whole roulade onto the platter with the seam underneath, and serve 2 slices per person with the beurre blanc on the side, garnished with tarragon.

Note: The roulade can be prepared ahead of time. Keep in the refrigerator wrapped in paper or foil, until ready to serve. Slice before reheating—in a 400-degree oven for 6 to 7 minutes, or in a microwave for 1 minute. Serve immediately with beurre blanc and tarragon.

Taramasalata

Taramasalata is a tasty first course of Greek origin. In Greece, where it is often served for *meze* with a drink, it is usually made with salted and dried gray mullet roe. Now that smoked cod roe, a good substitute, is imported from Scotland by the United States, we can make a delicious version of this paste—a big improvement over the insipid version of taramasalata available in jars.

For cocktail snacks, the taramasalata can be piped or spread on small pieces of celery or used to fill very small profiteroles.
SERVES 6

> ¾ *pound smoked cod roe*
> 6 *½-inch-thick slices white bread, crusts removed*
> 1 *cup milk*
> 1 *clove garlic, finely minced*
> *juice of 2 lemons*
> ½ *cup olive oil*
> *lettuce leaves*
> *pita bread*
> 16 *Greek black olives*

With a spoon scrape the roe from its thin casing into a medium bowl. Soak the bread in the milk and then squeeze it dry with your hands. Add the bread, garlic, and lemon juice to the roe and mix well. Put in a food processor or blender and process for 1 minute, scraping down the sides once. With the motor running, add the oil in a thin stream through the feed tube.

I suggest serving it on lettuce leaves and garnishing it with olives. Accompany with toasted pita fingers.

Layered Raw Fish with Pickled Ginger and Wasabi

This is an elegant, somewhat westernized, sort of sashimi platter, spectacular as a first course to a special dinner, or alone for lunch or supper. In most large cities where there are Japanese fish markets one can find reliably fresh fish with which to make this dish. For this preparation, choose fish with colorful flesh; tuna, tilefish, red snapper, porgy, flounder, salmon, mackerel, and yellowtail are among those that are especially good raw, if very fresh. Particular attention to freshness is needed for mackerel, tuna, and salmon due to their high oil content.

Abalone, conch, and geoduck clam can be served raw after they have been tenderized. Among shellfish, squid and scallops are also served raw, while octopus must be cooked, because it is tough, and crab is always cooked. Shrimp are usually served cooked, although in Japan some eat freshly peeled shrimp live. Herring roe, seaweed with herring roe, salmon, mullet, sea urchin, and flying fish roe can also be part of the dish.

The dish is embellished with scallions, spinach, daikon (white radish), seedless cucumber, nori (dried seaweed), and sesame seeds and accompanied by pickled ginger slices—which should be made at least the day before—a wasabi paste, and a dipping sauce. Make a selection of about four of the recommended fish and at least two of the shellfish, some flying fish roe or salmon roe, and for richness some sea urchin roe if possible. Feel free to expand on the suggested ingredients.
SERVES 6

> 6 ounces squid or abalone
> 6 ounces conch or geoduck clam
> 6 ounces skin-on salmon fillet
> 6 ounces skin-on mackerel fillet
> 6 ounces tuna fillet
> 6 ounces yellowtail, flounder, fluke, tilefish, or red snapper fillet, skinned
> 4 ounces flying fish or salmon roe
> 4 ounces sea urchin roe or 3 sea urchins

PICKLED GINGER SLICES
> 4 ounces fresh ginger
> ¼ cup plus 2 tablespoons raspberry vinegar

WASABI PASTE

    1 ounce canned wasabi, available in Oriental markets
    7 teaspoons heavy cream

DIPPING SAUCE

    1 cup rice vinegar
    6 tablespoons light soy sauce
    2 teaspoons sugar

    ½ seedless cucumber, peeled and sliced very thin
    2 tablespoons white wine or rice vinegar
    2 tablespoons sugar
    1 teaspoon salt
    1 8-ounce daikon (Japanese white radish), peeled and finely grated
    4 scallions, cut into fine julienne
    4 ounces spinach, stemmed, rinsed twice, and dried
    3 tablespoons toasted sesame seeds
    3 sheets nori (dried seaweed)

One day or more before serving start pickling the ginger. Peel the ginger, slice it razor-thin across the grain, and put it into a pint-size screw-top jar. Pour the raspberry vinegar into a 2-cup measuring container and add enough cold water to measure 1½ cups. Pour this liquid into the jar, screw the lid on, and refrigerate. Pickled ginger will keep well for months.

About one hour before serving, make the wasabi paste. Put the wasabi powder in a bowl, add the cream, and mix thoroughly with a fork until you have a thick paste, adding more cream if necessary.

To make the dipping sauce mix all the ingredients together well and set aside.

To marinate the cucumber slices, place them in a bowl and add cold water to cover; add the vinegar, sugar, and salt. Marinate for one hour.

Assemble the platter just before serving. If using abalone, conch, or geoduck, cut into 2-inch slices and tenderize gently with a smooth mallet. (Or score them in several lines, close together, taking care not to cut all the way through.) Halve the squid lengthwise and score in a criss-cross pattern. Scale the salmon. To remove the skin, put the fillet, skin side down, on a board. Hold the end of the fillet with your fingertips and with a heavy knife held at a slight angle cut away the skin; do not cut too closely, as you want to leave a bit of flesh attached to the skin. Score the salmon skin on both sides, toast for a few minutes under a broiler and serve sliced into ¼-inch strips.

The mackerel skin should be peeled off by pulling with your fingers, leaving some of the silver and blue color on the flesh—this is for taste and looks. Discard skin.

Remove small bones from all the fish with pin nose pliers or tweezers (page 62). Slice the fish across the grain as thin as possible; try to achieve slices about 3 by 2 inches.

Place the grated daikon in the middle of a large platter with the scallions arranged around the daikon.

Make layered stacks by alternating different varieties of fish slices with spinach leaves, one layer of sesame seeds, and ending with a bit of roe on top. Lay these little stacks on the platter. Some of the fish can be rolled up in nori and arranged on the platter. Fan out the slices of shellfish, including fish slices if desired. Place teaspoonfuls of roe near the fish in a decorative fashion. Drain the cucumber slices and put around the edge of the platter. Garnish with any leftover daikon, spinach, and scallions.

Put portions of wasabi paste and pickled ginger slices on individual plates, with individual saucers of dipping sauce on the side. Let everyone help himself to the sashimi.

Smoked Fish Plate with Cucumber and Ginger

All sorts of fish and shellfish can be smoked to very good effect. As long as the brine in which it has been cured is not too strong or salty, smoked fish is a delight. When buying smoked fish, ask the clerk to let you have a little taste to determine what fish you like best.

Some of the smoked fish available are salmon, trout, mackerel, bluefish, tuna, sturgeon, sablefish (black cod), whitefish, chub, blackfish (wrasse), dogfish, halibut, mussels, shrimp, and scallops. Select three or four smoked fish for this dish, as I did for the purposes of this recipe.

SERVES 6

¾ pound smoked salmon, sliced
6 ounces smoked dogfish, thinly sliced
6 ounces smoked sablefish, thinly sliced
6 ounces smoked mussels
1 12-inch seedless cucumber
2 tablespoons freshly grated ginger
2 tablespoons fresh lemon juice
½ teaspoon salt
6 small lettuce leaves and 6 small radicchio leaves, rinsed and dried
6 square slices Danish pumpernickel, lightly buttered

With a vegetable peeler, peel the cucumber so that some peel remains. Coarsely grate the cucumber and leave to drain in a fine strainer for 1 hour. Then put the cucumber in a bowl and add the ginger, lemon juice, and salt.

Arrange the lettuce and radicchio leaves around the edge of a platter or on individual plates. Place the smoked fish and shellfish in a decorative fashion on the platter or plates, perhaps curling the salmon slices around a bit of cucumber and ginger. Cut the bread slices into triangles and serve on the side.

Soufflés

Notes on Making Soufflés

Smoked Sablefish (Black Cod) or Smoked Haddock
(Finnan Haddie) Soufflé

Smoked Trout Soufflé with Red Lumpfish Caviar

Oyster and Clam Soufflé

Sea Urchin Roe Soufflé

Seafood Soufflés

Notes on Making Soufflés

As soufflés seem to present problems for some, I shall seek to dispel your doubts, ensure success and make you feel at ease about cooking this delightful dish.

A soufflé usually takes between 30 and 35 minutes to cook. If it is to be served as a first course, or as a main course without appetizer, put it in the oven as soon as you have greeted the last guest. If it is to be served as a second course, put it in the oven before you sit down to a leisurely first course and the fully risen soufflé will be ready when you are.

At the risk of repeating myself in the soufflé recipes following, I give the following tips and instructions on how I make successful soufflés.

I like to use a Cousances soufflé dish, which is made in France, because it gives better results than the usual porcelain soufflé dish. This heavy dish is made of cast iron and covered with white enamel.

The soufflé base can be made hours beforehand, as long as you reheat it a little before folding in freshly beaten egg whites.

Put a baking sheet on the middle rack of the oven before preheating the oven to 375 degrees. Butter the soufflé dish and dust with cornmeal.

Beat the egg whites—with a wire whisk in a copper bowl; using a Kitchen Aid mixer; or with an electric hand beater—until stiff, but *only* until they hold soft peaks and still look grainy. If they become too stiff and dry they will lose some of their airiness when folded into the base. First stir a large spoonful or two of the beaten egg whites into the base. Then fold in the rest carefully, using a rubber spatula and turning the bowl to incorporate the whites. Avoid overmixing. It does not matter if there are a few small lumps of egg white in the mixture; they will disappear during cooking.

Place the soufflé dish on the baking sheet in the oven. The hot baking sheet will provide additional heat to the bottom of the soufflé dish and in turn will help the soufflé rise spectacularly.

Bake for 25 to 30 minutes if using the Cousances (cast-iron) soufflé dish, 35 to 40 minutes if using a porcelain soufflé dish, depending on how creamy you like the center to be. It is quite permissible to open the oven door and look in after 25 or 30 minutes to see how the soufflé is rising and to cook longer if necessary.

Smoked Sablefish (Black Cod) or Smoked Haddock (Finnan Haddie) Soufflé

The look and taste of this dish are greatly enhanced by sprinkling the soufflé with caviar just after cooking. Use black lumpfish caviar if economy necessitates.

If you choose to use smoked haddock, try to buy it on the bone. I think the flavor is better this way.

SERVES 4 AS A MAIN COURSE; 6 AS AN APPETIZER

¾ pound smoked sablefish or haddock (1½ pounds if haddock on the bone)
2 tablespoons black caviar
1¼ cups milk, plus more as necessary
5 tablespoons unsalted butter
5 tablespoons all-purpose flour
freshly ground white pepper to taste
pinch cayenne
grated zest of 1 lemon
2 tablespoons grated Parmesan cheese
5 large eggs, separated, plus 1 egg white
2 tablespoons coarsely ground cornmeal

Preheat the oven to 375 degrees. Lay the smoked fish in a roasting pan and pour the milk over. Bake for 20 minutes. Strain off the milk; measure it and add additional milk if necessary to make 1¼ cups.

When the fish is cool enough to handle, pick off all the flesh from the bones and skin. Put the flesh in a bowl and flake with a fork. Look for and remove any bones you may have missed.

Melt the butter in a medium saucepan over medium heat. Add the flour and stir with a wire whisk until smooth. Slowly add the milk, continuing to whisk until the mixture thickens. Lower the heat and cook for another 2 minutes, whisking occasionally.

Take the saucepan off the heat, add the smoked fish, pepper, cayenne, lemon zest, and Parmesan. Mix well. Whisk the egg yolks in a small bowl. Turn the soufflé base into a large bowl, stir in the egg yolks, and let rest for 10 minutes.

Put a baking sheet on the middle rack of the oven and preheat to 375 degrees. Butter a 10-cup soufflé dish and dust with cornmeal. Beat the 6 egg whites until stiff, but only until they hold soft peaks and still look grainy. If they become too stiff and dry, they will lose some of their airiness when folded into the base.

Stir a large spoonful or 2 of the beaten egg whites into the base. Fold in the rest carefully, using a rubber spatula and turning the bowl to incorporate the whites. Avoid overmixing; it does not matter if there are a few small lumps of egg white in the mixture.

Turn the mixture into the prepared soufflé dish. Place the dish on the baking sheet in the oven. Bake for 25 to 30 minutes if using the Cousances soufflé dish, or 35 to 40 minutes if using a porcelain soufflé dish. If you like the center creamy, cook it for the shorter time. Sprinkle it with caviar. Serve at once.

Smoked Trout Soufflé with Red Lumpfish Caviar

SERVES 4 AS A MAIN COURSE; 6 AS AN APPETIZER

2 smoked trout (each about 8 ounces)
2 tablespoons red lumpfish caviar
2 tablespoons prepared horseradish
5 tablespoons unsalted butter
5 tablespoons all-purpose flour
1¼ cups milk
freshly ground white pepper to taste
pinch cayenne
5 large eggs, separated, plus 1 egg white
2 tablespoons coarse cornmeal

Remove and discard the trout heads and skins. Carefully pull the flesh away from the bones. Put the flesh in a bowl and flake with a fork. Look for and remove any bones you may have missed. Add the horseradish and mix well.

Melt the butter in a medium saucepan over medium heat. Add the flour and stir with a wire whisk until smooth. Slowly add the milk, continuing to whisk until the mixture has thickened. Lower the heat and cook for another 2 minutes, whisking occasionally.

Take the saucepan off the heat and add the pepper, cayenne, and trout. Mix well. Whisk the egg yolks in a small bowl. Turn the soufflé base into a large bowl, stir in the egg yolks, and let rest for 10 minutes.

Put a baking sheet on the middle rack of the oven and preheat to 375 degrees. Butter a 10-cup soufflé dish and dust with cornmeal. Beat the 6 egg whites until stiff, but only until they hold soft peaks and still look grainy. If they become too stiff and dry, they will lose some of their airiness when folded into the base.

Stir a large spoonful or 2 of the beaten egg whites into the base. Carefully fold in the rest, using a rubber spatula and turning the bowl to incorporate the whites. Avoid overmixing; it does not matter if there are a few small lumps of egg white in the mixture.

Turn the mixture into the prepared soufflé dish. Place the dish on the baking sheet in the oven. Bake for 25 to 30 minutes if using the Cousances soufflé dish, or 35 to 40 minutes if using a porcelain soufflé dish. If you like the center creamy, cook it for the shorter time. Sprinkle with caviar. Serve at once.

Oyster and Clam Soufflé

In this recipe the soufflé base is layered with oysters, clams, and bacon bits.

I serve this soufflé with a shallot and wine sauce, but it may be served without the sauce if you wish.

SERVES 4 AS A MAIN COURSE; 6 AS AN APPETIZER

12 oysters, shucked and juice reserved (page 44)
12 littleneck clams, shucked and juice reserved (page 28)
½ pound sliced bacon
5 tablespoons unsalted butter
5 tablespoons all-purpose flour
¾ cup milk
½ teaspoon salt
½ teaspoon freshly ground black pepper
5 large eggs, separated, plus 1 large egg white
1 cup fine Dry Bread Crumbs (page 308)
2 tablespoons coarse cornmeal
1 recipe Shallot and Wine Sauce (page 268) (optional)

Fry the bacon until crisp. Set aside to drain on paper towels, and break into ½-inch bits when cool.

Melt the butter in a medium saucepan over medium heat. Add the flour and stir with a wire whisk until smooth. Add the milk and ¼ cup each reserved oyster and clam juices (strained through cheesecloth or a very fine chinois or strainer). Continue to cook, whisking constantly, until the mixture thickens. Lower the heat and cook for another 2 minutes, whisking occasionally.

Take the saucepan off the heat, add the salt and pepper, and mix well. In a small bowl whisk the egg yolks. Turn the soufflé base into a large bowl, stir in the egg yolks, and let rest for 10 minutes. Meanwhile, coat each oyster and clam with the bread crumbs.

Put a baking sheet on the middle rack of the oven and preheat to 375 degrees. Butter a 10-cup soufflé dish and dust with cornmeal.

Beat the 6 egg whites until stiff, but only until they hold soft peaks and still look grainy. If they become too stiff and dry, they will lose some of their airiness when folded into the base.

Stir a large spoonful or 2 of the beaten egg whites into the base. Fold in the rest carefully, using a rubber spatula and turning the bowl to incorporate the whites. Avoid overmixing; it does not matter if there are a few small lumps of egg white in the mixture.

Spoon one third of the soufflé base into the bottom of the prepared soufflé dish, to a depth of 1 inch. Carefully lay 4 oysters and 4 clams on the soufflé base. Sprinkle with one third of the bacon bits. Alternate 2 more layers of soufflé base with layers of 4 oysters, 4 clams, and bacon bits.

Place the soufflé dish on the baking sheet in the oven. Bake for 25 to 30 minutes if using the Cousances soufflé dish, or 35 to 40 minutes if using a porcelain soufflé dish. If you like the center creamy, cook it for the shorter time. Warm the shallot and wine sauce, if using. Serve soufflé at once with optional sauce passed separately.

Sea Urchin Roe Soufflé

If you like the slightly sweet, unctuous taste of sea urchin roe, you will find this soufflé special.
SERVES 4 AS A MAIN COURSE; 6 AS AN APPETIZER

8 ounces sea urchin roe, from 15 to 20 sea urchins (page 48)
5 tablespoons unsalted butter
5 tablespoons all-purpose flour
1¼ cups milk
1 tablespoon fresh lemon juice
¼ teaspoon salt
¼ teaspoon freshly ground white pepper
5 large eggs, separated, plus 1 large egg white
2 tablespoons coarsely ground cornmeal

Melt the butter in a medium saucepan over medium heat. Add the flour and stir with a wire whisk until smooth. Add the milk and continue to cook, whisking constantly, until the mixture thickens. Lower the heat and cook for another 2 minutes, whisking occasionally.

Take the saucepan off the heat and add the lemon juice, salt, and pepper. Mix well. Whisk the egg yolks in a small bowl. Turn the soufflé base into a large bowl, whisk in the egg yolks, and let rest for 10 minutes.

Put a baking sheet on the middle rack of the oven and preheat to 375 degrees. Butter a 10-cup soufflé dish and dust with cornmeal.

Put the sea urchin roe into a food processor or blender and process until smooth, about 30 seconds. Beat the 6 egg whites until stiff, but only until they hold soft peaks and still look grainy. If they become too stiff and dry, they will lose some of their airiness when folded into the base.

Stir a large spoonful or 2 of the beaten egg whites into the base. Fold in the rest carefully, using a rubber spatula and turning the bowl to incorporate the whites. Avoid overmixing; it does not matter if there are a few small lumps of egg white in the mixture.

Turn the mixture into the prepared soufflé dish. Place the soufflé dish on the baking sheet in the oven. Bake for 25 to 30 minutes if using the Cousances soufflé dish, or 35 to 40 minutes if using a porcelain soufflé dish. If you like the center creamy, cook it for the shorter time. Serve at once.

Seafood Soufflés

These are not strictly soufflés, but rather a light custard mixed with seafood and baked in ramekins. They look like soufflés because they puff up in the oven.

I think the use of frozen or canned shrimp and crab is appropriate here, so that it is a quickly made, but appetizing first course. There are some quality canned seafood products on the market, but I have not yet found tasty frozen shrimp or crab.
SERVES 6

> 10 ounces mixed tiny shrimp and chopped sea scallops, or 4 ounces
>   canned or frozen tiny peeled shrimp and 6 ounces canned or frozen
>   crab meat
> 3 large eggs, plus 3 large egg yolks
> 1 cup heavy cream
> ½ teaspoon salt
> freshly ground black pepper to taste
> pinch cayenne
> ¼ teaspoon sweet paprika
> 1 tablespoon fresh lemon juice

Put the eggs, egg yolks, cream, salt, pepper, cayenne, and paprika in a bowl and mix well with a wire whisk. Let stand at room temperature for 15 minutes.

Put the seafood in a fine strainer and rinse under cold running water for 30 seconds. Butter 6 ramekins, each 3 inches in diameter with ¾-cup capacity.

Preheat the oven to 400 degrees. Fill the ramekins with equal portions of seafood and sprinkle lemon juice over. Pour the egg and cream mixture over the seafood. Place the ramekins in a baking pan and pour ¼ inch hot water into it.

Bake the soufflés until puffed up and golden brown on the top, 25 to 30 minutes. Serve immediately.

Soups

Clam and Fennel Soup

Crawfish Bisque

Mediterranean-Style Fish Soup

Gumbo

Bourride

Lobster Bisque

Mussel Bisque

Oursinado

Oyster Bisque

Oyster and Artichoke Soup

Shrimp with Fennel and Wild Rice Soup

Clam and Fennel Soup

A simple and hearty soup for a winter's evening.

To make the soup look more decorative, add another fennel bulb to the list of ingredients and see Note at the end of the recipe. The soup will look handsome, with the whole fennel bulb in the center surrounded by the opened clams and soup.
SERVES 4

20 littleneck clams, rinsed (page 28)
1 large onion, very finely chopped
4 cloves garlic, very finely chopped
2 tablespoons vegetable oil
1 small bulb fennel, trimmed, hard core removed, and cut lengthwise
    into thin strips
3 medium tomatoes, peeled, seeded, and sliced into 1/4-inch strips
    (page 305), or 8 canned peeled tomatoes, seeds removed and sliced
    into strips
3 cups bottled clam juice
1/2 teaspoon freshly ground black pepper
pinch cayenne
1 tablespoon tomato paste
salt to taste
1 loaf French bread

In a large saucepan, sauté the onion and garlic in the oil, over medium heat, until they become glossy and slightly brown. Add the fennel strips and sauté for 2 minutes. Add the tomato strips, clam juice, pepper, cayenne, and tomato paste. Stir and bring to the boil.

Add the clams. As soon as the clams have opened, taste the soup and add salt only if necessary. Serve with French bread.

Note: If you would like to make a more decorative version of this soup, trim a second fennel bulb, cut out the hard core at the bottom, but leave whole. Bring a medium saucepan of lightly salted water to the boil, add the fennel bulb, and boil 10 minutes. To serve, put the whole fennel bulb in the center of a shallow soup tureen or casserole. Using a large spoon or ladle, spoon the clams and soup around the fennel bulb.

Crawfish Bisque

I used to make a version of this recipe when I worked at Barbara Kafka's Star Spangled Foods. Subsequently, when doing restaurant work in New York, I found I could have live crawfish flown up from New Orleans—lovely, large, lively crawfish that are the essential ingredient for this delicious bisque.

Those of you who live where crawfish abound are very lucky. There are so many uses for their sweet meat. In this recipe for bisque the whole creature is used one way or another.
SERVES 8

> 4 pounds live crawfish (crayfish)
> 12 cloves garlic, chopped
> 15 basil leaves, rinsed if necessary and dried, chopped
> 3½ cups dry white wine
> 6 tablespoons (¾ stick) unsalted butter
> 1 large onion, finely chopped (1¾ cups)
> 3 carrots, scraped and finely chopped
> 4 stalks celery, finely chopped
> 1 teaspoon salt, plus additional to taste
> 2 tablespoons sweet paprika
> 2 cups heavy cream
> roux (optional) made with 6 tablespoons unsalted butter and
>   6 tablespoons all-purpose flour
> freshly ground black pepper to taste
> ¼ teaspoon cayenne

Rinse the crawfish in several changes of water and let soak until the water runs clear, about 30 minutes.

Put half the garlic, basil, wine, and enough water to cover the crawfish in a large saucepan and bring to a boil. After 10 minutes, throw in the crawfish and cook for 1 minute after the liquid returns to the boil. Remove from heat and let the crawfish cool in the liquid for 15 minutes. Drain, reserving the liquid.

When the crawfish are cool enough to handle, pick off the claws and separate the heads from the tails. Peel the tails, removing the vein (page 33), and set aside. Put the tail shells with the heads.

In a food processor or blender, process the heads and tail shells in batches until they become mush. Put this mush in batches in a double thickness of cheesecloth and wring dry, reserving the juice that exudes from the shells.

Melt the butter in a large frying or sauté pan over medium heat. Sauté the rest of the garlic with the onion, carrots, celery, and 1 teaspoon salt. When they soften and start to brown, stir the paprika into the mixture. Lower the heat and cook for another 7 minutes. Add the crawfish mush, stir, and cook for 5 minutes.

Pour the crawfish liquid into a large saucepan with enough water to measure 2 quarts. Add the sautéed vegetables and crawfish mush. Bring to the boil and then lower the heat and boil gently, uncovered, for 40 minutes.

In the meantime, cook the cream in a saucepan over medium low heat until it is reduced to between 1¼ and 1½ cups.

Push the crawfish stock through the fine mesh of a food mill, discard the solids, and return to a large saucepan.

If you would like the bisque slightly thickened, make the optional roux. Melt the butter over medium heat in a large saucepan, then add the flour and stir with a wire whisk for 1 minute. Gradually add the crawfish stock, continuing to whisk, and bring to a gentle boil. Lower the heat and simmer for 15 minutes.

Divide the claws into 2 equal portions, larger and smaller. Save the larger ones for garnish. Purée the smaller claws with the juice obtained from squeezing the crawfish shell mush. Add to the bisque and season to taste with salt, pepper, and cayenne. Cook for 2 minutes longer. Pour slowly into the reduced cream, whisking all the while. Strain, add the rest of the tail meat, and serve with some of the larger claws as garnish.

Mediterranean Style Fish Soup

A light, summer alternative to the rich creamy bisques often served in winter, this soup is a rich tawny orange color with no sign of fish in it. Many restaurants in France and Spain along the Mediterranean coast serve a version of this scrumptious recipe.

In order to make the soup correctly you need to find a friendly fish store person who will save the heads and bones of various filleted fish for the stock. Also very important to the flavor of the soup is a substantial amount of uncooked shrimp shells and 4 uncooked empty lobster bodies. Be sure to give advance notice to the fish store of your needs.

In the south of France the fish markets sell rockfish by the kilo just for soup. They are a collection of tiny, ugly fish, very spiny and unusual looking—no need to gut them, just cook them with the vegetables, spices, water and wine and push the soup through a food mill.

SERVES 8

 4 pounds heads, bones, and skin from any of the following: cod,
   scrod, red snapper, whiting, flounder
 4 uncooked empty lobster bodies
 16 mussels (about 1 pound), cleaned (page 42)
 4 cups (6 ounces) uncooked shrimp shells
 3 cups dry white wine
 6 tablespoons olive oil
 2 medium onions, chopped (2 cups)
 ½ head garlic, peeled and chopped
 3 carrots, scraped and chopped
 1 leek, trimmed of its roots and some green leaves, halved lengthwise,
   rinsed and chopped
 ½ bulb fennel or 3 stalks celery, trimmed and chopped
 3 tablespoons sweet paprika
 ¼ cup cognac
 1 teaspoon fresh thyme leaves
 1 1-pound, 12-ounce can peeled tomatoes, chopped
 1 teaspoon saffron
 2 pinches cayenne
 5 drops Tabasco
 salt to taste
 freshly ground black pepper to taste
 2 tablespoons Pernod
 2 cups Rouille (page 72)
 1 loaf French bread

To make the stock, put the heads, bones, and skin in a large saucepan. Pour in 2 cups wine and 10 cups cold water.

Bring to the boil and boil gently for 30 minutes. Strain the stock through a fine sieve or chinois and reserve.

Put the oil in a large saucepan over medium heat. Add the onions, garlic, carrots, leek, and fennel or celery. Sauté until lightly browned, stirring occasionally. Lower the heat and add the paprika, stir, and cook for another 7 minutes.

Heat the lobster bodies in a medium frying pan over medium heat. When they are hot, pour over the cognac and flame. When the flames have died down, add the lobster bodies to the sautéed vegetables. Then add the shrimp shells, reserved fish stock, tomatoes, thyme, and remaining cup wine. Bring to the boil, then lower the heat and simmer gently for 1½ hours.

Remove the lobster bodies from the soup. With a slotted spoon extract the shrimp shells and vegetables from the soup, and in batches process these in the food processor. Then push them—also in batches—through the fine mesh of a food mill along with the soup, discarding the solids after each batch. Turn the food mill handle backward every now and again to facilitate the procedure.

Add the saffron, cayenne, Tabasco, salt, and pepper. Bring to the boil and then simmer gently for another 30 minutes. Taste for seasoning and adjust if necessary. For the final blending of tastes, add the Pernod and stir. Let stand for 10 minutes: if any oil has risen to the surface, skim off using a ladle. The soup may be made to this point beforehand. Cool to room temperature and refrigerate until needed.

When ready to serve, heat the soup; add the mussels and cook just until they open. Meanwhile, slice the bread and lightly toast. Rub the bread slices with a cut garlic clove. Serve the soup with rouille sauce on the side, to spread on the toast.

Gumbo

I remember enjoying this gumbo at—of all places—a party given in Paris for a group of visiting American artists on the occasion of a Jackson Pollock retrospective at the Musée d'Art Moderne in 1979. The friends of the late artist were represented in a show called "Autour Jackson Pollock."

Ernestine Lassaw, wife of the sculptor Ibram, is from Shreveport, Louisiana, and she managed to buy the essential ingredient of a gumbo—filé powder—in a Paris store. She found some okra (quingumbo is an African word for okra) in a little African store off the Boulevard St. Germain. "The dark, handsome owner was so pleased, he insisted on giving us two more bags of okra; much more than we could ever use!" My thanks to Ernestine for this recipe.

This gumbo is a clear soup, slightly thickened by the filé, added at the last moment. Other gumbos are thickened with a dark roux. Your guests can help themselves to as much filé as they wish.

Some people dislike the gelatinous quality of okra. I fry them in a little oil, until they are crisp and turn a bright dark green.

For looks and flavor, I like to add a little wild rice to the long-grain rice.

Start preparation the day before you serve it. First make a stock with the ham and chicken, then refrigerate it overnight and remove the congealed fat from the top the next day. At serving time it's just a matter of cooking the rice and okra (separately) and adding the other ingredients to the hot stock.

SERVES 8

1 pound lump crab meat

1 pound small shrimp (50 to the pound), shelled and deveined

8 or more oysters, shucked (page 44) (optional)

2 pounds smoked ham on the bone (shank end)

2 medium onions

1 teaspoon dried thyme

1 2½-pound chicken, rinsed

2 tablespoons wild rice

¾-cup long-grain rice

6 tablespoons (¾ stick) unsalted butter

3 tablespoons oil

1 pound okra, cut into ¾-inch lengths if very large

¼ cup fresh flat-leaf (Italian) parsley leaves

filé powder to taste

Put the ham in a large saucepan. Finely chop 1 onion and add with the thyme and 10 cups water. Bring to the boil, then lower the heat and simmer for 15 minutes. Add the chicken. Raise the heat until liquid returns to the boil, then lower the heat and simmer for 1 hour.

Remove the ham and chicken and let cool while the stock continues to simmer.

When the ham and chicken are cool enough to handle, remove the meat and flesh from the bones. Discard the ham fat and chicken skin. Return the ham bone and chicken carcass to the stock and simmer for another hour. Refrigerate the ham and chicken overnight in covered containers. Pour the finished stock through a fine strainer into a container; cool, cover, and refrigerate overnight.

The following day, cut the ham into ½-inch cubes and the chicken flesh into 1-inch pieces. Cook the rices separately; the wild rice will take about twice as long as the long-grain rice. Rinse the wild rice under cold water, put in a saucepan with 1 cup cold water and a pinch of salt, cover, and simmer until tender and fluffy, about 40 minutes. Avoid overcooking—it can turn to mush! Drain, mix together, stir in 2 tablespoons butter, and keep warm. While the rices are cooking, finely chop the remaining onion. Melt 4 tablespoons butter in a large saucepan and sauté the chopped onion over medium heat until it turns glossy. Remove the congealed fat from the top of the cold stock with a large spoon and discard. Measure the stock and pour it over the sautéed onion. Add enough water to add up to 8 cups of liquid and bring to the boil.

Heat the oil in a medium frying pan over high heat; add the okra and toss until they turn a bright green. Drain on paper towels and keep warm.

Add the ham, chicken, crab meat, shrimp, and oysters (if using) to the soup. When it returns to the boil, stir and cook for 2 more minutes. Take off the heat. Pour into a soup tureen and sprinkle with the flat-leaf parsley.

Let your guests put a spoonful or 2 of rice in their soup bowl, add a ladleful of soup, and help themselves to ½ to 1 teaspoon of filé powder, which should be stirred into the gumbo. Lastly let them help themselves to the fried okra.

Bourride

The traditional bourride served in France is a fish soup made with fish stock, vegetables, tiny potatoes, pieces of non-oily fish (such as cod, striped bass, or monkfish), and some shellfish. It goes well at an informal dinner party. The soup is slightly thickened with aïoli (a mayonnaise redolent of garlic) at the last moment.

Serve the soup with small slices of French bread, rubbed with garlic and toasted. Save some aïoli sauce to spread on the toast.

The soup base takes about an hour to make and can be prepared beforehand; the fish and shellfish and the aïoli are added ten minutes before serving. Unlike the traditional version, mine does not call for straining out the vegetables—the vegetables improve the bourride, in my opinion. It becomes a delicious vegetable soup with fish in it!

The recipe may seem long, but it is really simple. You need only serve a salad before or after the soup.

SERVES 8

STOCK

3 pounds heads, bones, and skin from several white fish (sole, Dover
  sole, cod, or flounder), plus skin from fish fillets to be added later
  with soup ingredients

3 stalks celery with leaves, coarsely chopped

1 medium onion, coarsely chopped

3 sprigs parsley

⅔ cup dry white wine

SOUP

2 pounds cod, scrod, or striped bass, skin reserved for stock, or monkfish (page 29)

1 pound small to medium shrimp (50 to the pound), shell on

1 pound cleaned squid (page 53)

1 pound mussels, cleaned (page 42)

8 cherrystone or littleneck clams, rinsed (page 28)

¼ cup olive oil

1 large onion, finely chopped (1¾ cups)

3 stalks celery, finely chopped

1 small fennel bulb, trimmed and chopped

1 large carrot, scraped and coarsely grated

2 cloves garlic, finely chopped

3 medium leeks, trimmed of their roots and some green leaves, halved
  lengthwise, rinsed, and finely chopped

6 medium tomatoes, peeled, seeded, and chopped (page 305)

salt to taste

freshly ground black pepper to taste

pinch dried thyme

pinch cayenne

1½ pounds tiny potatoes

zest of ½ orange, removed with vegetable peeler

zest of ½ lemon, removed with vegetable peeler

6 tablespoons dry vermouth

1 recipe Aïoli (page 287)

1 long loaf French bread

2 cloves garlic, peeled and halved crosswise

3 scallions, finely chopped

4 tablespoons finely chopped fresh parsley

To make the fish stock, remove the skin from the fish fillets and reserve for use in the fish stock. Cut the fillets into ½-inch chunks and set aside. Remove the gills (if any) from the fish heads and put the fish bones, skin, and heads with the celery, onion, parsley, wine, and enough water to cover (approximately 7 cups) in a medium saucepan. Bring to the boil, then lower the heat and simmer for 45 minutes.

To make the soup, heat the oil in a large heavy casserole or saucepan. Gently sauté the onion, celery, fennel, carrot, and garlic, stirring occasionally, for about 10 minutes. Add the leeks and cook another 5 minutes. Add the tomatoes and cook yet another 5 minutes. Stir in the salt, pepper, cayenne, and thyme and remove from the heat.

When the fish stock is done, strain into the cooked vegetables. Add the potatoes with the orange and lemon zests. Bring to the boil and simmer until the potatoes are just tender, about 15 minutes. The soup base may rest off heat until 10 minutes before serving time, at which point you will heat up the soup, add the vermouth, and cook the fish and shellfish. The aïoli and the garnish of chopped scallions and parsley are added at the last moment.

Put half the aïoli in a sauce bowl for the table and reserve the rest to flavor and thicken the soup.

Slice the bread ½ inch thick. Rub all over with the cut garlic. Briefly toast both sides under the broiler.

When ready to serve, heat the soup to boiling and add the vermouth and all the fish and shellfish, putting the clams in first. Boil until all the fish is cooked through, 7 to 10 minutes. Monkfish will take a little longer than cod, scrod, or striped bass. Remove from the heat.

Take 2 cups of the soup and gradually blend with half the aïoli, whisking with a wire whisk until smooth. Gently stir this into the soup. The soup should not cook any more, because the egg yolks in the aïoli will scramble in the soup.

Sprinkle with the chopped scallions and parsley and serve with the warm toast and remaining aïoli. Spread the aïoli on the bread and dip it into the soup as you eat.

Lobster Bisque

This delicious bisque is easily made. The lobster meat should be extracted when raw, but as I find this difficult I suggest that you kill, not cook, the lobster in a steam bath before extracting the uncooked meat.

SERVES 4

1 1-pound lobster, killed in steam bath (page 261)
2 tablespoons (¼ stick) unsalted butter
1 medium onion, finely chopped (1 cup)
2 carrots, scraped and finely chopped
2 celery stalks, finely chopped
1 medium tomato, skinned, seeded, and cut into ½-inch cubes (page 305)
1½ teaspoons sweet paprika
1 tablespoon cognac
2 cups dry white wine
4 cups Fish Stock (page 305)
3 tablespoons rice
1½ teaspoons salt
freshly ground white pepper to taste
pinch cayenne
½ cup heavy cream

When the lobster has been killed (not cooked), cut it in half and remove all tail meat and claw meat intact. Pick out as much meat as you can from where the legs join the body. Reserve the coral and/or tomalley. Refrigerate the flesh and the coral and tomalley in separate bowls covered with plastic wrap.

Put the shells and legs (not the claw shells) in a food processor or blender and process until well chopped.

Melt the butter in a large saucepan over medium heat and sauté the onion, carrots, and celery until glossy. Add the tomato, stir in the paprika, and cook for another 3 minutes. Add the chopped shells, cook 2 minutes, add the cognac, and flambé. Add the wine and 2 cups fish stock. Cover and cook for 20 minutes. In the meantime, gently boil the rice in the rest of the fish stock in a covered saucepan until rice is very soft, about 30 minutes. It will be used to thicken the bisque.

When the wine, stock, vegetables, and shells are done, push them through the fine mesh of a food mill. Discard the solids. Add the rice and stock and stir. Put the soup into a blender (in batches) to liquidize. Transfer soup to a saucepan, add salt, pepper, and cayenne, and bring slowly to the boil.

Cut the lobster tail flesh into thin escalopes and the rest of the flesh into ½-inch cubes. Whisk the coral and tomalley into the cream and, off heat, whisk this mixture into the bisque as soon as it has reached a boil. Taste and adjust seasoning. Add the lobster meat and serve at once.

Mussel Bisque

This sumptuous restaurant recipe can be easily prepared at home.

The bisque is made of mussel and fish stock and cream, both reduced separately then whisked together. If you prefer a thicker bisque, I advise thickening the stock with a roux (butter and flour cooked together).

SERVES 8

8 pounds mussels (cultivated preferred), cleaned (page 42)
4 cups heavy cream
6 tablespoons (¾ stick) unsalted butter
1 large onion, coarsely chopped
10 shallots (8 ounces), coarsely chopped
10 cloves garlic, coarsely chopped
3½ cups dry white wine
3 cups Fish Stock (page 305) (optional, depending on how rich you want the bisque to be), or 3 cups water
roux (optional) made with 6 tablespoons (¾ stick) unsalted butter and 6 tablespoons all-purpose flour

Put the cream in a large frying or sauté pan or large saucepan. Bring to the boil over medium high heat, then turn the heat to low and simmer until reduced to 2 cups.

Melt the butter in a large saucepan over medium heat, add the onion, shallots, and garlic and sauté until soft and translucent, 10 to 15 minutes.

Put the wine and mussels in another large saucepan. Cover and bring to a boil over high heat. Cook until the mussels have all opened, about 5 to 8 minutes. Remove from the heat and strain the mussels through a colander into the saucepan with the sautéed vegetables. Add the fish stock or water and bring to a boil over high heat, then lower the heat and gently boil for 15 minutes. Strain the mussel and fish stock through a fine chinois, pushing the vegetables against the chinois. Set the stock aside.

In the meantime, choose 16 nice-looking mussels (in their shells) and remove any beards. Allow 2 mussels per person as garnish for the bisque.

You may remove the rest of the mussels from their shells and debeard them for another recipe, such as Mussels in Puff Pastry Cases with Saffron Cream Sauce (page 113), Baked Mussels with Garlic and Tomato Butter (page 114),or Mussel and Green Bean Salad (page 168).

If desired, make a roux by melting the butter in a large saucepan, adding the flour and cooking over low heat, whisking with a wire whisk, for 1 minute. Slowly add the stock, bring to a gentle boil, and cook for 15 minutes, whisking from time to time.

When the cream has reduced to 2 cups, add the mussel and fish stock by the cupful to the cream, constantly whisking with a wire whisk.

Reheat the bisque with the 16 mussels in their shells and serve immediately.

Oursinado

Oursin is the French word for sea urchin. Oursinado is a fish soup/stew made in Provence in the south of France. Part of the liquid is thickened with egg yolks, butter, and puréed sea urchin roe and then poured over slices of stale bread previously soaked in the soup. The fish is served separately. This is a rich dish and a meal unto itself.

I suggest using sea bass and whiting, cut into steaks, and cod fillet.

SERVES 6

> *2 pounds black sea bass and whiting sliced into 1¼-inch thick steaks*
> *1 pound skinned fillet of cod*
> *4 ounces roe from about 12 sea urchins (page 48)*
> *2 tablespoons olive oil*
> *1 medium onion, very finely sliced*
> *1 carrot, scraped and very finely sliced*
> *1 stalk celery, cut into fine julienne*
> *2 tablespoons finely chopped fresh parsley*
> *pinch dried thyme*
> *½ teaspoon salt*
> *¼ teaspoon freshly ground black pepper*
> *1 bay leaf*
> *1½ cups dry white wine*
> *4 tablespoons (½ stick) unsalted butter*
> *5 large egg yolks*
> *1 baguette or loaf French bread, cut into 1-inch slices and left to dry*
> *   out for a few hours*

Heat the oil in a large saucepan or casserole over medium low heat. Add the onion, carrot, and celery, and sweat for 7 minutes, stirring occasionally. Add the fish steaks and sprinkle with parsley, thyme, salt, and pepper. Place the fish fillet on top (it needs less cooking time). Add the bay leaf, wine, and 2½ cups water and swirl the liquid around. Cook over low heat until the fish are cooked but not falling apart, about 10 minutes. Remove from the heat and pour off 3 cups of soup.

Put 6 or 12 slices of stale bread (depending on their size) in a shallow casserole and pour over 1 of the 3 reserved cups of soup. Warm over very low heat while you make the sea urchin cream.

Purée the sea urchin roe in a food processor until smooth, about 30 seconds.

Fit a bowl over a saucepan one third full of simmering water. Place the butter and egg yolks in the bowl and beat with a wire whisk until hot and thick. Gradually add the remaining 2 cups reserved soup and cook, whisking constantly, until thick enough to coat the back of a wooden spoon.

Reheat the fish steaks and fillet in their liquid and carefully transfer all to a warmed serving dish.

Whisk the sea urchin purée into the thickened sauce and pour over the bread. Serve the sauced bread and the fish in separate dishes.

Oyster Bisque

SERVES 6

24 oysters, shucked and juice reserved (page 44)
3 shallots, finely chopped (5 tablespoons)
2 cups dry white wine
8 ounces pleurotes or oyster mushrooms
2 tablespoons (¼ stick) unsalted butter
1 small sprig thyme
4 cups half-and-half
freshly ground white pepper to taste
salt to taste
1 teaspoon sweet paprika

Put the shallots and wine in a medium saucepan and cook over medium heat until the wine has reduced to ¾ cup.

In the meantime, cut the *pleurotes* into 1-inch pieces. Melt the butter in a frying pan over medium high heat; add the mushrooms and thyme. Cook, turning often, until they lose their moisture. Remove pan from the heat.

When the wine has reduced, strain off the shallots and return the wine to the saucepan. Add the oysters and their liquor and cook over medium heat until their edges curl. Transfer the mushrooms with a slotted spoon to the saucepan with the oysters. Discard the thyme sprig. Add the half-and-half and a little pepper. Stir and slowly bring just to a boil; taste the liquid for seasoning and add a little salt and more pepper if desired. Pour the bisque into a warm soup tureen or soup bowls and sprinkle with paprika before serving.

Oyster and Artichoke Soup

When artichokes are cheap and even past their prime, usually in late spring, is the time to make this soup, for all you will be using are the bottoms of the artichokes. They have a fine sweet flavor and combined with oysters produce something very special. Many different versions of this soup are served in New Orleans.
SERVES 4

20 oysters
8 medium or 6 large artichokes
4 tablespoons (½ stick) unsalted butter
3 tablespoons all-purpose flour
½ cup dry white wine
4 cups mild chicken stock
½ cup heavy cream
¾ cup finely chopped celery
pinch thyme
salt to taste
freshly ground white pepper to taste
3 scallions, very finely chopped

Wash the artichokes. Bring a large saucepan of salted water (to cover the artichokes) to a boil. Add the artichokes and boil, loosely covered, until the leaves easily pull away, 35 to 40 minutes. Remove the artichokes from the water and drain upside down. When they are cool enough to handle, pull off all the leaves and cut away the choke. Trim the bottom of the artichoke and cut the stem (if necessary) to 1½ inches and peel it. Chop coarsely and put aside in a covered bowl. Eat the leaves or discard them.

Shuck the oysters, reserving and straining their liquor through a fine chinois or cheesecloth.

Melt the butter in a medium saucepan and whisk in the flour. Cook for 1 minute over very low heat, stirring occasionally. Add the white wine, chicken stock, heavy cream, celery, thyme, salt, and pepper and stir. Bring to the simmering point and simmer for 20 minutes.

Off the heat, add the artichoke bottoms and stems, the oyster liquor, and 8 oysters. Let cool for 5 minutes. Liquidize the soup in a blender until fairly smooth, but with some texture remaining. (This may be done ahead of time.)

When ready to serve, bring the soup to a boil and add the chopped scallions. Boil for 30 seconds, then add the remaining 12 oysters and cook just until their edges curl. Serve immediately.

Shrimp with Fennel and Wild Rice Soup

You can substitute celery for the fennel in this recipe, if fennel is not available, but of course it will give a different flavor.
SERVES 6

> ¾ pound small shrimp (50 to a pound), shell on
> ¼ cup (4 tablespoons) wild rice
> 1 cup dry white wine
> 2 tablespoons sweet paprika
> 2 cups bottled clam juice
> 1 bulb fennel or 6 stalks celery
> salt to taste
> freshly ground black pepper to taste
> juice of ½ lemon

Rinse the wild rice under cold water, put in a saucepan with 1½ cups water and 1 teaspoon salt, cover, and simmer until tender and fluffy, about 40 minutes. Avoid overcooking—it can turn to mush! Drain and set aside.

Shell and devein the shrimp, reserving the shells for the stock.

To make the stock, in a medium saucepan bring 6 cups water and the wine to a boil. Add the shrimp shells and paprika and boil gently for 20 minutes. Strain the liquid through the fine mesh of a food mill, pushing the shrimp shells against the mesh and then discarding.

Return the stock to the medium saucepan and add the clam juice. Bring to a boil.

Trim and cut the fennel into thin strips, discarding the hard core (or trim and wash the celery and thinly slice on the diagonal).

Boil the fennel (or celery) for 3 minutes in the stock. Add the cooked wild rice, shrimp, salt, pepper, and lemon juice. Bring to the boil, stir, and taste for seasoning. Serve immediately.

Pies

Shrimp or Crawfish Custard Pie

Anchovy and Cheese Pie

Clam or Squid Pie

Skate (or Ray) and Spinach (or Swiss Chard) Pie

Shrimp or Crawfish Custard Pie

Tiny shelled shrimp can be bought precooked, frozen, or canned; for convenience, you can use any of them, but be sure the quality is high, for all too often the shrimp are tasteless and limp.

Crawfish tail meat is sometimes available without the rest of the carapace; although it is convenient, it is usually not as fine as freshly cooked crawfish.

SERVES 8 AS AN APPETIZER; 4 AS A MAIN COURSE

1 pound tiny shelled shrimp (60 to the pound) fresh, precooked,
  frozen, or canned, or *4 pounds live crawfish (page 33)*
1 recipe Pastry (page 306), using 1 stick (4 ounces) butter
¼ cup all-purpose flour
3 large eggs, plus 3 large egg yolks
½ cup milk
1 cup heavy cream
1 teaspoon salt
pinch cayenne
2 tablespoons tomato paste
2 tablespoons Dijon mustard
3 tablespoons unsalted butter
¼ teaspoon ground nutmeg
¼ teaspoon freshly ground black pepper
1 teaspoon dried tarragon
1 teaspoon dried oregano
⅓ cup dry white vermouth
4 scallions, trimmed of their roots and some green leaves, finely
  chopped
2 tablespoons chopped fresh chives

Defrost shrimp, if frozen, in the refrigerator for 4 hours.

Refrigerate pastry for 1 hour. Let stand at room temperature for 30 minutes.

If using crawfish, extract the tail meat by peeling off the shells and removing the vein.

Sprinkle flour on a clean board or counter and roll the pastry ⅛ inch thick. Then roll the pastry around the rolling pin and drape over a 10-inch pie dish. Press the pastry into the pan and up the sides. Trim the pastry ¾ inch wider than the edge. Crimp the pastry at ½-inch intervals all around the edge of the pie pan. Refrigerate for 30 minutes.

Preheat the oven to 350 degrees. Prick the bottom and sides of the pastry with a fork and cut a piece of aluminum foil to fit inside the pie pan. Press the foil onto the pastry, up the sides, and over the crimped edges. Bake for 20 to 25 minutes until golden brown, removing the foil during the last 5 minutes to crisp the bottom of the pie.

In the meantime, put the eggs, egg yolks, milk, cream, salt, cayenne, tomato paste, and mustard in a medium bowl and beat together with a wire whisk.

Melt the butter in a medium frying or sauté pan over high heat. Add the nutmeg, pepper, tarragon, oregano, and the shrimp or crawfish and cook, tossing frequently for 2 minutes if the shrimp or crawfish are fresh but less if they're precooked.

Deglaze the pan with vermouth and cook for 2 minutes. Remove the shrimp or crawfish from the pan with a slotted spoon and lay in the bottom of the baked pie shell. Sprinkle with chopped scallions.

Add the pan juices to the egg and cream mixture and whisk well. Pour this mixture over the shrimp or crawfish. Cut 3-inch-wide strips of aluminum foil and cover the exposed edges of the pie crust. Carefully put the pie in the 350-degree oven and bake until the custard has set and the top is golden brown, 35 to 40 minutes, sprinkling with the chives after 30 minutes of baking.

You may serve this pie hot or at room temperature.

Anchovy and Cheese Pie

I have invented this recipe based on an idea mentioned by M.F.K. Fisher in her book *With Bold Knife and Fork:* "I think one of my most useful kitchen capers with anchovies is to lay them in a half-baked pie shell, with a cheesy custard and perhaps some sliced olives, and bake them to serve warm or cold."

The pie will resemble a pissaladière, with the anchovy fillets and black olives crisscrossed on top.

SERVES 8

> *4 ounces canned flat-filleted anchovies (about 24 fillets) (see Note)*
> *1 recipe Pastry (page 306), using 1 stick (4 ounces) butter*
> *6 ounces aged Cheddar cheese, finely grated*
> *2 tablespoons finely grated Romano cheese (Pecorino)*
> *4 large eggs, plus 2 large egg yolks*
> *1 cup light cream*
> *freshly ground white pepper to taste*
> *pinch cayenne*
> *2 scallions, trimmed of their roots and some green leaves, finely*
> *   chopped*
> *10 black olives, pitted and halved*

Let the pastry soften nearly to room temperature, about 20 minutes. On a lightly floured surface, roll the pastry out in a large circle ⅛ inch thick. Then roll it up on the rolling pin and drape over a 10- inch fluted-edged metal pie pan. Push the pastry down into the pan. Trim the edge of the pastry, leaving enough so the pastry protrudes ½ inch straight up above the edge of the pie pan. Refrigerate for 30 minutes.

Preheat the oven to 350 degrees. Take the pie pan from the refrigerator and prick the bottom of the pastry lightly with the tines of a fork. Cut a piece of aluminum foil large enough to cover the pie and press it down on top of the pastry and up over the protruding edge of pastry.

Bake for 25 minutes, then remove the foil and cook until the crust is golden brown.

In the meantime, put the eggs, egg yolks, cream, pepper, and cayenne in a medium bowl and whisk together well.

Sprinkle the grated cheeses in the partly cooked pie shell and then the chopped scallion. Pour the egg and cream mixture on top of the cheeses and return the pie to the oven. Bake for 20 minutes. When the custard is nearly set, remove the pie from the oven and place the anchovy fillets in a crisscross fashion on top of the custard. Place the olive halves in between and bake until the top is light brown, about 20 minutes.

Note: If you are not so keen on anchovies, it is possible to use only 2 ounces by cutting the fillets in half lengthwise, instead of using whole ones.

Clam or Squid Pie

On the East Coast of the United States, clams are in plentiful supply, especially in the summer. The native "Bonackers" of East Hampton produce a lovely clam pie.

I sometimes substitute squid for variety. Take your choice!
SERVES 8 AS AN APPETIZER; 4 AS A MAIN COURSE

24 *large cherrystone clams (2 cups shucked), or 2½ pounds squid*
(heads and tentacles included), cleaned (page 53)
1 *recipe Pastry (page 306), using ¾ cup (1½ sticks) butter, and*
mixing 1½ tablespoons coarse cornmeal with the flour
¾ *pound potatoes, peeled and cut into ¼-inch cubes*
1 *large onion, finely chopped (3 cups)*
6 *slices bacon, fried and crumbled*
2 *large eggs, plus 1 large egg yolk for the pastry glaze*
⅔ *cup heavy cream*
2 *tablespoons (¼ stick) unsalted butter, melted*
3 *tablespoons finely chopped fresh parsley*
1 *teaspoon salt*
freshly ground black pepper to taste
¼ *teaspoon dried thyme leaves*
¼ *teaspoon dried marjoram*

Take the pastry out of the refrigerator to soften.

Shuck the clams, if using, and drain them following directions on page 28. Save the juice for another purpose. Chop the clams or squid fine, or if you have a grinder put them through the medium cutter plate.

Put the whole eggs in a medium bowl and beat with a wire whisk. Add all remaining ingredients.

Roll out just over half the pastry and fit into a 10-inch pie pan or dish, with a ¾-inch overlap. Press the overlapping pastry around the edge of the pie pan or dish. Moisten the overlapping pastry with water.

Preheat the oven to 350 degrees. Pour the filling into the pie dish and roll out the other half of the pastry to fit over the filling. Crimp the edges together and prick several (10) small holes in the top of the pastry with a small, sharp knife. Decorate with leftover pieces of pastry in leaf or some other shapes. Make a glaze by beating the egg yolk with 1 tablespoon cold water. Brush the entire pie top with the glaze.

Bake the pie in the oven until the pastry top is nicely browned, 1 hour to 1 hour 10 minutes.

Skate (or Ray) and Spinach (or Swiss Chard) Pie

Layers of spinach or swiss chard and skate make up this pie covered with puff pastry. It looks spectacular and tastes wonderful.

SERVES 8

2½ pounds skinned skate or ray
6 tablespoons (¾ stick) unsalted butter
5 shallots, finely chopped
2½ pounds spinach, stemmed, rinsed twice, and dried (14 cups lightly packed) or 1½ pounds swiss chard, rinsed and cut crosswise into 2-inch slices
1 tablespoon finely chopped chives
2 tablespoons pine nuts (pignoli)
1 cup heavy cream
½ teaspoon salt
¼ teaspoon freshly ground black pepper
1 pound Puff Pastry (page 307) or frozen prepared puff pastry (Saucier makes a good one), thawed
1 large egg, separated

Bring a large saucepan of water to a boil. If the skate has not been skinned, put it in the water for 1 or 2 minutes; then remove it and pull off the skin and any membrane. Rinse off any blood. Put the skate back in the water and, when the water returns to the boil, cook for 7 minutes. Drain. When cool enough to handle, cut the flesh away from both sides of the central cartilage in as many large pieces as possible. Set aside.

Melt the butter in a large sauté or frying pan or large shallow casserole over medium heat. Add the chopped shallots and sauté for 2 minutes. Add the spinach or swiss chard and turn the leaves in the butter until all are wilted. Add the chives, pine nuts, cream, salt, and pepper. Stir together and simmer over low heat until the cream and liquids have reduced to ¾ cup.

Spread a third of the spinach mixture in the bottom of a 10-inch glass pie plate. Spread half the skate on the spinach, add another layer of spinach, then the remaining skate, and finally the rest of the spinach or swiss chard.

Lightly flour a chopping board and roll the puff pastry into a 12-inch square, ³⁄₁₆ inch thick. Roll the pastry around the rolling pin and drape over the pie dish. Trim the pastry, leaving a ½-inch overhang. Brush the underside of the edge of the pastry and edge of the pie plate with egg white and crimp the edges.

Preheat the oven to 350 degrees.

Using the pastry trimmings, cut out decorative pieces and attach these to the top of the pastry with egg white. Brush the pastry with the egg yolk mixed with 1 tablespoon cold water. Make several slits in the pastry with a sharp knife so that steam can escape. Put the pie in the oven and bake until the pastry is nicely risen and golden brown, about 45 minutes.

Salads

Bluefish Salad

Mussel and Green Bean Salad

Conch Salad

Lobster Salad with Virgin Olive Oil, Garlic, and Basil

Shrimp, Celery, and Dill Salad

Bluefish Salad

This is a fitting dish to include in a cold summer buffet.
SERVES 8 TO 10

> 3 pounds bluefish fillets, skin on, or 6 pounds whole bluefish
> 1¼ pounds small red-skin potatoes
> 1 medium carrot, scraped and coarsely grated   .
> 3 stalks celery, chopped into ¼-inch pieces
> 4 tablespoons finely chopped fresh parsley
> 3 tablespoons chopped fresh dill weed
> ¾ cup light olive oil
> ⅔ cup fresh lemon juice
> 2 teaspoons salt
> 1 teaspoon freshly ground black pepper
> lettuce leaves
> lemon wedges

Wash the potatoes, put in a medium saucepan, and cover with cold water. Boil until tender, about 20 minutes. When they are cool enough to handle, peel and cut into ½-inch cubes. Set aside to cool.

If using fillets, put them in a shallow casserole or frying pan and cover with lightly salted water. Poach the fillets over medium heat for 15 minutes, depending on their thickness. As soon as they are cooked through, transfer to a large bowl with a slotted spoon. When cool enough to handle, remove the skin and any bones. Discard the dark part of the flesh.

If using whole fish, poach or bake in foil at 400 degrees for 45 minutes and when cool enough to handle pick off all the flesh from the skin and bones. Discard the skin and bones.

Place the fish, potatoes, carrot, celery, parsley, and dill in a large bowl. In a separate small bowl, whisk together the oil, lemon juice, salt, and pepper. Pour over the fish and mix together carefully, trying not to flake the fish too much. Chill until serving time.

Serve the fish salad at room temperature on a bed of lettuce leaves and garnish with lemon wedges.

Mussel and Green Bean Salad

This is a good dish to include in a buffet-style meal. It serves just as well as an appetizer.
SERVES 20 IN A BUFFET; 10 AS AN APPETIZER

8 pounds mussels (cultivated preferred), cleaned (page 42)
2 cups dry white wine
2 pounds fresh green beans
2 medium red onions
35 large basil leaves, rinsed if necessary and dried
1½ cups light olive oil
1 tablespoon Dijon mustard
½ cup fresh lemon juice
1 teaspoon salt
freshly ground black pepper to taste

Put the wine and mussels in a large saucepan. Cover and bring to a boil over high heat. Steam until the mussels open, about 5 to 8 minutes. Remove from the heat and strain the mussels through a fine sieve or chinois. Reserve the stock for another use, such as Mussel Bisque (page 150).

As soon as the mussels are cool enough to handle, pick them from their shells and remove any beards.

Remove the stalk end of the beans and cut them in half if they are longer than 2 inches. Fill a medium saucepan with lightly salted water and bring to a boil. Add the green beans and boil until they are tender but still crisp, about 5 minutes. Drain in a colander and refresh by running cold water over them.

Slice or finely chop the red onions. Make a pile of 25 basil leaves, one on top of the other, fold them down the center, and cut them on the diagonal into ⅛-inch strips.

Put the oil in a large bowl with the mustard and beat with a wire whisk. Then add the lemon juice, salt, and pepper and whisk until opaque.

Add the mussels, green beans, red onions, and basil strips to the dressing and mix together well.

Spoon the mussel salad onto a large serving platter or individual plates and garnish with the remaining basil leaves.

Conch Salad

Begin the preparation of this salad the day before you serve it because the conch must marinate at least overnight. Prepare the red pepper and watercress just before serving.
SERVES 4

1½ pounds conch, fresh or precooked
1 cup vegetable oil
¼ cup fresh lime juice
1 or 2 cloves garlic, finely minced
¼ teaspoon salt
freshly ground black pepper to taste
1 bunch watercress
1 sweet red pepper, stems, seeds, and ribs removed, cut into ¼-inch
  cubes

If the conch has not been cooked, rinse and put in a saucepan of lightly salted water. Bring to the boil. Lower the heat and cook until tender, about 1½ hours. Drain and cool.

Clean and trim the conch of tough skin as directed on page 31. Cut the conch lengthwise into very thin slices and put in a shal-·low bowl. Whisk the oil, lime juice, garlic, salt, and pepper together in a bowl and pour over the conch. Cover with plastic wrap and refrigerate overnight.

The next day, pick the leaves from the stalks of half the watercress. Add the watercress leaves and the chopped red pepper to the marinated conch. Arrange the rest of the watercress around the edge of a platter and spoon the conch salad in the middle.

Lobster Salad with Virgin Olive Oil, Garlic, and Basil

SERVES 2

> 2 1¼-pound lobsters
> ¼ cup virgin olive oil
> 1½ cloves garlic
> 8 basil leaves, rinsed if necessary and dried
> 3 cans (4½ cups) light (not dark) beer

Put the olive oil in a medium bowl. Purée the garlic using a garlic press with very small perforations. Finely chop 4 leaves of basil; they should resemble fine green dust. Add the garlic and chopped basil to the olive oil.

Cook lobsters following the directions on page 261. Run some cold water on them as they drain in the kitchen sink.

It is advisable to remove the meat from the shells as soon as they are cool enough to handle to avoid the fat congealing around the meat. Detach the tail from the body; with kitchen scissors cut through the shell down the middle of the underside and remove the meat intact. Turn the tail meat over and take out the vein after making a shallow incision down the back. Cut through the body lengthwise and from each side pull away the leg section and attached meat in one piece. Remove the feathery gills. Save the green tomalley and any red coral. Crack the claws and the knuckles leading up to them with nutcrackers or a hammer and remove the pieces of meat intact.

Cut the tail meat crosswise into 4 slices. Put all the lobster meat except the legs into the bowl of olive oil, garlic, and basil. Move the pieces around so they are covered all over with the flavored oil.

To serve, spoon the tomalley and any coral into the center of a serving platter; surround with the remaining basil leaves, arrange the leg sections around the edge of the plate, and place the marinated lobster meat in between.

Serve with a tossed green salad and toasted whole-grain bread.

Shrimp, Celery, and Dill Salad

SERVES 8

2½ pounds medium to large shrimp (16 to 20 per pound)
1 cup light olive oil
juice of 2 lemons
salt to taste
freshly ground white pepper to taste
2 cans (3 cups) light (not dark) beer
4 cloves garlic, finely chopped
1 teaspoon celery seeds
pinch cayenne
6 stalks celery, trimmed and rinsed
¼ cup chopped dill weed (¼-inch lengths)
8 lemon wedges

Shell and devein the shrimp, leaving on the tails. Put the oil, lemon juice, salt, and pepper in a small bowl and beat with a fork.

Bring the beer, garlic, celery seeds, and cayenne to a boil in a medium saucepan. Boil for 7 minutes and then drop in the shrimp. When the liquid returns to a boil, stir the shrimp and cook for just 30 seconds. There is nothing worse than tough shrimp.

Drain the shrimp and put in a medium bowl. Whisk the dressing again with a fork and add to the shrimp while they are still warm. Mix thoroughly and let cool. Refrigerate for 30 minutes.

Before serving, thinly slice the celery on the diagonal. Add the celery and dill to the shrimp and mix again. Spoon the salad onto individual plates or a serving platter. Serve with lemon wedges.

Pasta and Risotto

Spinach Fazzoletti Filled with Sole and Shrimp

Clam Sauce with Linguine

Pasta with Smoked Salmon, Salmon Roe,
and Cream

Black Risotto

Mussel Risotto

Spinach Fazzoletti Filled with Sole and Shrimp

For this dish you make your own pasta sheets, cut them into squares, and parboil them. They are then filled with a mixture of sole and shrimp, and the pasta folded like a handkerchief. (The Italian word for handkerchief is *fazzoletto*.) The packages are then steamed and sauced with brown butter.

This recipe was inspired by one of the most delicious appetizers I have ever eaten, at a magnificent dinner given in the Ruffino Chianti Vineyard in Italy for The Sunday Times (London) Wine Club. It was a small portion of the lightest-ever pasta, with a cheese filling and sauced with brown butter. Of course you can vary the filling in this recipe if you choose.

Although not necessary, if you own a spaghetti machine the job of making the pasta is simplified. Elbow grease and a rolling pin are also necessary for this recipe.

SERVES 6 AS AN APPETIZER

> ¾ *pound skinned fillets of gray or other sole, or flounder, rough tissue removed (page 59)*
> ¾ *pound small shrimp (40 to 50 per pound), shelled*
> 12 *ounces fresh spinach, stemmed, rinsed twice, and dried (4 cups lightly packed)*
> ¼ *teaspoon ground nutmeg*
> *scant 1½ cups all-purpose flour*
> 1 *large egg, room temperature*
> 2 *tablespoons heavy cream, room temperature*
> *salt to taste*
> *freshly ground white pepper to taste*
> 2 *tablespoons fresh lemon juice*
> ¾ *cup (1½ sticks) unsalted butter*

Put the spinach in a medium frying or sauté pan and cook over medium heat, turning occasionally, until all the leaves have wilted. Transfer the spinach to a chopping board and chop it as fine as you can. When cool enough, with your hands, squeeze batches of it to rid of all liquid. Put in a food processor or blender, and process with nutmeg until the spinach is puréed.

Place the flour in a mound on a board. Make a well in the center and into it put the egg, cream, and spinach. Stir the spinach, egg, and cream mixture with a fork, gradually incorporating the flour. Once the mixture becomes difficult to handle with the fork, use a rubber spatula to incorporate the remaining flour. With your hands squeeze all together to form a ball. If the mixture is too moist to form into a ball, knead in a little more flour. If the mixture is too dry and the ball crumbles, dip your hands in water as you work. Knead until it becomes a smooth and elastic ball, 5 to 10 minutes.

The rest of the kneading can be done by inserting the dough through the widest opening (#6) of a pasta machine. Cut off a sixth of the dough. Flatten it and sprinkle with a little flour. Pass it through the rollers, then fold it in thirds and repeat the operation. Do this 4 times, until the dough is pliable and elastic; lay on a floured board.

Now change the setting of the rollers by one stop (#5) to attain a thinner sheet and pass through once. Change the setting down again (#4) to get a thinner sheet and pass the sheet through once. Then pass the sheet through #3 and #2 rollers. Cut the sheet in half crosswise and, using a rolling pin, roll out each half into an 8-inch, nearly transparent square. Lay the squares on a floured board. You will need 6 squares, so repeat the preceding operation with 2 more sixths of the dough. (See Note below about what you can do with the remaining dough.)

Bring a large saucepan of lightly salted water to the boil and cook the squares, 2 or 3 at a time, for 5 minutes. Remove the squares from the boiling water carefully with a wooden or rubber spatula, so as not to tear them. Drain and spread out flat on a cloth.

Divide the fillets into 6 portions, fold each in 2, and lay it in the center of each square of pasta; season with salt and pepper. Put some shrimp on top of the fillets, sprinkled with lemon juice. Gather up the edges of the pasta and bring together over the filling.

Preheat the oven to 200 degrees.

Using either a metal steamer or a bamboo steamer, fill a saucepan or wok one third full of hot water and bring the water to a boil. If using a metal steamer, lightly oil the bottom surface. Place the fazzoletti in the steamer and steam for 20 minutes. When the fazzoletti are tender transfer carefully (with a wide, thin metal spatula) to an ovenproof serving dish. It will probably be possible to cook only 2 at a time, so keep the cooked fazzoletti loosely covered with aluminum foil in the warm oven until all are ready to serve.

In the meantime, put the butter in a medium frying or sauté pan over medium heat to melt the butter. Continue to cook until the butter turns a golden brown. Pour it immediately into a small pitcher, discarding the milk solids at the bottom of the pan.

Serve the fazzoletti with the brown butter poured over.

Note: The recipe for the pasta produces more than you need for 6 fazzoletti. It is difficult to make less pasta, so use the rest for noodles or double the filling ingredients and the butter and make 12 fazzoletti for a main course—2 fazzoletti per person.

Clam Sauce with Linguine

Out in East Hampton, Long Island—and in fact all along the East Coast—clams are abundantly available in the summer from fish stores and local fishermen. If directed correctly you can have the fun of digging in the sand with your toes and collecting them yourself. Sometimes this is a squeamish business, for the sand is unusually soft where they live.

One summer when I was head chef of a restaurant in East Hampton, a friend of mine, Bill Cole, often prepared this simple but delectable dish for me on my one day off. Thanks to Bill, this was no busman's holiday!

SERVES 4

24 cherrystone clams
5 tablespoons olive oil
4 cloves garlic, finely chopped
4 tablespoons finely chopped fresh parsley
1 pound linguine

Pry open the clamshells with a clam knife and remove the clams, reserving the juice separately. Strain the juice into a bowl through a fine sieve, chinois, or cheesecloth. Cut the clams in half or into quarters if they are large.

Bring a large saucepan of salted water to a boil for the linguine. Add 1 tablespoon olive oil to the water.

Heat the remaining oil in a frying pan over medium heat, and add the garlic and clam juice. As the liquid boils, skim off any scum; continue to cook until the liquid is reduced by half.

In the meantime, cook the linguine until *al dente*, about 5 to 7 minutes. Add some cold water to the saucepan to stop the cooking and drain in a colander.

Add the chopped clams to the broth to warm through; then add the chopped parsley. Transfer the linguine to a serving dish and pour the sauce over. (I don't believe in serving grated Parmesan cheese with fish sauce on pasta. The two just don't go together.)

Pasta with Smoked Salmon, Salmon Roe, and Cream

For this dish you need scraps of smoked salmon. I have found that friendly people in stores that sell smoked salmon will save the belly and other parts of the smoked salmon they cannot sell and give them to me for free. This can be an economical meal, yet elegant and good-tasting. This is not an authentic Italian dish—I don't think the Italians would ever use smoked salmon, salmon roe, and cream with pasta! Even so, it is delicious.
SERVES 4

> *8 ounces sliced smoked salmon or smoked salmon scraps*
> *2 ounces preserved salmon roe*
> *¾ pound fresh linguine*
> *1 cup heavy cream*
> *1 teaspoon freshly ground black pepper*

Whether using smoked salmon slices or scraps, cut salmon into strips about 1 by ¼ inch.

Bring a large saucepan of lightly salted water to a boil. Put the cream and salmon strips in a smaller saucepan over low heat.

When the water comes to a boil, add the pasta and cook until *al dente,* 1 to 5 minutes. Remove from heat, add a cup of cold water to stop the cooking, and then drain well in a colander. Put linguine in a bowl and add the cream and smoked salmon, then the salmon roe and pepper. Toss gently and serve at once.

Black Risotto

This recipe, so-called because it uses squid ink, is adapted from an amusing book, *Venus in the Kitchen*, by Pilaff Bey and edited by Norman Douglas. It is a most interesting book using unusual ingredients and containing all sorts of recipes designed as "approved aphrodisiacs"!

There is a recipe for Pie of Bull's Testicles and an amazing recipe called Rôti Sans Pareil, in which you stuff a bird into a bird ad infinitum—sixteen birds! I once made a version of this using seven birds, and it was most successful. I started with a snipe and ended with a turkey—all boned out and with stuffing in between.

When you can get hold of fresh squid or cuttlefish that still contain their ink sacs, take advantage and make this recipe. (Although of course for a less impressive effect you could forget the ink and make the risotto with cleaned squid.)
SERVES 6

> 2 pounds fresh whole squid with ink sacs (see instructions on page 54 to clean the squid; be sure to retrieve the ink sacs intact from inside the body)
> ¼ cup tomato paste
> ½ cup olive oil
> 1 medium onion, finely chopped (1 cup)
> 3 cloves garlic, finely minced
> 1 pound Italian round rice (Arborio)
> 1 sweet red pepper, stems, seeds, and ribs removed, finely chopped
> 1 cup red wine
> 2 teaspoons salt
> ½ teaspoon freshly ground black pepper
> 1 pound spinach, stemmed, rinsed twice, dried, and cut in ¼ inch shreds (5 cups)
> 4 tablespoons (½ stick) unsalted butter

Cut the squid bodies into ¼-inch rounds and chop the tentacles, if large, into 1½-inch lengths. Save the ink sacs, and also the little dark sacs in the heads, which look somewhat like eyes with a tiny transparent ball in each. You can add the sacs whole when required in the recipe or pierce each sac with a knife over a bowl filled with ¼ cup water. Squeeze the ink out of the sacs into the water and remove the tiny transparent marblelike balls.

Dilute the tomato paste in 8 cups of hot water in a saucepan and put on low heat.

Heat the oil in a large sauté or frying pan or shallow flameproof casserole over medium heat. Sauté the onion and garlic until translucent. Move the onion and garlic to the side of the pan and over higher heat toss the squid rounds and tentacles quickly in the oil until they become opaque—just a few minutes, otherwise they will toughen. Remove the squid and tentacles with a slotted spoon and reserve.

Lower the heat to low; add the rice, stirring it with the onion, garlic, and oil. Cook for 1 minute. Then add the chopped red pepper, wine, salt, and pepper. Let bubble 1 minute and add the spinach. Mix all together and when the spinach has wilted stir in 2 cups of the diluted tomato paste. Continue to cook, with the liquid just simmering, adding more diluted tomato paste as necessary to keep the rice moist. Stir occasionally. The rice should be tender in 30 minutes; at this point add the ink and water (or the ink sacs, breaking them up with a wooden spoon and stirring them into the rice). Add the squid rounds and tentacles and lastly the butter. Heat through, taste for seasoning, and serve.

Mussel Risotto

SERVES 6

> 5 pounds mussels (cultivated preferred), cleaned (page 42)
> 2 cups dry white wine
> ½ teaspoon saffron threads (lightly packed)
> 1 stick (4 ounces) unsalted butter
> 1 large onion, finely chopped (3 cups)
> 4 cloves garlic, finely chopped
> 2 cups (1 pound) Italian round rice (Arborio)
> salt to taste
> freshly ground white pepper to taste

Put the mussels and wine in a large saucepan. Cover and bring to a boil over high heat. Steam until the mussels open, about 5 minutes. Remove from the heat, strain the mussels through a fine sieve or chinois, and reserve the stock. Steep the saffron in ¼ cup stock.

As soon as the mussels are cool enough to handle, pick all but 12 mussels out of their shells and remove any beards. Set aside, covered with plastic wrap. Check the 12 mussels in their shells to be sure they have no beards.

Put the remaining mussel stock in a medium saucepan and place over low heat. Have ready about 4 cups water in another saucepan over low heat.

In a large frying pan or shallow casserole, melt the butter over medium heat. Add the chopped onion and garlic and cook until they are translucent. Stir the rice into the chopped vegetables and cook for 1 minute. Pour 2 cups warm mussel stock into the rice and lower the heat so the liquid barely simmers. Just before the stock has been absorbed, add another 2 cups stock, stirring the rice occasionally.

When the stock is all absorbed, add the hot water, a cupful at a time as it is absorbed, stirring occasionally, for 35 to 40 minutes, at which point the rice should be moist and tender. Add the saffron and the stock it has been soaking in. Season with salt and pepper, keeping in mind the mussel stock is naturally quite salty. Stir in the reserved mussels and cook until warmed through.

Warm the 12 mussels in their shells in a saucepan with a little water. Pour the risotto onto a large warm serving platter or individual plates and garnish with the mussels in their shells.

Fish

Sautéed Blowfish with a Touch of Garlic, Lemon, and
Parsley

Baked Bluefish with Sweet Red Pepper and Pernod

Gratin of Catfish with Potatoes and Pesto

Broiled Fillet of Cod or Scrod with Tomato Coulis
Flavored with Star Anise

Baked Cod with Spinach Butter

Baked Halibut Wrapped in Lettuce Leaves with
Hollandaise

Broiled Halibut Printanière (with Julienned Vegetables)

Broiled Halibut with Tomatoes and Aïoli Sauce

Broiled Lingcod with Onion, Curry, and Green Chili
Pepper Sauce

Baked Lingcod with Black Olives and Onions

Broiled Mackerel with Rhubarb and Tomato Sauce

Poached Monkfish with Raspberry Vinegar Sauce

Monkfish à l'Americaine

Monkfish and Fennel Tagine

Broiled Pollock with Lime Sabayon

Baked Pompano Wrapped in Grape Leaves with
Tomatillos and Beurre Blanc

Broiled Red Snapper with Rosemary and Pernod Sauce

Broiled Red Snapper with Garlic and Vinegar Sauce

Red Snapper with Sake and Black Bean Sauce

Baked Red Snapper en Papillote with Orange Juice,
Zest, and Nutmeg

Broiled Baby Coho Salmon with Scallops and Black
Caviar on a Fine Tomato Glaze

Broiled Escalopes of Salmon with Sauternes Sauce

Broiled Salmon with Ginger Hollandaise

Baked Stuffed Salmon

Baked Salmon with Sorrel Leaves and Beurre Blanc

Baked Salmon with Red Wine Sauce

Poached Salmon with Brandy Paprika Sauce

Cold Poached Salmon with Sorrel Mayonnaise

Broiled and Baked Stuffed Sardines

Shad and Shad Roe with Garlic and Tarragon

Shad and Shad Roe with Paprika, Butter, and Lemon

Poached Skate or Ray with Caper and Parsley
Vinaigrette

Fried Smelt Fillets with Garlic, Mustard, and Lemon

Broiled Whole or Fillets of Dover Sole with Lemon and
Parsley Sauce

Gray Sole Stuffed with Shrimp, with Tomato, Basil, and
Cream Sauce

Sautéed Gray Sole or Flounder with Ginger Meunière

Gray Sole with Mustard Dill Beurre Blanc

Broiled Whole Striped Bass with Scallions, Garlic,
Lemon, and Teriyaki

Striped Bass Fillets with Mussel, Tarragon, and White
Wine Sauce

Baked Sturgeon with Duxelles

Broiled Sturgeon with Pistachio-Basil Butter

Broiled Swordfish with Sweet Red Pepper, Oregano,
and Lemon Sauce

Broiled Swordfish with Brown Butter and Capers

Broiled Swordfish with Pesto and Tomato Concassé

Broiled Swordfish or Mako en Brochette

Broiled Swordfish with Lemon Beurre Blanc

Fried Trout with Mint and Garlic Stuffing and
Brown Butter

Marinated Trout

Trout with Cider and Tarragon

Speckled Trout with Pecan Sauce

Broiled Tuna with Onion and Black Olive Confit

Albacore with Tomato, Green Pepper, and Basil Sauce

Broiled Whole Turbotin with Tabasco Hollandaise

Baked Whole Fish with Saffron Mayonnaise

Baked or Broiled Fish with Sun-Dried Tomato Sauce

Broiled Fish Fillets with Citrus and Fennel Sauce

Harlequin

Panache of Fish and Shellfish

Fish and Vegetable Tempura

Gefilte Fish

Cold Broiled Fish with Gazpacho Sauce

Cold Broiled Fish Fillets with Coronation Curry
Mayonnaise

Sautéed Blowfish with a Touch of Garlic, Lemon, and Parsley

Blowfish, or the puffer fish, is sold as sea squab or chicken of the sea nowadays. The fish is skinned and only the tail section is sold, consisting of a central spine with plump flesh around it.

The blowfish puffs up when taken from the water. The first and last time I caught one, I was fishing alone in an aluminum canoe not far from the shore of a small inlet off Sag Harbor. Knowing that I should try to kill it by hitting it on the back of the head, I started whacking it with the only heavy object in the canoe—the paddle. The blowfish blew up and up, until I thought it would explode. I wasn't killing it—the paddle mostly hit the bottom of the canoe—and the noise was so loud my friends came down to the shore wildly amused, urging me to come in.

The flesh is sometimes toxic in Japan, where highly courageous, specially trained chefs play a type of Russian roulette when preparing them. On the East Coast of the United States, it is advisable to wear gardening gloves to remove the tough, rough skin. Once the skin is stripped off, the precious sweet meat that surrounds the central spine can be eaten, much like a chicken drumstick.

Blowfish used to be in plentiful supply but are now less readily available, and of course more expensive. I buy them anytime I see them, for they are so delicious. This preparation is simplicity itself.

SERVES 4

> 2 pounds skinned blowfish tails
> 1 cup all-purpose flour
> 1 teaspoon salt
> ½ teaspoon freshly ground black pepper
> 3 tablespoons Clarified Butter (page 304)
> 2 cloves garlic, finely minced
> juice of ½ lemon
> 3 tablespoons fresh parsley, finely chopped
> 4 lemon wedges

Preheat the oven to 250 degrees.

Put the flour in a shallow dish and mix in the salt and pepper. Lightly coat the fish fillets and shake off the excess. Melt the clarified butter in a large frying or sauté pan over medium to high heat. Sauté the blowfish, sprinkling the chopped garlic over them as they brown. Turn them so they brown on all sides. Remove from the pan and keep warm in the oven. Add the lemon juice and parsley to the butter in the frying or sauté pan and swirl around. Remove the fish from the oven and pour the sauce over.

Garnish with lemon wedges. Accompany with zucchini cooked with chopped mint, poured over flat egg noodles.

Baked Bluefish with Sweet Red Pepper and Pernod

This is a favorite dish that my friend Jane de Rochemont prepares for her friends.
SERVES 4

  1½ pounds skin-on fillets of bluefish, or 3 pounds whole bluefish,
    filleted
  ¼ cup Pernod
  1 small onion, finely chopped (½ cup)
  salt to taste
  freshly ground black pepper to taste
  2 pinches dried thyme leaves
  1 large sweet red pepper, stems, seeds and ribs removed, and cut into
    ¼-inch-wide strips

Preheat the oven to 425 degrees.

Mix the Pernod with ¼ cup cold water. Pour half the diluted Pernod into the bottom of an ovenproof serving dish. Lay the bluefish fillets skin side down in the Pernod.

Sprinkle the fish with the onion, salt, pepper, and thyme and lay the red pepper strips over the fish decoratively. Pour over the rest of the diluted Pernod and bake for 20 minutes, depending on the thickness of the fillets.

Serve the fillets with a little of the liquid left in the pan poured over them.

Gratin of Catfish with Potatoes and Pesto

This dish can also be made with flounder, smelt, or petrale sole fillets.

SERVES 4

2 pounds skinned fillets of catfish

¾ pound red-skin potatoes

4 tablespoons (½ stick) unsalted butter, melted

½ cup Pesto (page 294), or 3 to 4 ounces storebought pesto

1 large ripe tomato, skinned, seeded, and cut into ¼-inch cubes (page 305), drained

freshly ground white pepper to taste

Wash the potatoes and slice ⅛ inch thick (don't peel them); you can do this by hand, with a mandolin, or in a food processor fitted with a metal slicing blade. Drop the potato slices in a bowl of cold water. Bring a medium saucepan of lightly salted water to a boil. Drain the potatoes and boil until just tender but not over-cooked, about 5 minutes. Drain, put in a bowl, and cover with the melted butter.

Preheat the oven to 400 degrees.

Lightly oil a shallow, round gratin dish. Arrange the fish fillets in a circle interspersing them with slices of potato. Spread the pesto over all and sprinkle with tomato and pepper. Bake for 25 minutes, depending on the thickness of the fillets. It is advisable to check for doneness after 20 minutes.

Broiled Fillet of Cod or Scrod with Tomato Coulis Flavored with Star Anise

Star anise and tomato sauce are a fascinating combination. The star anise gives a slight licorice taste to the sauce, almost as if you had added Pernod or Ricard. This sauce is equally good with broiled or baked chicken.

SERVES 6

> 3 pounds skinned fillets of cod or scrod
> 1 recipe Tomato Coulis (page 298)
> 8 pieces star anise (available in specialty and Chinese grocery stores)
> dry white wine
> 4 tablespoons (½ stick) unsalted butter, melted
> salt to taste
> freshly ground black pepper to taste
> juice of ½ lemon

Prepare the tomato coulis, adding the star anise 5 minutes after the tomatoes. Keep warm.

Preheat the broiler and pour white wine into a broiler pan to a depth of ⅛ inch. Lay the fillets in the wine and spoon melted butter over them. Sprinkle with salt, pepper, and lemon juice. Broil the fish for 15 to 20 minutes, depending on the thickness of the fillets. Remove the fish to a warmed serving platter or place on indvidual plates. Pour the sauce around the fish.

I suggest serving this dish with steamed carrot sticks and plain white rice.

Baked Cod with Spinach Butter

This dish may be made with other white-fleshed fish, such as pollock, orange roughy, lingcod, cusk, weakfish, or wolffish.
SERVES 4

2 pounds skinned fillet of cod
¾ pound spinach, stemmed, rinsed twice, and dried (4 cups lightly packed)
1 stick (4 ounces) unsalted butter
½ teaspoon salt, plus additional to taste
¼ teaspoon ground nutmeg
1 teaspoon fresh lemon juice
dry white wine
freshly ground white pepper to taste
4 lemon wedges

Stack about 20 spinach leaves together at a time, fold in half lengthwise, and cut the spinach diagonally into ¼-inch strips. Bring a medium saucepan of lightly salted water to a boil. When the water is at a boil, add the spinach and blanch for 30 seconds after the water returns to the boil. Drain in a fine strainer and refresh by running cold water over. Scatter the spinach strips on a cloth or double layer of paper towels and pat dry. Let stand for 1 hour to dry further.

Melt 6 tablespoons butter in a saucepan; add ½ teaspoon salt, nutmeg, and lemon juice. Remove butter from the heat and add the spinach strips. Toss the spinach to coat well. Transfer the spinach butter to a bowl.

Preheat the oven to 400 degrees. Pour wine to a depth of ¼ inch in a baking pan and place the fillet in the wine. Melt the rest of the butter in a small pan and brush it over the cod. Sprinkle with a little salt and pepper. Bake the cod for 10 to 15 minutes, depending on the thickness of the fillet. Spread the spinach butter over the fish halfway through the cooking time. Transfer the fish to a warmed platter and pour any spinach butter left in the pan over it. Serve with lemon wedges.

Baked Halibut Wrapped in Lettuce Leaves with Hollandaise

As halibut is usually sold in steaks, you will have to ask a special favor from the fish man—to cut fillets for you. (It would be horrid to find the center bone under the lettuce-wrapped fish!) Or you could buy a piece of halibut and fillet it yourself, following the instructions on page 59.
SERVES 4

4 halibut skinned fillets, (each 7 to 8 ounces)
dry white wine
salt to taste
freshly ground white pepper to taste
4 large lettuce leaves, rinsed, dried, and center ribs removed
1 cup Blender Hollandaise Sauce (page 285)

Preheat the oven to 450 degrees. Set some water to boil in a medium saucepan.

Into a shallow oven pan large enough to hold the 4 fillets, pour white wine to a depth of ⅛ inch. Place the fillets on top of the wine and sprinkle with salt and pepper. Bake for about 12 minutes, depending on the thickness of the fillets.

Dip the lettuce leaves in the boiling water until the leaves turn bright green and lose some of their crispness. This should be timed with the removal of the cooked fish from the oven. Shake the water off the lettuce leaves, then quickly wrap the fish with the warm leaves just before serving.

Let your guests help themselves to the hollandaise. Accompany with steamed tiny potatoes and broccoli (so good with hollandaise!).

Broiled Halibut Printanière (with Julienned Vegetables)

White halibut, when broiled to a golden brown, bedded on a blanched lettuce leaf, and topped with julienned cucumber and leek, is a very simple and pretty dish. This is not a fattening dish. A little butter is used to brown the fish (and can be eliminated, if you wish). Lemon juice mixed with the fish juices makes the sauce.

SERVES 4

> 4 halibut skinned fillets, or skin-on steaks (each 7 to 8 ounces)
> ¼ seedless cucumber, peeled
> 1 leek, trimmed of its roots and tough green leaves, halved lengthwise
>   and rinsed
> dry white wine
> 3 tablespoons unsalted butter, melted
> 2 tablespoons fine Dry Bread Crumbs (page 308)
> salt to taste
> freshly ground white pepper to taste
> 4 large leaves green-leaf or other lettuce, rinsed and dried
> 4 tablespoons fresh lemon juice

To julienne the vegetables proceed as follows. Cut the cucumber lengthwise into ¼-inch slices; then cut these slices into 2½-inch lengths and then into ¼-inch-thick matchsticks. Cut the leek into 2½-inch lengths and slice them as thinly as you can—like hay or straw. Place the julienned vegetables in a bowl of cold water.

Preheat the broiler and bring a medium saucepan of lightly salted water to the boil for the vegetables.

Pour wine to a depth of ⅛ inch into the broiler pan and lay the halibut in the wine. Spoon the butter onto the fish and sprinkle with salt and pepper. Broil the fish for 4 minutes. Sprinkle with bread crumbs and broil until the fish is golden brown.

While the fish is cooking, place the vegetables in a strainer and blanch, removing after 3 minutes. Blanch the lettuce leaves in the boiling water for 2 seconds, lift them out, and shake off the water. Spread the leaves on a warmed serving platter or individual plates and place the fish on top. Mix the lemon juice with the liquid in the broiler pan. Place little bunches of vegetables on top of the fish and pour the liquid from the broiler pan over all. Serve with steamed parsleyed carrots and potatoes.

Broiled Halibut with Tomatoes and Aïoli Sauce

Because it has a somewhat bland taste, halibut is a good fish to serve with a colorful and pungent sauce.
SERVES 4

4 halibut skin-on steaks or skinned fillets (each 7 to 8 ounces)
dry white wine
4 tablespoons (½ stick) unsalted butter, melted
salt to taste
freshly ground white pepper to taste
2 medium tomatoes
½ recipe Aïoli (page 287)

Cut the tomatoes into 8 slices, ⅜ inch thick.

Preheat the broiler. Pour wine to a depth of ⅛ inch into the broiler pan. Lay the halibut in the wine. Spoon 2 tablespoons of the butter over the halibut and sprinkle with salt and pepper. Put the fish under the broiler and broil for 3 minutes. Place the tomato slices beside the fish, spoon the remaining butter over the tomatoes, and sprinkle with salt and pepper. Broil the fish and tomatoes until the fish is cooked through, about 2 more minutes, depending on how thick the fish is. Place 2 tomato slices on each of 4 warmed plates. Place the fish on the plates, slightly overlapping the tomato, and spoon the aïoli beside the fish.

Broiled Lingcod with Onion, Curry, and Green Chili Pepper Sauce

The lightly curried sauce may be used with other fish, such as rockfish, bass, cod, or pollock.
SERVES 4

    2 pounds lingcod skinned fillet
    1 tablespoon vegetable oil
    2 tablespoons (¼ stick) unsalted butter
    1 medium onion, thinly sliced
    1 tablespoon curry powder
    ½ teaspoon ground ginger
    1 cup chicken stock (homemade preferred)
    1½ teaspoons canned chopped mild green chili peppers
    dry white wine
    4 tablespoons Clarified Butter, melted (page 304)
    salt to taste
    freshly ground black pepper to taste

Heat the oil and 2 tablespoons butter in a medium frying or sauté pan over medium high heat. Add the onion and cook until it starts to brown. Lower the heat, add the curry powder and ginger, and stir thoroughly. Cook for 3 more minutes, then add the chicken stock and chopped green chili peppers. Cook for another 3 minutes; turn off the heat and set aside.

Preheat the broiler. Pour wine to a depth of ⅛ inch into a broiler pan and lay the filleted lingcod in the wine. Pour clarified butter over the fish and sprinkle lightly with salt and pepper. Broil for 5 to 7 minutes, depending on the thickness of the fillet.

In the meantime, reheat the sauce and taste for seasoning. Add salt and pepper if desired. When the lingcod is cooked, place it on a warmed serving platter and pour the sauce over it.

Baked Lingcod with Black Olives and Onions

This is also a good way to cook the tail end of a large fish like cod, pollock, or haddock.
SERVES 6

> *3-pound piece of skin-on lingcod (tail end)*
> *1 tablespoon olive oil*
> *2 tablespoons (¼ stick) unsalted butter*
> *1 medium onion, finely chopped (1 cup)*
> *6 ounces drained canned colossal pitted California black olives,*
>   *chopped*
> *¼ teaspoon fresh rosemary*
> *1 tablespoon fresh lime juice*
> *salt to taste*
> *freshly ground black pepper to taste*
> *dry white wine*

Heat the oil and butter in a medium frying or sauté pan over medium high heat. Add the chopped onion and fry until translucent and tender. Lower the heat and add the olives, rosemary, lime juice, salt, and pepper. Cook for 2 minutes longer, adding a little hot water if the mixture gets too dry.

Preheat the oven to 400 degrees. Pour wine to a depth of ⅛ inch into a baking pan and lay the tail piece of fish in it. Bake for 15 minutes, then remove from the oven, pull off the skin, and turn the fish. Cover the fish with the onion and olive mixture. Bake until cooked through, another 5 minutes or so, depending on the thickness of the tail end. Serve on a warmed serving platter.

Broiled Mackerel with Rhubarb and Tomato Sauce

The sauce may sound like a strange one with fish, but in fact its acidity contrasts nicely with the slightly oily mackerel.
SERVES 6

> 6 mackerel skin-on fillets (each 8 ounces), small bones removed with
> pin nose pliers
> 2 tablespoons (¼ stick) unsalted butter
> 3 tablespoons finely chopped onion
> ¾ pound rhubarb, trimmed and cut into ¾-inch slices
> 1 medium to large tomato, skinned, seeded, and cut into ¼-inch
> cubes (page 305)
> 1 tablespoon sugar
> salt to taste
> freshly ground black pepper to taste
> 2 tablespoons vegetable oil
> 6 pinches dried thyme

Melt the butter in a medium saucepan over medium heat and add the onion. Cook until the onion is translucent, a minute or 2. Add the rhubarb, tomato, sugar, and pinches of salt and pepper and cover the saucepan. Lower the heat and cook, stirring occasionally, for 6 minutes.

In the meantime, preheat the broiler. Pour half the oil into the broiler pan and lay the mackerel fillets, skin side down, in the oil. Sprinkle the rest of the oil over the mackerel with a little salt, pepper, and a pinch or 2 of thyme. Broil until cooked through and lightly browned on top, about 5 minutes. Cooking time will depend on how thick the fillets are.

Serve the rhubarb and tomato sauce alongside the broiled mackerel fillets.

Poached Monkfish with Raspberry Vinegar Sauce

The sauce for this dish is quickly made, once the beurre blanc has been prepared. Monkfish takes a little longer to cook than other fish; it has a dense texture that is sometimes compared to lobster.

I also like this sauce poured over baked chicken breasts and with poached sea scallops.

SERVES 4

> 2½-pound piece of skinned monkfish, or 2 pounds skinned fillet (page 41)
> 1 recipe Poaching Liquid (page 304)
> ¾ cup raspberry vinegar
> 4 tablespoons chopped shallots
> 3 teaspoons green peppercorns
> ¾ cup Beurre Blanc (page 289)

Remove the central spine, if necessary, from the monkfish. Cut the fillets on the diagonal into slices 1 inch thick.

Bring the poaching liquid to a simmer and lower the slices of monkfish in a sieve into the liquid. Cook for 8 to 10 minutes.

In the meantime, put the raspberry vinegar, shallots, and green peppercorns in a sauté pan. Cook over medium heat until the vinegar has totally evaporated. Add the beurre blanc and stir thoroughly with a spoon.

Drain the monkfish and place on a warm serving platter or individual plates. Pour the sauce over the fish and serve immediately.

Monkfish à l'Americaine

The sauce, usually served with lobster, is typically Provençale with its tomatoes and garlic. Pierre Fraisse, a restaurateur born in Sête, in the south of France, opened a restaurant in Chicago and named the sauce for his American clients.

SERVES 4

2 pounds monkfish skinned fillet (3 pounds on the bone), (page 41)
6 medium tomatoes, skinned, seeded, and coarsely chopped (page 305)
4 tablespoons Clarified Butter (page 304)
2 tablespoons olive oil
2 tablespoons cognac
4 shallots, finely chopped
4 cloves garlic, finely chopped
1 small leek (white part only) trimmed of its roots, quartered lengthwise, rinsed and finely chopped
1 small carrot, scraped, finely chopped
3 tablespoons finely chopped fresh parsley
1 tablespoon chopped fresh tarragon
1 tablespoon tomato paste
⅔ cup dry white wine
salt to taste
freshly ground black pepper to taste
pinch cayenne

Cut the monkfish fillets crosswise into 1½-inch-thick slices.

Process the tomatoes in a food processor or blender until finely chopped, about 20 seconds.

Preheat the oven to 200 degrees.

Heat the butter and oil in a large frying pan, sauté pan, or shallow casserole over high heat. Add the pieces of monkfish and cook for 7 minutes, turning the pieces occasionally so that they brown on all sides. Lower the heat to medium, sprinkle the cognac over the fish, and flame. When the flames have died down, transfer the monkfish to a medium baking dish and keep warm in the oven.

Add the shallots, garlic, leek, carrot, and parsley to the frying pan and sauté over medium heat, stirring occasionally, for 5 minutes. Stir in the tomatoes, tarragon, tomato paste, wine, salt, pepper, and cayenne. Simmer for 10 minutes, stirring occasionally.

Add the monkfish to the sauce and cook for another 2 minutes. Serve with steamed rice.

Monkfish and Fennel Tagine

Tagine is the name given to a Moroccan or North African stew traditionally cooked in a round earthenware dish with a conical lid of the same name.

The flavors of this dish, which resembles a sauté more than a stew, are typical of Moroccan fare. I think the mixture of fennel, black olives and lemon juice is a fabulous combination with fish.

This recipe can be made with any firm-fleshed fish, such as grouper, tilefish, or conger eel, and is wonderful with couscous.
SERVES 4

>2 pounds monkfish skinned fillet (3½ pounds on the bone)
>1 pound fennel, trimmed and quartered
>¼ cup vegetable oil
>2 cloves garlic, finely minced
>1 tablespoon freshly grated ginger
>1 tablespoon coriander seeds, crushed with a mortar and pestle or
>   coffee grinder
>salt to taste
>freshly ground black pepper to taste
>½ cup black Moroccan or other olives
>¼ cup dry vermouth
>¼ cup fresh lemon juice

Bring a medium saucepan of lightly salted water to a boil, add the fennel pieces, and boil until tender, but still crunchy, about 5 minutes. Drain and refresh in cold water.

Slice the fish crosswise into 2-inch pieces.

In a shallow casserole or frying or sauté pan large enough to hold all the fish in a single layer, heat the oil over medium high heat. Add the fish and brown on all sides. Lower the heat and add the garlic, ginger, and coriander; stir. Scatter the fennel pieces among the pieces of fish. Sprinkle all with salt and pepper. Add the olives, vermouth, and lemon juice and cover the casserole or pan.

Cook 7 minutes longer, turning the pieces of fish and fennel once.

Broiled Pollock with Lime Sabayon

This dish may be made with other filleted fish, such as striped bass or red snapper.
SERVES 4

2 pounds pollock skinned fillet, small bones removed with pin nose
   pliers
dry white wine
2 tablespoons unsalted butter, melted
½ teaspoon salt
freshly ground white pepper to taste
1 tablespoon freshly grated ginger
6 large egg yolks
2 tablespoons fresh lime juice

Cut the fish into 4 portions, or leave whole and portion at the table. Pour wine to a depth of ⅛ inch into a broiler pan. Lay the fish in the wine. Brush with butter and sprinkle with salt, pepper, and grated ginger.

Preheat the broiler.

Put the egg yolks and 2 tablespoons cold water in a metal bowl that will fit over a saucepan. Fill the saucepan one third full of hot water. Put it over medium heat and when the water comes to a boil, lower the heat so the water barely simmers. Stir the egg yolks and water briskly with a wire whisk, then put the bowl over the saucepan. Whisk until the mixture becomes light and airy and the egg yolks are very hot, but not scrambled! When the egg yolks and water become very thick, add the lime juice and a pinch of salt, and whisk some more. Transfer the sabayon immediately to a serving bowl and set aside.

Broil the fish for 5 to 7 minutes, depending on the thickness. Place on a warmed serving platter and serve with lime sabayon on the side.

Baked Pompano Wrapped in Grape Leaves with Tomatillos and Beurre Blanc

Pompano are harvested from Florida waters and also are imported from New Zealand, where they are known as trevalley. The grape leaves go wonderfully with the flavor of the fish and show off its beautiful skin.

SERVES 6

> 6 pompano skin-on fillets (each 8 ounces), small bones removed with pin nose pliers
> 6 grape leaves (fresh or bottled)
> ½ pound tomatillos (available in Spanish specialty or other good produce stores)
> 1 recipe Beurre Blanc (page 289)
> 1 cup dry white wine, plus additional for broiler pan

Put the grape leaves in a bowl and over them pour enough boiling water to cover. Let stand 10 minutes and drain. Repeat this operation.

Peel the tomatillos of their outer dry skin and cut into quarters. Put with 1 cup wine in a small saucepan and bring to the boil. Lower the heat and cook for 7 minutes. Reserve.

Preheat the oven to 425 degrees.

Wrap one end of each fillet with a grape leaf, exposing the pretty skin. Pour wine to a depth of ⅛ inch into a baking pan and lay the wrapped fillets in the wine. Bake for 5 to 7 minutes, depending on the thickness of the fillets.

In the meantime, gently reheat the tomatillos. When the fillets are cooked, place them on a warmed serving platter or individual plates. Using a slotted spoon, portion the tomatillos onto the fish. Spoon the beurre blanc over all.

Broiled Red Snapper with Rosemary and Pernod Sauce

With thanks to chef Jane Russell, I present a recipe of hers that was very popular at Wilkinson's Seafood Café in the summer of 1983. This dish is prepared in minutes; advantageous for restaurant serving and also for you!
SERVES 4

> 4 red snapper skin-on fillets (each 8 ounces), small bones removed
>   with pin nose pliers
> dry white wine
> 4 tablespoons Clarified Butter, melted (page 304)
> salt to taste
> freshly ground white pepper to taste
> 4 small sprigs fresh rosemary
> 6 tablespoons Pernod mixed with 2 tablespoons water

Preheat the broiler.

Into the bottom of a broiler pan pour white wine to a depth of ⅛ inch. Lay the fillets on the wine, skin side down. Brush them with the butter and sprinkle with salt and pepper. Stick 4 small rosemary sprigs into each fillet, making a nice design.

Broil until lightly browned on top and cooked through, 5 to 7 minutes. Now place the broiler pan on top of a burner at high heat. Pour over the Pernod and water mixture. Ignite with a match and when the flames have subsided remove the fillets with a metal spatula to a warmed serving dish and pour the sauce over.

This is delicious with steamed carrots and puréed potatoes.

Broiled Red Snapper with Garlic and Vinegar Sauce

The garlic and vinegar sauce is virtually fat-free. It takes about 1½ hours to complete; however, as its preparation entails simple reducing, you are free to do other things at the same time. This sauce should be prepared beforehand, for the fish takes only a few minutes to broil.

SERVES 4

> 2 2-pound red snappers, filleted, bones and heads reserved for stock
> 2 cups dry white wine, plus wine for the broiler pan
> ½ cup red wine vinegar
> 2 tablespoons sugar
> salt to taste
> freshly ground white pepper to taste
> 1 head garlic, ⅔ of the cloves peeled, the rest left unpeeled
> 2 tablespoons (¼ stick) unsalted butter, melted

To make the fish stock, place the fish heads and bones in a medium saucepan and cover with cold water. Bring to a boil over medium heat, uncovered. Lower the heat and cook for 30 minutes. Strain the liquid through a fine sieve and discard the heads and bones. Reserve 2 cups of stock for the sauce. If any stock remains, save or freeze for another use.

Put the strained fish stock, wine, vinegar, sugar, salt, and pepper into a medium saucepan. Bring to a boil, then lower the heat and boil gently for 25 minutes. Add the garlic cloves and simmer until they are tender, about 30 minutes. (This will depend on their freshness. Old garlic takes longer to cook than new.) Keep warm.

Preheat the broiler. Pour wine into a broiler pan to a depth of ⅛ inch. Remove the small bones down the middle of the fillets with pin nose pliers. Place the fillets, skin side down, in the wine, pour melted butter on top, and sprinkle with salt and pepper.

Broil the fillets for 5 to 7 minutes, basting the fish with the sauce and garlic for the last 2 minutes of cooking. Cook until the snapper and garlic cloves are slightly browned.

Accompany with steamed snow peas, tiny carrots, and peeled small potatoes.

Red Snapper with Sake and Black Bean Sauce

This dish is sensational to look at and the sauce is very special. People love it. Pacific rockfish or striped bass can be used instead of red snapper.
SERVES 6

> 6 red snapper skin-on fillets (each 8 ounces), small bones removed
>   with pin nose pliers
> dry white wine
> 1 cup sake
> 3 tablespoons dried black beans (available in Chinese grocery stores)
> 3 tablespoons finely chopped shallots
> 2 tablespoons finely grated ginger
> 4 teaspoons soy sauce
> 2 tablespoons sesame oil
> 1½ cups Beurre Blanc (page 289)
> 12 orange segments (Cut off all peel and pith from an orange. Use a
>   sharp thin knife to cut down against the inside of the membrane of
>   each segment. Then cut against the membrane on the left side of
>   each segment and, without removing the knife, turn the blade up
>   against the membrane on the right side, releasing it.)

Preheat the oven to 425 degrees.

Pour wine to a depth of ⅛ inch into an oven pan large enough to hold the fish in one layer. Lay the fillets skin side up on the wine and bake them for 10 minutes, depending on their thickness.

In the meantime, put the sake, black beans, shallots, ginger, soy sauce, and sesame oil in a sauté or frying pan over medium high heat and reduce (that is, boil fairly hard, shaking the pan now and again, until the contents of the pan are nearly dry). Remove from the heat and, just before serving, add the beurre blanc. Stir thoroughly.

Remove the fillets from the oven and using a wide metal spatula place them, skin side up, on a warm platter or individual plates. Pour the sauce to the side, with 2 orange segments at the tail end of each fillet. Serve with blanched snow peas and steamed wild rice.

Baked Red Snapper en Papillote with Orange Juice, Zest, and Nutmeg

Baking fish in a package of parchment paper helps retain all its juices and flavor. It is a delight to savor the delicious aroma when opening the package.
SERVES 4

> 4 red snapper skin-on fillets (each about 8 ounces), small bones
>   removed with pin nose pliers
> freshly squeezed juice of 2 oranges
> finely grated zest of 1 orange
> 1 teaspoon freshly grated nutmeg
> salt to taste
> freshly ground white pepper to taste

Taste the orange juice and if it is not very sweet stir in 1 table-spoon sugar. Put the juice, zest, nutmeg, salt, and pepper in a small bowl.

Cut 4 pieces of parchment paper 24 by 16 inches. Fold each piece of parchment paper in half and cut into a large heart shape.

Preheat the oven to 450 degrees.

Lay the fillets on one half of each heart-shaped paper and sprinkle with equal amounts of the orange juice mixture. Fold over the other half of the heart shape and crimp the edges of the paper together, ending with a tight twist. Place the packages on a baking sheet and bake for 20 minutes.

When the paper is nicely puffed up and starting to brown, transfer the packets to warm serving plates and let each person open his or her own with little scissors, savoring the wonderful aroma.

I suggest serving this dish with steamed fennel and wild rice.

Broiled Baby Coho Salmon with Scallops and Black Caviar on a Fine Tomato Glaze

Color is important to this dish, so I suggest that you find a baby coho salmon or a pink trout. The boned-out fish are spread flat and look lovely on a tomato glaze, garnished with white scallops and sprinkled with black caviar.
SERVES 6

> 6 baby coho salmon or pink trout (each about 8 ounces), boned
> 6 sea scallops
> 3 teaspoons black caviar (black lumpfish caviar acceptable)
> 1 recipe Tomato Coulis (page 298), using larger amount of tomatoes
> dry white wine
> 4 tablespoons (½ stick) unsalted butter, melted
> salt to taste
> freshly ground white pepper to taste
> 6 lemon curls (Thinly slice a lemon, then make a cut from the center
>   of each slice outward; twist into a curl.)

Drain the tomato coulis through a food mill using the fine mesh, letting just a thin, gloriously transparent red glaze fall through the mesh into a small saucepan. Turn the handle backward every so often to facilitate this process. Do not rub through any pulp. You should have 1¼ cups tomato glaze. Reserve the pulp for another use. Keep the glaze warm.

Cut the heads, tails, and fins from the boned-out fish with kitchen scissors.

Preheat the broiler. Pour wine to a depth of ⅛ inch into a broiler pan. Lay the fish flat in the wine. Brush with melted butter and sprinkle with a little salt and pepper. Place a scallop in the middle of each fish and broil for 5 to 8 minutes, depending on the thickness of the fish. Turn the scallops over halfway through cooking, to be sure they cook through.

Pour the warm tomato glaze on individual warmed plates or a larger warmed platter. Place the fish on top of the glaze and a ½ teaspoon of black caviar atop each scallop.

Garnish with lemon curls.

I suggest serving sautéed sliced zucchini and some steamed new potatoes with this dish. Place one steamed potato each side of the tails and the zucchini alongside the fish.

Broiled Escalopes of Salmon with Sauternes Sauce

Sauternes is a luscious, golden sweet wine from the Bordeaux district in France. This sauce complements the salmon most deliciously.
SERVES 4

> 2 pounds salmon skinned fillet, small bones removed with pin nose
>   pliers
> 3 shallots, finely chopped
> 1½ cups Sauternes
> 2 cups heavy cream
> salt to taste
> 1 teaspoon fresh lemon juice
> 4 tablespoons Clarified Butter, melted (page 304)
> 4 teaspoons finely chopped fresh chives

Wrap the fillet with plastic wrap and refrigerate.

Put the shallots and Sauternes in a small sauté or frying pan over low heat. Cook until the wine has reduced and become syrupy, about 20 minutes. Add the cream and continue to cook over low heat until the cream becomes thick, about 20 minutes. Add a pinch of salt and the lemon juice. Strain through a chinois or fine strainer and put aside.

Preheat the broiler. Pour a teaspoon of clarified butter on 4 ovenproof plates. Cut the salmon fillet against the grain into slices ¼ inch thick. Arrange these slices on the clarified butter on the plates so that you have a nice round circle of salmon in the center of the plate. Place another teaspoon of clarified butter on top of the salmon. Broil the salmon until it just starts to brown, about 3 minutes. In the meantime, warm the sauce gently in a small saucepan over low heat.

Remove the salmon from under the broiler, and with a wide metal spatula slide onto clean individual warmed plates. Spoon the sauce over the top of the salmon and sprinkle each helping with a teaspoon of chopped chives.

Broiled Salmon with Ginger Hollandaise

SERVES 4

1½ pounds skinned salmon fillet, small bones removed with pin nose
    pliers
2 tablespoons finely grated ginger
1 cup Blender Hollandaise Sauce (page 285)
dry white wine
3 tablespoons unsalted butter, melted
salt to taste
freshly ground white pepper to taste

Cut 4 slices of salmon, on the diagonal. Fold the grated ginger
into the hollandaise.

Preheat the broiler. Pour white wine to a depth of ⅛ inch into
a broiler pan. Place the salmon fillets in the wine, pour over the
butter, and sprinkle with salt and pepper.

Broil the salmon for 5 to 7 minutes, depending on the thickness
of the fillet. Serve with ginger hollandaise.

Baked Stuffed Salmon

SERVES 8

5-pound piece skin-on Norwegian (Atlantic) or king or Chinook
    (Pacific) salmon, preferably a thick piece 8 inches long. (Ask the
    fish store to remove the center and rib bones.)
salt to taste
freshly ground black pepper to taste
juice of 1 lemon
1 medium onion, thinly sliced
1 large tomato, thinly sliced from top to bottom
6 to 10 basil leaves, rinsed if necessary and dried, thinly sliced

Preheat the oven to 400 degrees

In order to stuff the salmon, slice partly through the salmon so
that you can open it up and lay it flat, skin side down, and then

close it over after stuffing. Remove the thin bones running down the center of each fillet with pin nose pliers or tweezers. Sprinkle the inside of the fish with salt and pepper and half the lemon juice. Place two thirds of the onion, tomato, and basil leaves on one of the fillets.

Cut a piece of heavy aluminum foil 6 inches longer than the fish and lightly oil the foil. Close up the fish with the stuffing inside and place it in the middle of the foil. Arrange the remaining onion, tomato, and basil on top and sprinkle with the rest of the lemon juice. Bring the two edges of the foil up over the fish and make a double fold at the top for a tight seal. Fold the ends over the fish.

Bake for 50 minutes if the piece of salmon is thick (4 to 5 inches), less if it is thinner, turning the package over after 30 minutes. To check the salmon, open up the foil and insert a thin sharp knife into the center to see if it is still raw.

To serve, unfold the foil and slide the salmon and its juices onto a warmed serving platter. Cut the salmon into 8 slices.

Baked Salmon with Sorrel Leaves and Beurre Blanc

The pink salmon, the pale brown cooked sorrel leaves, and the pale yellow beurre blanc make a symphony of spring colors.
SERVES 6

> 3 pounds skinned fillet of Norwegian (Atlantic) or king or Chinook
>   (Pacific) salmon, small bones removed with pin nose pliers
> dry white wine
> salt to taste
> freshly ground white pepper to taste
> 6 lettuce leaves (use slightly wilted outer leaves)
> 12 sorrel leaves, rinsed, blanched for 5 seconds, and stems removed
> 1½ cups Beurre Blanc (page 289)

Preheat the oven to 450 degrees.

Slice the fish on the diagonal into 6 pieces.

Into a shallow baking pan pour the wine to a depth of ⅛ inch. Lay the fish in the wine, sprinkle with salt and a little white pepper, and cover each piece with a lettuce leaf to keep the moisture in.

Bake for about 7 minutes, depending on how thick the fillets are. Remove the lettuce leaves and carefully lay 2 sorrel leaves on a slant on top of each piece of salmon. Return to the oven for 1 minute. The leaves will turn a lovely pale brown.

Serve immediately with some beurre blanc partially covering the sorrel leaves.

Accompany with steamed tiny potatoes and green beans.

Baked Salmon with Red Wine Sauce

This was a popular winter dish at Wilkinson's Seafood Café. The rich garnet-colored sauce goes well with the pink salmon.
SERVES 6

> *3 pounds skinned fillets of Norwegian (Atlantic) or king (Pacific)*
> *salmon, small bones removed with pin nose pliers*
> *¾ cup finely chopped shallots*
> *2¼ cups Merlot wine*
> *1 tablespoon tomato paste*
> *2 tablespoons homemade beef or veal glaze or 1 ounce frozen beef stock*
> *concentrate (Saucier)*
> *¼ teaspoon salt*
> *freshly ground white pepper*
> *dry white wine*
> *6 lettuce leaves (use the slightly wilted outer leaves)*

Put the shallots, Merlot, tomato paste, meat glaze, salt, and pepper in a medium saucepan and bring to a boil over medium high heat. Reduce the heat to low and simmer until the sauce is reduced to 1½ cups, about 45 minutes.

In the meantime, slice the fish diagonally into 6 pieces.

Preheat the oven to 425 degrees. Pour white wine into a shallow baking dish to a depth of ⅛ inch. Place the salmon in the wine. Cover with lettuce leaves to keep the moisture in. Bake until cooked through, about 15 minutes. Place the salmon on a warmed serving platter or individual plates and pour the sauce partly on the salmon, partly on the plate.

8/98- OK but not great

Poached Salmon with Brandy Paprika Sauce

This dish is equally good served hot or cold

If serving cold, nearly all the preparation can be done in advance; just the final assemblage needs to be taken care of at the last moment.

SERVES 6

> 3 pounds skinned fillet of Norwegian (Atlantic) or king (Pacific)
>   salmon, small bones removed with pin nose pliers
> ⅓ cup cognac
> ½ cup dry white wine
> 1 cup Fish Stock (page 305), or 1½ cups water
> 1 tablespoon sweet paprika
> 2 tablespoons Dijon mustard
> ⅛ teaspoon salt
> freshly ground white pepper to taste
> 1 tablespoon finely chopped fresh tarragon, or 1 teaspoon dried
>   tarragon
> 1 tablespoon finely chopped fresh dill weed
> 1½ cups heavy cream
> 1 recipe Poaching Liquid (page 304), using 2 cups wine and 6 cups
>   water
> If serving cold: several razor-thin slices of seedless cucumber
>   dill sprigs
> lemon wedges

Put cognac, wine, stock, paprika, mustard, salt, pepper, tarragon, and dill weed in a medium saucepan set over medium high heat and bring to a boil. Turn heat to low and simmer until reduced to ½ cup, about 45 minutes.

In the meantime, reduce the cream in a frying or sauté pan until there is 1 cup, about 30 minutes.

Preheat the oven to 350 degrees.

Cutting on the diagonal, slice the fish into 6 pieces.

Reheat the poaching liquid and pour into a baking pan large enough to hold the 6 pieces of salmon. Lay the salmon in the poaching liquid, skin side up. Cover with a sheet of aluminum foil. Bake for 10 minutes. Remove the salmon, brushing off any vegetables that may have adhered to the pieces. Let cool. If not serving at once, cover with plastic wrap and refrigerate. Before serving, allow the fish to come to room temperature.

To finish the sauce, whisk the cognac–fish stock reduction into the cream. Let cool to room temperature and refrigerate if not serving at once.

To serve cold, spoon some sauce in the center of 6 individual plates or 1 large serving platter. Arrange pieces of salmon on the sauce. Cover the salmon with cucumber slices, overlapping them to resemble the scales of a fish. Top each portion with a sprig of dill. Serve with cold steamed potatoes and steamed snow peas, garnished with lemon wedges.

To serve hot, arrange the poached salmon pieces on individual plates or a serving platter. Spoon reheated sauce over the salmon and top with dill sprigs. Serve with small steamed potatoes and blanched snow peas, garnished with lemon wedges.

Cold Poached Salmon with Sorrel Mayonnaise

SERVES 6

3 pounds skinned fillet of Norwegian (Atlantic) or king (Pacific)
    salmon, small bones removed with pin nose pliers
30 sorrel leaves, stemmed, rinsed, and dried
1½ cups Mayonnaise (page 286)
1 recipe Poaching Liquid (page 304)
6 lemon wedges

Blanch the sorrel leaves in boiling water for 5 seconds; drain and refresh in cold water. Drain again and pat dry on a cloth or paper towels. Finely chop the leaves, add to the mayonnaise, and blend well.

Cut the salmon into 6 portions on the diagonal. Poach the salmon as for Poached Salmon with Brandy and Paprika Sauce on page 212.

Place the cold poached salmon portions on individual plates or on a serving platter. Spoon the sauce over one end of the fish and garnish with lemon wedges.

Broiled and Baked Stuffed Sardines

Occasionally fresh or frozen sardines from the Mediterranean are available. They are cheap and tasty. This dish will evoke memories of the south of France if you have ever been there. I have eaten delicious charcoal-grilled sardines by the dozen in Portugal, but they were generally a smaller variety than the ones in this recipe.

The recipe may sound complicated but it really is not, and the final presentation is surprisingly elegant.

Serve three sardines per person. One is left whole, stuffed with fresh mint, and broiled; the other two are boned, stuffed, rolled and baked.

SERVES 6

18 sardines (each 3 to 4 ounces)
1½ cups Fresh Bread Crumbs (page 308)
6 flat-filleted canned anchovies, finely chopped
finely grated zest of 2 lemons
3 cloves garlic, finely chopped
salt to taste
freshly ground black pepper to taste
1 bunch mint
coarse salt to taste
6 lemon wedges
4 ounces black Niçoise olives
1 recipe Anchovy Butter (page 291)

Using a fairly blunt knife, scale the sardines, being careful not to cut through their delicate skin. With a small sharp knife, make a slit from the ventral opening up to the head and remove the insides. Wash under running water and pat dry.

Cut the heads off 12 sardines. Remove the backbones from these fish: continue the slit down to the point just above the tail. Insert the tip of the knife at this point and sever the backbone from the tail. Grasp the backbone with your fingers and pull it free. Spread the sardines out flat, flesh side up.

In a small bowl make the stuffing by mixing together the bread crumbs, anchovies, lemon zest, garlic, salt, and pepper. Chop enough mint leaves to make 4 tablespoons and add to mixture.

Spread the stuffing mixture evenly over the flattened sardines. Roll each up crosswise, starting at the head end, and fasten with a toothpick inserted just below the tail. With kitchen scissors cut off the little back fin.

If you have 2 ovens or a separate broiler, preheat the broiler and preheat an oven to 400 degrees. Otherwise, simply preheat the broiler. In either case, oil a sheet of foil that fits the broiler pan and tuck it into place.

Stuff the whole sardines with chopped mint. There is no need to fasten the openings. Sprinkle all the sardines with coarse salt.

If you do not have a separate broiler, broil the mint-stuffed whole sardines, removing them when done to a warmed serving dish. To bake the rolled and stuffed sardines, adjust the oven to 400 degrees and bake for 15 minutes. During the last 5 minutes place the broiled whole fish in the oven to warm through.

If using a separate broiler, bake the stuffed sardines in the oven for 15 minutes, and broil the whole mint-stuffed sardines, without turning, until the skins are crisp and they are cooked through, about 10 minutes.

Garnish each portion with 2 lemon wedges, 5 black olives, and a slice or 2 of anchovy butter. Accompany with steamed green beans and fried straw potatoes.

Shad and Shad Roe with Garlic and Tarragon

The shad is a sweet and somewhat rich fish, only available during its spawning season. The season begins as early as mid-January on southern coasts; by March the shad have traveled up along the Carolina coast, reaching New York by April or May.

The fish is a marvelous silvery color with multiple bones. Only an experienced shad boner can fillet the fish properly. I have talked to such an expert in the Fulton Fish Market, who explained, to my astonishment, that the shad has 365 bones. One way to avoid boning the fish is to cook it for a long time; this tenderizes the bones and makes them edible.

The roe is a delicacy treasured by many. You can serve the shad fillet on its own or with the roe, or a pair of the roe by itself.

Handle the roe with care, for the membrane around the eggs is fragile.
SERVES 2

> 2 shad skinned fillets (each 6 ounces)
> 1 pair medium shad roe
> dry white wine
> 2 tablespoons unsalted butter, melted
> salt to taste
> freshly ground white pepper to taste
> 2 cloves garlic, finely minced
> 2 tablespoons fresh tarragon leaves

Preheat the oven to 450 degrees.

Into an oven pan large enough to fit the fish and roe, pour wine to a depth of ⅛ inch. Lay the fillets and the roe (separated in 2) in the wine. Pour the melted butter over, then sprinkle with salt, pepper, garlic, and tarragon.

Bake until the fillets are slightly browned on top, about 20 minutes. Press the roe with your index finger to establish whether it is cooked through. Be careful not to overcook as they tend to dry out and become tough.

Slice the roe on the diagonal, if you like, to improve its appearance and arrange on warmed plates or a platter with the fillets. Serve with the liquid from the pan poured over the fish and roe.

Shad and Shad Roe with Paprika, Butter, and Lemon

The shad and roe are cooked exactly as in the preceding recipe; only the sauce is different.
SERVES 2

> 2 shad skinned fillets (each 6 ounces)
> 1 pair medium shad roe
> 2 tablespoons unsalted butter, melted
> salt to taste
> freshly ground white pepper to taste
> 1 tablespoon sweet paprika
> juice of ½ lemon

Follow instructions in previous recipe but instead of using garlic and tarragon, pour on the melted butter, then sprinkle with salt, pepper, paprika, and lemon juice. Cook and serve as before.

Poached Skate or Ray with Caper and Parsley Vinaigrette

SERVES 4

> 3 pounds skate or ray, preferably skinned, cut into 4 portions
> 1 large egg yolk
> 2 teaspoons Dijon mustard
> 1 cup olive oil
> 3 tablespoons fresh lemon juice
> ¼ cup nonpareil (small) capers
> ¼ cup finely chopped fresh parsley
> 2 scallions, finely chopped
> ½ teaspoon salt
> pinch freshly ground black pepper

Put the egg yolk and mustard in a medium bowl; with an electric hand-held mixer or a wire whisk, beat until thick. Add a few drops of oil, beating continuously, until an emulsion begins to form; then continuing to whisk, pour the rest of the oil in a fine trickle to make a mayonnaise. Stir in the lemon juice, capers, parsley, scallions, salt, and pepper. Then add ½ cup lukewarm water to thin the mayonnaise. Set aside at room temperature.

Prepare the skate as directed for the skate pie on page 162.

Serve the skate hot with the sauce at room temperature.

Fried Smelt Fillets with Garlic, Mustard, and Lemon

When smelt are in season, take the opportunity to savor these sweet white-fleshed little fish. Herring could also be used.
SERVES 4

2 pounds smelt, cleaned
½ cup all-purpose flour
2 tablespoons dry English mustard
½ teaspoon salt
¼ teaspoon freshly ground white pepper
6 tablespoons (¾ stick) unsalted butter
2 cloves garlic, finely minced
¼ cup fresh lemon juice

Cut the heads off the smelt. Bone the smelt. Slip a thin pointed knife under the backbone at the head end of 1 smelt and then loosen the rib bones from the flesh. Pull the backbone off and flatten the fillets, leaving on the tail. Repeat with the rest of the smelt.

Mix the flour with the mustard, salt, and pepper.

Heat the butter in a large frying or sauté pan over medium-high heat. Add the chopped garlic and swirl around the pan. Add the smelt and fry for 1 minute on each side. Remove to a warmed serving dish. Mix the lemon juice with ¼ cup water and pour into the pan. Deglaze the pan by cooking for 1 minute. Pour the pan liquid over the smelt and serve immediately.

Broiled Whole or Fillets of Dover Sole with Lemon and Parsley Sauce

I am a great believer in eating certain fish whole. They cook and taste better. Flatfish have a central spine with sturdy flat rib bones that fan out from each side of the spine. The flesh is easily lifted off with knife and fork at the table and the central spine can be lifted out whole and put to the side. Simplicity itself. The spine together with the ribs becomes so sturdy that you could comb your hair with it! Still, there are those who find boning difficult

(which it is not), and I continue to encourage more people not to insist on filleted fish every time.
SERVES 4

> 4 *whole Dover sole or gray sole, lemon sole, petrale sole, or flounder (each about 1 pound), or 2 pounds skinned fillets, rough tissue removed (page 59)*
> *freshly ground white pepper to taste*
> *dry white wine*
> 4 *tablespoons Clarified Butter, melted (page 304)*

LEMON AND PARSLEY SAUCE
> 6 *tablespoons (¾ stick) unsalted butter, cut into pieces*
> 2 *tablespoons fresh lemon juice*
> *pinch salt*
> 2 *tablespoons finely chopped fresh parsley*

> 4 *lemon curls (Slice a lemon, then make a cut from the center of each slice outward; twist into a curl.)*

Remove the heads and insides (which are negligible) of the whole fish and trim the side fins with a pair of kitchen scissors. Make a slit down the middle of the dark side of the fish from head to tail, and cut the fillets away from the central spine, but not completely off. Open up the fillets a little and sprinkle with pepper.

Preheat the broiler. Pour wine to a depth of ⅛ inch into a broiler pan. Lay the fish in the wine and pour 1 tablespoon melted clarified butter into the opening of each fish. If using fillets, lay the fish in the wine. Spoon clarified butter over them and sprinkle with pepper.

Broil the whole fish for 5 to 7 minutes. Broil the fillets for 3 to 5 minutes, depending on the thickness of the fillets. Transfer the fish to hot serving plates or a platter.

In the meantime, make the lemon-parsley sauce. Melt the butter in a frying or sauté pan over medium high heat, shaking the pan occasionally, until the butter melts and foams. Add the lemon juice and salt. Remove from the heat and add the chopped parsley just before pouring it over the cooked fish. Garnish with lemon curls.

Gray Sole Stuffed with Shrimp, with Tomato, Basil, and Cream Sauce

SERVES 4

> 4 gray sole skinned fillets (each 6 to 8 ounces), rough tissue removed (page 59), producing 8 fillets
> 8 medium to large shrimp, (16 to 20 per pound), shell on

SAUCE
> 1½ cups Tomato Coulis (page 298,) using smaller amount of canned tomatoes with ½ cup of the juice
> ¼ cup heavy cream
> 15 basil leaves, rinsed if necessary and dried
> dry white wine
> salt to taste
> freshly ground white pepper to taste

> 2 slices tomato, cut in half

Liquidize the tomato coulis in a blender until it is smooth, a few seconds. Add the cream and 1 tablespoon chopped basil. Blend another 5 seconds.

Shell and devein the shrimp, leaving on the tails. Bring some lightly salted water to a boil in a small saucepan. Drop the shrimp into the boiling water; when the water returns to the boil, immediately drain the shrimp.

Preheat the oven to 425 degrees. Pour white wine to a depth of ⅛ inch into a baking pan.

Lay the fillets on a flat surface and place 1 shrimp on each. Starting with the thin end of each fillet, roll to enclose the shrimp. Place each rolled fillet upright in the baking pan with the shrimp tails protruding from the top. Sprinkle with salt and pepper.

Bake the rolled fillets for 10 to 15 minutes. Meanwhile, heat the sauce gently and have a warmed serving platter ready.

Fold the rest of the basil leaves in half and cut on the diagonal into ⅛-inch strips.

Pour the sauce onto the serving platter, scatter the basil leaves decoratively on the sauce, and then with the aid of a wide spatula place the rolled fillets on the sauce. Garnish with the tomato slices.

Sautéed Gray Sole or Flounder with Ginger Meunière

SERVES 4

4 gray sole skinned fillets (each 6 to 8 ounces), rough tissue removed
    (page 59), producing 8 smaller fillets
½ teaspoon salt
freshly ground white pepper to taste
½ cup all-purpose flour
1 stick (4 ounces) unsalted butter
1 tablespoon freshly grated ginger
4 scallions, finely chopped
3 tablespoons lemon juice

Mix the salt and pepper with the flour in a shallow pan or dish.
Lay the fillets in the flour and coat both sides, shaking off the
excess flour.

Melt the butter in 1 large or 2 small frying pans over medium
high heat. Sauté the fillets 2 minutes on each side. Remove to a
warm serving platter.

Swirl the ginger, scallions, and lemon juice in the remaining
butter and pour over the fish.

Gray Sole with Mustard Dill Beurre Blanc

SERVES 4

8 gray sole skinned fillets (each 3 to 4 ounces), rough tissue removed
    (page 59), producing 16 smaller fillets
dry white wine
4 tablespoons Clarified Butter, melted (page 304)
salt to taste
freshly ground white pepper to taste
1 cup Beurre Blanc (page 289)
2 tablespoons Dijon mustard
3 tablespoons fresh dill weed, cut into ½-inch lengths

Preheat the oven to 450 degrees.

For each serving, take 4 pieces of fish and lay them side by
side, slightly overlapping. Fold the ends up to the middle, then

fold the top ends down onto the bottom ends, so that it looks rather like a croissant. Pour the wine into a baking pan to a depth of ⅛ inch. Place the rolled fillets on top, spoon the butter over the fish, and sprinkle with salt and pepper. Bake for 7 to 10 minutes.

Stir the mustard and dill into the beurre blanc and spoon over the fish before serving.

Broiled Whole Striped Bass with Scallions, Garlic, Lemon, and Teriyaki

One early-summer evening in East Hampton, the artist Norman Bluhm invited me to a dinner where he served his version of this dish. It seems to me a fine way to season and cook a fresh whole striped bass. My thanks to Norman for this recipe.
SERVES 6

> 1 6-pound striped bass, scaled, cleaned, head and tail left on
> 3 scallions, trimmed of their roots and some green leaves, cut
>   lengthwise in half, then into 4-inch-long pieces
> 3 cloves garlic, finely minced
> zest of ½ lemon, cut into ⅛-inch-wide strips
> ¼ cup vegetable oil
> ¼ cup teriyaki sauce
> salt to taste
> freshly ground black pepper to taste
> dry white wine

Preheat the broiler. It might be necessary to finish the cooking in an oven, so preheat the oven to 400 degrees.

Make 5 or 6 diagonal slashes in the skin of the fish on both sides. Insert scallion strips, garlic, and lemon zest in the slits and some of all of these inside the fish. Mix the oil and teriyaki sauce and sprinkle both sides of the fish with half the mixture and salt and pepper.

Pour dry white wine to a depth of ⅛ inch into the broiler pan and lay the whole fish in the wine. Broil for 10 minutes on one side, sprinkling on more oil and teriyaki after 5 minutes. Then turn the fish over carefully, using 2 wide metal spatulas, and sprinkle with more oil and teriyaki. Broil, basting occasionally with the pan juices, until the fish is cooked, about 10 more minutes. If the skin is getting burned and the fish is still raw on the central spine (check by inserting a knife through the thickest part of the fish), finish the cooking in the oven; it shouldn't take more than another 10 minutes or so.

Remove the fish to a warmed serving platter and pour the juices over it.

I suggest serving the fish with a mixture of steamed wild and white rice and steamed whole leeks.

Striped Bass Fillets with Mussel, Tarragon, and White Wine Sauce

SERVES 6

> 6 8-ounce striped bass skin-on fillets, or 1 6-pound striped bass, filleted and small bones removed with pin nose pliers
> 1 pound (cultivated preferred) mussels, cleaned (page 42)
> ½ cup dry white wine, plus some for baking fish
> 5 tablespoons unsalted butter
> 1½ tablespoons all-purpose flour
> ¾ cup milk
> ½ cup heavy cream
> juice of ½ lemon
> salt to taste
> freshly ground white pepper to taste
> 2 tablespoons chopped fresh tarragon, or 1 teaspoon dried tarragon

Put the cleaned mussels in a medium saucepan with ½ cup white wine. Cover and bring to a boil over medium high heat. As soon as the mussels have opened, after a few minutes, remove pan from heat. Strain the juice through a fine strainer, chinois, or cheesecloth and reserve. When the mussels are cool enough to handle, take the mussels out of their shells, remove any beards, and set aside.

Make the sauce. Melt 2 tablespoons butter in a medium saucepan over medium heat, add the flour, and cook for a minute or 2, beating with a wire whisk. Add the reserved wine and mussel stock and stir. Then add the milk and cook over low heat for another 3 minutes, stirring occasionally. Add the cream, lemon juice, salt, and pepper and simmer very gently for 5 minutes. Set aside.

Preheat the oven to 450 degrees. Pour wine to a depth of ⅛ inch into a baking pan. Lay the fillets, skin side up, in the wine. Bake for 15 minutes, depending on the thickness of the fillets. In the meantime, add the mussels and tarragon to the sauce and gently reheat.

Place the fillets on a warmed serving platter or individual plates, with the sauce ladled next to the fish.

Try serving steamed peeled potatoes and sautéed spinach with this dish.

Baked Sturgeon with Duxelles

This is a rich dish that needs little embellishment.
SERVES 4

4 skinned sturgeon fillets (each 6 to 8 ounces)
4 tablespoons (½ stick) unsalted butter
1 medium onion, finely chopped (1 cup)
6 ounces mushrooms, finely chopped
½ teaspoon salt, plus additional to taste
¼ teaspoon freshly ground black pepper, plus additional to taste
¼ cup heavy cream
dry white wine
4 tablespoons Clarified Butter (page 304)

Melt 4 tablespoons butter in a medium frying or sauté pan over medium high heat. Add the onion and sauté until it starts to brown. Stir the mushrooms into the onions and cook until they lose all their moisture and turn dark. Add the salt, pepper, and cream. Stir and heat through. Set aside.

Preheat the oven to 400 degrees. Pour wine to a depth of ⅛ inch into a baking pan. Lay the sturgeon in the wine and pour the clarified butter over. Sprinkle with a little salt and pepper. Bake until they are cooked through, 10 to 15 minutes.

At the same time, gently reheat the duxelles sauce to serve with the baked sturgeon.

Broiled Sturgeon with Pistachio-Basil Butter

The recipe for this delicious compound butter came from Curt Stimpson, president of the Crystal Nordic Fresh Fish Company in Seattle, Washington. The butter can also be used with swordfish, rockfish, cod, pollock, and bass (see Note).
SERVES 6

> 3 pounds skin-on sturgeon, on the bone
> ½ cup (2 ounces) pink (red) pistachios, in the shell
> 10 basil leaves, rinsed if necessary and dried
> 1 stick (4 ounces) unsalted butter, room temperature
> 1 clove garlic, finely minced
> ¼ teaspoon salt
> ½ teaspoon freshly ground black pepper
> 1 teaspoon sugar
> 1 tablespoon fresh lime juice
> dry white wine

Shell the pistachios and put them in the bowl of a food processor or blender. Process the pistachios until finely chopped. Finely chop the basil leaves. Add the basil, butter, garlic, salt, pepper, sugar, and lime juice and process until well blended. Put the pistachio-basil butter in a bowl.

Cut the sturgeon flesh from the central spine and rib bones, producing 2 pieces of flesh. Skin the fish and cut the flesh into ¼-inch-thick escalopes.

Preheat the broiler. Pour wine to a depth of ¹⁄₁₆ inch into a broiler pan and place the fish in the wine. Broil the fish escalopes for 1 minute; then spread some of the pistachio butter on top of them. Broil until the sturgeon is just cooked through, 1 to 2 minutes. Transfer the sturgeon to a warmed serving platter or individual plates.

In the meantime, heat the rest of the pistachio butter and serve in a warmed sauceboat.

Note: If you plan to serve the pistachio butter with another fish, shape it into a 2-inch round on a piece of plastic wrap, roll it into a log shape, and refrigerate or freeze until needed. When broiling or baking fish, cut slices of the butter and lay them on top of the fish halfway through the cooking time.

Broiled Swordfish with Sweet Red Pepper, Oregano, and Lemon Sauce

SERVES 6

6 swordfish steaks (each 8 ounces and 1 inch thick)
1 large sweet red pepper, stems, seeds, and ribs removed, cut into
   ¼-inch cubes
juice of 2 lemons
1 cup olive oil
1 teaspoon salt
½ teaspoon freshly ground black pepper
3 tablespoons fresh oregano leaves, picked from their stems
dry white wine

Put the pepper in a bowl with the lemon juice, oil, salt, pepper and oregano and mix well.

Preheat the broiler and pour wine to a depth of ⅛ inch into the broiler pan. Lay the swordfish steaks in the wine and broil for 3 minutes. Pour the sauce over the fish and continue to broil until the fish is cooked through and lightly browned, 3 to 4 more minutes. Immediately transfer to a warmed serving platter or individual plates. Pour the sauce in the pan over the fish.

Broiled Swordfish with Brown Butter and Capers

This sauce also goes well with skate or ray and just about any flatfish, such as sole or flounder.
SERVES 4

4 swordfish steaks (each 8 ounces and 1 inch thick)
dry white wine
1 stick (4 ounces) unsalted butter
1 tablespoon fresh lemon juice
pinch salt
¼ cup nonpareil (small) capers

Preheat the broiler. Pour wine to a depth of ⅛ inch into the broiler pan and lay the swordfish steaks in the wine.

Melt the butter in a medium frying pan over medium to high heat. When it bubbles, keep your eye on it and wait until it turns a light brown. As soon as this happens, take the pan off the heat. After 30 seconds pour the clear brown butter into a saucepan; discard the burned milk solids at the bottom of the pan. Keep the butter warm.

Spoon a little of the brown butter over the swordfish steaks and broil until the steaks are lightly browned and cooked through, 6 to 7 minutes.

Place the swordfish steaks on a warmed serving platter or on individual plates. Add the lemon juice, salt, and capers to the remaining warm brown butter, stir, and pour over the fish.

Broiled Swordfish with Pesto and Tomato Concassé

SERVES 6

6 swordfish steaks (each 8 ounces and 1 inch thick)
3 medium ripe tomatoes, skinned, seeded, and cut into ¼-inch cubes
    (page 305)
pinch salt
dry white wine
3 tablespoons Clarified Butter, melted (page 304)
1 recipe Pesto (page 294)
6 lemon wedges

Put the tomato concassé in a sieve, add a pinch of salt, and let drain for 45 minutes.

Preheat the broiler and pour wine to a depth of ⅛ inch into a broiler pan. Lay the swordfish steaks in the wine, top with a little clarified butter, and broil for 3 minutes. Then spread pesto on the steaks and broil until the fish is cooked through, 3 to 4 more minutes.

Transfer to a warm serving platter or individual plates, and serve immediately with the tomato concassé on the side. Garnish with lemon wedges.

Broiled Swordfish or Mako en Brochette

This dish can be cooked under a broiler or on a charcoal grill, which provides added flavor. You could also use a combination of mako and swordfish.
SERVES 6

> 3 pounds swordfish or mako shark steak
> 1 cup olive oil
> juice of 1½ lemons
> 2 tablespoons fresh oregano leaves
> 1 teaspoon salt
> 1 teaspoon freshly ground black pepper
> 2 sweet red peppers, stems, seeds, and ribs removed, cut into
>   1½-inch squares

Mix together the olive oil, lemon juice, oregano, salt, and pepper in a small bowl.

Remove the skin from the fish and cut into 1-inch cubes. Using 10-inch skewers, spear the fish, alternating with pieces of red pepper. Marinate in the olive oil mixture for at least 10 minutes.

Preheat the broiler or prepare a charcoal fire.

Broil or grill for 8 to 10 minutes, depending on the available heat, turning occasionally.

Serve with some of the remaining marinade poured over.

Broiled Swordfish with Lemon Beurre Blanc

SERVES 4

> 4 swordfish steaks (each 8 ounces and 1 inch thick)
> dry white wine
> 2 tablespoons Clarified Butter (page 304)
> ¼ cup fresh lemon juice
> 1 cup Beurre Blanc (page 289)
> salt to taste
> freshly ground black pepper to taste

Preheat the broiler and pour wine to a depth of ⅛ inch into the broiler pan. Lay the swordfish steaks in the wine and brush with the butter. Season with salt and pepper. Broil until the fish is slightly browned and cooked through, 5 to 6 minutes.

In the meantime, put the lemon juice in a frying pan and reduce it over medium heat to a thick syrup. Remove from heat, add the beurre blanc, and whisk thoroughly. Serve the swordfish on a warmed serving platter or individual plates with the lemon beurre blanc poured over one end of each steak.

Fried Trout with Mint and Garlic Stuffing and Brown Butter

SERVES 4

> 4 brook trout (each about 8 ounces) boned
> 4 cloves garlic
> 4 finely chopped tablespoons fresh mint
> salt to taste
> 1 cup all-purpose flour
> 1 tablespoon sweet paprika
> freshly ground black pepper to taste
> 8 tablespoons Clarified Butter (page 304)
> 2 tablespoons fresh lemon juice
> 1 lemon, cut into quarters

Cut the heads, tails, and fins from the boned trout with kitchen scissors.

Boil the garlic cloves in water until they are tender, about 20 minutes, depending on how fresh they are. This removes the raw taste of the garlic and consequent breath odor, but it still retains flavor.

Mash the garlic cloves on a chopping board with the flat of a heavy knife; add the mint and a pinch of salt. With the fish spread open flat, spread this mixture on the flesh. Fold each fish back into its original shape.

Mix the flour, paprika, salt, and pepper together in a shallow dish or pan. Heat the butter in a large frying pan over medium high heat. Coat both sides of the fish with the flour and shake off the excess. Lay them in the hot butter and fry for 4 minutes each side. Remove the fish carefully with a large spatula to a warm serving platter. Cook the butter remaining in the pan until it turns a light brown color. Remove from heat, add the lemon juice and a pinch of salt, and pour over the fish. Garnish with lemon quarters.

Marinated Trout

The trout need to marinate 24 hours before serving, so start this recipe the day before serving.
SERVES 4

> 4 trout (each 8 ounces), boned, with heads and tails left on
> ¾ cup dry white wine
> ¾ cup light olive oil
> 1 clove garlic, thinly sliced
> 1 tablespoon coriander seeds, crushed with a mortar and pestle or
>   coffee grinder
> 1 teaspoon salt
> 10 black peppercorns
> pinch dried thyme
> 1 bay leaf
> 4 slices lemon

Cut the small fins off the trout with kitchen scissors.

Lay the trout head to tail in a shallow casserole or frying or sauté pan in which the trout will fit closely together.

Combine the wine and oil in a small bowl and pour over the fish. Sprinkle on the garlic, coriander seeds, salt, peppercorns, and thyme. Place the bay leaf in the center and a slice of lemon on each fish.

Cover the pan and cook over low heat for 25 minutes, basting with the liquid after 15 minutes. Let the trout cool in the liquid in the casserole (or if cooked in a frying pan or sauté pan transfer all to a serving dish). Cool, cover with plastic wrap, and refrigerate overnight.

Serve at room temperature.

Trout with Cider and Tarragon

This is a beautiful way to serve trout, and the recipe is easily and quickly made.

SERVES 4

4 trout (each 8 ounces), boned, heads and tails left on
2 cups fresh apple cider
1 tablespoon fresh tarragon
salt to taste
freshly ground white pepper to taste
2 teaspoons cornstarch

Put the trout in a large frying or sauté pan, or use 2 pans, so that the trout can lay head to tail comfortably. Pour the cider over them and bring to the boil over medium heat. Lower the heat and simmer for 5 minutes, then turn the trout over carefully and simmer for another 5 minutes. Remove to a cutting board.

Pour out ½ cup cider into a bowl. Add tarragon to the rest of the cider and continue to simmer for 5 minutes, adding a pinch of salt and pepper. Whisk the cornstarch into the cooled cider in the bowl.

In the meantime quickly remove the skin and fins from both sides of the trout, leaving the heads and tails intact. Place the trout on a warmed serving dish. Whisk the cider and cornstarch mixture into the simmering cider, and continue to simmer until the sauce thickens. Spoon the sauce over the trout and serve immediately.

Speckled Trout with Pecan Sauce

I have enjoyed this dish at Paul Prudhomme's K-Paul's in New Orleans, and with thanks to the great Chef Prudhomme here is my version. I admit this recipe is pale compared to Paul's: less cayenne, less butter, and fewer pecans. His is a rubust, gutsy conception, a little too rich and caloric for me. But if you are ever near the restaurant I urge you to have it there!

Speckled trout comes from the Gulf; you can use another sweet, firm white fish, such as pollock, sea bass, or red snapper.
SERVES 6

6 skinned speckled trout fillets (each 6 to 8 ounces)

SAUCE
1 stick (4 ounces) unsalted butter, softened
1 medium onion, finely chopped (1 cup)
3 cloves garlic, finely minced
2 tablespoons fresh lemon juice
½ cup pecan meal, or 2 ounces pecan halves, very finely chopped
½ teaspoon salt
10 drops Tabasco

¼ cup cornflour (available in health food stores)
¼ cup all-purpose flour
½ teaspoon salt
¼ teaspoon freshly ground black pepper
1 teaspoon sweet paprika
pinch cayenne
8 tablespoons Clarified Butter (page 304)
18 pecan halves

In a food processor or blender, make the sauce by processing the butter, onion, garlic, lemon juice, pecan meal, salt, and Tabasco. Set aside.

Sift the cornflour, flour, salt, pepper, paprika, and cayenne into a shallow dish.

Preheat the broiler.

Heat the clarified butter in a frying pan large enough to hold all 6 fillets, or use 2 pans, over high heat. Put the sauce mixture into a small saucepan set over very low heat and let sauce simmer gently while you fry the fish.

Lightly coat the fillets with the seasoned flour and shake off excess. When the clarified butter is hot, fry the fillets until golden brown, 3 to 5 minutes each side, depending on the thickness of the fillets.

Lay the fillets in the broiler pan, top with equal portions of the sauce, and broil for 30 seconds. Remove the fillets to a warmed serving dish and place 3 pecan halves on top of each fillet. Serve with the remaining sauce from the broiler pan poured beside the fillets.

Broiled Tuna with Onion and Black Olive Confit

This sauce is a perfect accompaniment to broiled albacore tuna or sturgeon. The long, slow cooking of the sliced onions sweetens them, and their flavor is set off by the chopped black olives.
SERVES 6

> 1 3-pound skinned piece of tuna or 6 8-ounce skinned steaks
> 3 large onions (1½ pounds), thinly sliced
> 2½ cups dry white wine
> 1 tablespoon dark brown sugar
> ½ teaspoon salt
> 10 large black olives (preferably French, Greek, or Moroccan,
>   preserved in oil and herbs), pitted and chopped
> freshly ground white pepper to taste

Put the onions in a medium saucepan. Add 2 cups wine and enough water to cover the onions by 1 inch. Cover the saucepan and cook over medium heat until the onions are tender, about 2 hours. The cooking time will depend on the freshness of the onions.

Uncover, add the sugar and salt, and cook until the liquid evaporates. (If the onions are very tender and have started to turn a pale brown, pour off most of the liquid but leave the onions moist.) Stir in the olives.

Preheat the broiler. Cut the tuna into 6 slices if bought in one piece. Pour the rest of the wine into the broiler pan and place the tuna in the wine. Sprinkle with pepper.

Broil until the tuna is just firm to the touch, about 5 minutes, for tuna tends to dry out quickly. At the same time, reheat the onion and black olive confit. Serve the confit with the tuna.

Albacore with Tomato, Green Pepper, and Basil Sauce

I ate a wonderful version of this dish in The Way Station Restaurant in Cayucos, California, during the summer of 1984. The fish was fresh from the Pacific and the tomatoes, luscious sun-ripened beauties. Frozen albacore is also excellent, if properly executed on board as done by several fish companies on the West Coast.
SERVES 6

> 3 pounds albacore
> ¼ cup olive oil
> 1 medium onion, finely chopped (1 cup)
> 3 cloves garlic, finely chopped
> 1 green pepper, stems, seeds, and ribs removed, finely chopped
> 4 medium to large tomatoes, skinned, seeded, and cut into ½-inch
>   cubes (page 305)
> salt to taste
> freshly ground black pepper to taste
> dry white wine
> 3 tablespoons Clarified Butter, melted (page 304)
> ½ cup fresh basil leaves, rinsed if necessary and dried

Heat the oil in a medium saucepan over medium heat. Add the onion and garlic and sauté, stirring occasionally, until glossy. Add the green pepper and sauté for 3 minutes. Add the tomatoes, salt, pepper. Cover the pan and lower the heat. Simmer the sauce for 10 minutes.

In the meantime, preheat the broiler. Pour white wine to a depth of ⅛ inch into a broiler pan. Cut the albacore into 6 thick slices and place in the wine. Spoon the butter over the fish.

Fold the basil leaves lengthwise in half and cut them diagonally into ⅛-inch strips.

Broil the albacore until cooked through, 5 to 7 minutes. Make sure it doesn't dry out. Stir the basil strips into the sauce. Serve the albacore with the sauce on the side.

Broiled Whole Turbotin with Tabasco Hollandaise

At the time of writing, small turbot (*turbotin* in French) are being imported to these shores from Europe and New Zealand through restaurant suppliers. This fine fish, with its firm sweet white flesh, will assuredly find its way to fish stores soon.

In this recipe, you broil the turbotin, dark skin up and sprinkled with oil and paprika. When they are cooked the skin turns a luscious dark brown–reddish color. Sole could also be used.
SERVES 4

    4 turbotin (each about 1 pound)
    8 drops Tabasco
    1 cup Blender Hollandaise (page 285)
    4 teaspoons olive oil
    4 teaspoons sweet paprika

Add the Tabasco to the hollandaise sauce. Taste the sauce and add more Tabasco if you would like it hotter.

Cut off the fish heads and remove the insides (which are negligible). Trim the side fins with kitchen scissors.

Preheat the broiler and coat a broiler pan with a little oil. Place the fish, dark skin up, in the pan and pour a little oil on the skin. Sprinkle lightly with paprika. Broil for 5 to 7 minutes, depending on the thickness of the fish.

Serve with Tabasco hollandaise.

Baked Whole Fish with Saffron Mayonnaise

This is a dish suggested to me by my friend Jane de Rochemont. Because the fish is served at room temperature, it can be prepared several hours in advance.
SERVES 6

> 1 6-pound striped bass, red snapper, or pollock, cleaned and scaled,
>   head and tail left on
> ½ teaspoon saffron steeped in 2 tablespoons dry white wine
>   for 1 hour
> ¼ cup dry white wine
> 1½ cups Mayonnaise (page 286)
> ¼ cup Pernod
> salt to taste
> freshly ground white pepper to taste
> 1 lemon, cut into razor-thin slices and then in half

Stir the saffron and wine into the mayonnaise.

Preheat the oven to 400 degrees.

Cut a length of heavy aluminum foil 6 inches longer than the fish. Mix the Pernod and wine and pour a little on the foil. Place the fish on top and sprinkle the inside of the fish with salt and pepper. Pour the rest of the Pernod and wine over the fish. Bring the 2 edges of the foil up over the fish and make a double fold for a tight seal. Also fold the ends over the head and tail.

Pour a little water onto a baking sheet with ½-inch sides. Place the fish on the baking sheet and bake for 35 minutes. Remove from the oven, open the package, and insert a thin knife into the thickest part of the flesh to test for doneness. Bake a few more minutes if necessary.

When the fish is cooked, open up the foil and let cool for 10 minutes. Pour the fish juices into a bowl. Carefully peel off the skin, also removing the fins and the brownish flesh. Turn the fish over and repeat this operation. Place the fish, still in the aluminum foil, on a serving platter and very carefully slide the foil from under the fish (or tear the foil from each side without damaging the fish). Let cool to room temperature.

Arrange the lemon slices on the fish, to resemble fish scales, and serve with the saffron mayonnaise.

Baked or Broiled Fish with Sun-Dried Tomato Sauce

This flavorful sauce goes well with a variety of fish. Baked or broiled grouper, halibut, red snapper, tuna, weakfish (sea trout), tilefish, or gray sole can be served with this easily made sauce.

Sun-dried tomatoes, sold in oil or simply in a dry state, are obtainable in specialty stores, the dry tomatoes costing far less than the ones in oil. Sometimes dry-state sun-dried tomatoes are extremely salty—taste one before purchasing.

This sauce is finished with beurre blanc or heavy cream.
SERVES 4

4 fish skin-on fillets (each 8 ounces), small bones removed
2 ounces sun-dried tomatoes (dry state)
1 cup dry white wine
1 bay leaf
2 tablespoons olive oil
¼ teaspoon dried oregano
¼ teaspoon dried basil
½ cup Beurre Blanc (page 289), or ½ cup heavy cream

Put the tomatoes in a small saucepan with 1 cup water, ½ cup wine, the bay leaf, oil, oregano, and basil. Bring to a boil over medium heat, then turn the heat down to low and simmer uncovered for 45 minutes. Add more water if mixture gets too dry. When the tomatoes are cooked, take off the heat. Let them cool somewhat, then put them and whatever liquid remains in a food processor or blender and process until they become a fairly smooth purée, 1 minute or more.

For Baked Fish. Preheat the oven to 450 degrees. Pour wine to a depth of ⅛ inch into a baking dish. Lay the fish fillets in the wine, sprinkle with white pepper, and cover each fillet with a wilted lettuce leaf. Bake for 15 minutes, depending on the thickness of the fillets. Remove the lettuce leaves before serving.

To finish the sauce, 7 minutes before the fish has cooked, heat the sun-dried tomato purée with ½ cup wine in a frying or sauté pan over medium heat until the wine has almost evaporated. Off heat, add the beurre blanc or cream and stir together well before spooning the sauce over one end of the fish fillets.

For Broiled Fish. Preheat the broiler. Pour wine to a depth of ⅛ inch into a broiler pan. Lay the fish fillets in the wine, spoon a little melted clarified butter on the fillets, and sprinkle with a little white pepper.

Broil for 7 to 10 minutes, depending on the thickness of the fillets. Finish the sauce and serve for baked fish.

Broiled Fish Fillets with Citrus and Fennel Sauce

Although I do not often combine fruit with fish, this sauce is a beautiful complement to grouper, tilefish, gray sole, and red mullet (imported).
SERVES 4

> 4 skinned fillets of grouper, tilefish, gray sole, or red mullet (each 8 ounces), small bones removed with pin nose pliers; or in case of sole, see page 59
> ¾ cup fresh orange juice
> ¼ cup fresh lemon juice
> dry white wine
> 3 tablespoons Clarified Butter, melted (page 304)
> salt to taste
> freshly ground white pepper to taste
> 1 small bulb fennel, halved, hard core removed, then cut into ¼-inch strips
> 8 orange segments (Cut off all peel and pith from an orange. Use a sharp thin knife to cut down against the inside of the membrane of each segment. Then cut against the membrane on the left side of each segment and, without removing the knife, turn the blade up against the membrane on the right side, releasing it.)

Preheat the broiler.

Mix the orange and lemon juices together in a small bowl.

Pour wine to a depth of ⅛ inch into a broiler pan. Lay the fish fillets in the wine. If cooking sole fillets, fold them in half. Spoon clarified butter on the fillets and sprinkle with salt and pepper. Broil the fillets for 4 minutes, then pour the mixed juices over the fillets and scatter the fennel strips around the fish. Finish broiling, another 3 to 4 minutes, keeping in mind that grouper takes longer than the other fish.

Remove the fillets, fennel, and juices to a warm serving platter or individual plates. Garnish with orange segments.

Harlequin

Harlequin refers to the multicolored aspect of this dish. A pink-skinned fish is served skin side up with a pale yellow beurre blanc, and a silver-skinned fish is served with a red bordelaise sauce.

SERVES 6

1½ pounds skin-on fillets of red snapper, rockfish, or red mullet
1½ pounds skin-on fillets of striped bass, sea bass, or sea trout

BORDELAISE SAUCE (1½ CUPS)
2 cups red wine
8 shallots, finely chopped
1 teaspoon dried thyme
1 bay leaf
salt to taste
freshly ground black pepper to taste
2 cups veal or chicken stock (preferably homemade)
1 tablespoon tomato paste

1½ cups Beurre Blanc (page 289)
4 tablespoons light olive oil
4 tablespoons Clarified Butter (page 304)

Prepare the bordelaise sauce before the beurre blanc as it takes the longer of the two. For the bordelaise, put all the ingredients in a medium saucepan and bring to the boil. Boil gently until reduced to 1½ cups. Remove the bay leaf and taste for seasoning. Strain through a fine strainer or chinois if you wish a smooth sauce.

Remove the small bones with pin nose pliers from the fish fillets. Cut both types of fish into 6 equal portions each.

Preheat the broiler.

Using 2 large frying pans, put the oil in one to cook the pink-skinned fish, and clarified butter in the other to cook the silver-skinned fish.

Heat the oil and butter over medium heat and put the fish fillets skin side up in their pans. Fry for 3 to 5 minutes, depending on the thickness of the fillets. Spoon some oil and butter from the frying pans on top of the fish. Put the frying pans under the broiler for 1 minute to bring out the color of the skin.

To serve, place one fillet of each fish on warmed individual plates and spoon bordelaise sauce over one end of the silver-skinned fish and beurre blanc over one end of the pink-skinned fish.

Panache of Fish and Shellfish

If you want to produce an unusual and elaborate dish to please your guests, this will fill your requirements. Three different types of fish are poached and served with three different sauces, thereby suggesting the word panache with its parti-colored, variegated appearance.

You may use any combination of fish suitable for poaching. I suggest the following only as a guide.
SERVES 6

> 1 2-pound lobster
> 1 pound skinned monkfish fillet (page 41)
> 1 pound striped bass skin-on fillet, small bones removed with pin
>   nose pliers
> 1 recipe Poaching Liquid (page 304)
> 1 recipe Tomato, Basil, and Cream Sauce (page 220)
> 1 recipe Spinach Sauce (page 297)
> 1 cup Beurre Blanc (page 289)

Refer to the recipe on page 261 to obtain raw lobster meat. Slice the tail meat into 6 portions and use the knuckle and claw meat.

Slice the monkfish and striped bass into 6 portions each.

Bring the poaching liquid to a gentle simmer in a large shallow saucepan. Heat the tomato, basil, and cream and spinach sauces separately in small saucepans. The beurre blanc should be warm.

Put the monkfish in a strainer into the hot poaching liquid and cook for 3 minutes. Add the lobster pieces and the striped bass. Poach for 5 more minutes.

Drain and arrange the different fish on warmed serving plates.

Cover the lobster with beurre blanc, the monkfish with the tomato, basil, and cream sauce, and the striped bass (skin side up) with spinach sauce.

Fish and Vegetable Tempura

Little bundles of finely cut vegetables and fish are coated with a light flavored batter and then deep-fried. I got the idea to make these after buying vegetable tempura from one of the Korean vegetable markets in my neighborhood. I don't know how they make them, but here is my version with fish.
SERVES 5

1 pound skinned monkfish fillet (2 pounds on the bone) (page 41)
1 large egg white
1 cup all-purpose flour
½ teaspoon salt
freshly ground white pepper to taste
pinch cayenne
½ pound eggplant
½ pound zucchini, rinsed
¼ bulb fennel, trimmed
1 medium carrot, scraped
4 scallions, trimmed of their roots and some green leaves
2 tablespoons freshly grated ginger
1 quart oil (Crisco preferred)

To make the batter, beat the egg white in a bowl with a wire whisk and stir in 1 scant cup cold water. Then stir in the flour, salt, white pepper, and cayenne. Set aside.

Cut the eggplant, zucchini, and fennel into ¼-inch sticks, 3 inches long. Cut the carrot into ⅛-inch sticks, 3 inches long. Cut the scallions into 3-inch lengths, and in half lengthwise if large.

Cut the monkfish into ½-inch sticks, 3 inches long. Put the vegetable sticks in a medium bowl and toss together lightly with your hands. Add the monkfish sticks and grated ginger and toss with the vegetables.

Heat the oil in an electric fryer, wok, or saucepan to 375 degrees. Preheat the oven to 200 degrees.

Pour the batter over the vegetable and fish mixture and stir together so that all the pieces are coated. With a slotted spoon, form bundles of the mixture with the vegetables sticking out this way and that. Form 10 bundles with the mixture, 2 for each serving. Fry 2 bundles at a time for 5 minutes, turning halfway through the cooking time. Drain on paper towels and keep warm in the oven while you fry the remaining bundles. Be sure the oil returns to 375 degrees before frying the next batch.

The tempura bundles can be prepared in advance and reheated in a 350-degree oven for 5 minutes just before serving.

Gefilte Fish

This recipe is a Polish version given to me by my writer friend Bruce Stutz. Of course, gefilte fish can be eaten anytime, but the traditional time to eat it is at Passover at the first Seder. Drink a little slivovitz beforehand to promote appetite and then serve the gefilte fish with freshly grated horseradish mixed with beet. It is made with various freshwater fish, such as whitefish, pike, and carp. The fish are cut into steaks and the flesh is carefully cut away, leaving the central spine, rib bones, and skin intact. Then a stuffing (*gefilte* means stuffed) is made with the flesh. The steaks are reassembled and then poached-steamed. They are served cool with jellied stock and sliced carrots. I have been told that any bones found in the gefilte fish are stuck into the carrot slices.

The fish must be very fresh, indeed, even alive—they can be kept in the bathtub and stunned at the last moment! The fish can command a high price at Passover time so this is a fairly expensive and laborious dish to make but well worth the effort. It is so much better than storebought—in looks, taste, and texture!

Make the gefilte fish the day before you serve it, so they chill well and the stock has time to gel.

SERVES 6

> *5 to 6 pounds cleaned whole freshwater fish, such as: 2½ pounds*
> *whitefish, 1½ pounds pike, and 1-pound piece of carp, all with*
> *skin on*
> *3 carrots*
> *1 large yellow onion (skin reserved), thinly sliced*
> *3 stalks celery, diagonally sliced into 1-inch slices*
> *1 medium onion, finely chopped (1 cup)*
> *1 large egg, lightly beaten*
> *1 teaspoon salt*
> *freshly ground white pepper to taste*
> *2 tablespoons finely chopped fresh parsley*
> *freshly grated horseradish mixed with chopped cooked beet*

Cut the heads off the whitefish and pike behind the pectoral fin; then cut the fish into 1-inch-thick steaks. When you reach about

3 inches from the tail, put the tails aside for the moment. Using a sharp knife, carefully cut away all the flesh from the steaks, leaving the skin and bones intact. (Be especially sure to keep the skin intact. The skin will flop to the sides of the central bone.) Extract the flesh from the tail ends. Fillet the carp and skin the fillets; save the bones for the stock but discard the carp skin. Put all the fish flesh in a bowl. You should have about 2½ cups.

Scrape the carrots and carve 3 lengthwise small grooves down each carrot, so that when they are sliced they will look pretty. Slice the carrots ⅛ inch thick.

Put the carrot, yellow onion and its skin (for color), and celery in a large pot. Choose 6 of the largest and best-looking emptied fish steaks to stuff and set these aside. Add the rest of the emptied steaks to the stockpot with enough water to cover. Bring to a boil, lower the heat, and simmer for 20 minutes. Skim off any scum as it rises to the surface with a fine strainer. When the stock is done, turn off the heat and let it stand until you are ready to poach-steam the gefilte fish.

Using the fine cutting plate of a meat grinder, grind the fish flesh into a bowl. Add the chopped onion to the bowl and put the mixture through again. Add the egg to the fish and mix well. Mix in the salt and a fair amount of pepper. You can taste the mixture raw or cook a spoonful of the mixture in a little simmering water for 2 to 3 minutes and taste for seasoning.

Lay the emptied fish skins on a wet surface and, using a table knife dipped in cold water, fill the skins with the ground fish. Curve the belly flaps together and fill these hollows as well. Pile the filling higher in the middle and smooth the surface with the knife. Bring the stock to a simmer over medium heat, lower the heat, and lay the stuffed fish slices on top of the bones and vegetables in the stock. Cover the pot and poach-steam for 10 to 15 minutes. The gefilte fish are cooked when firm to the touch.

Carefully lift the gefilte fish out of the stock and cool on a serving platter with 2-inch sides. Hunt through the stock and pick out as many carrot slices as you can find and put them on the serving platter. Strain the stock through a fine strainer or chinois (use paper towels or cheesecloth if you have neither of these). Pour the stock on top of the gefilte fish and carrots and let cool. Cover and refrigerate overnight.

Serve your company a small shot of slivovitz. Sprinkle the gefilte fish with chopped parsley and serve with the freshly grated horseradish mixed with beet.

Cold Broiled Fish with Gazpacho Sauce

This is a simple summer dish that can be prepared in advance. Any of several fish can be used. The sauce is made with the basic ingredients of a gazpacho soup; however, it is not soupy—just a vibrantly flavored garnish to set off the fish.
SERVES 6

> 1 3-pound skinned fillet or 6 8-ounce skinned fillets of any of the
>   following: scrod, cod, striped bass, swordfish, grouper, or bluefish,
>   small bones removed with pin nose pliers

GAZPACHO SAUCE
>   ½ seedless cucumber, peeled and coarsley grated
>   2 large sun-ripened tomatoes, skinned, seeded, and cut into ¼-inch
>   cubes (page 305)
>   1 green bell pepper, stems, seeds and ribs removed, coarsely chopped
>   3 stalks celery, coarsely chopped
>   2 scallions, trimmed of their roots and some green leaves, finely
>   chopped
>   3 tablespoons finely chopped fresh parsley
>   2 cloves garlic, finely minced
>   salt to taste
>   freshly ground black pepper to taste
>   1 teaspoon fresh marjoram or oregano, finely chopped
>   1 tablespoon fresh basil, finely chopped
>   2 tablespoons olive oil
>   1 teaspoon red wine vinegar
>   juice of ½ lemon

>   dry white wine
>   3 tablespoons Clarified Butter, melted (page 304)
>   salt to taste
>   freshly ground white pepper to taste

Drain the grated cucumber in a sieve for 20 minutes.
   Put the tomato concassé in a medium bowl.
   Put the green pepper and celery in a food processor or blender and process until finely chopped, but don't let them become mush! Add to the tomato concassé with all of the other sauce

ingredients. Mix well and let rest uncovered in the refrigerator for 30 minutes.

Preheat the broiler. Pour wine to a depth of ⅛ inch into the broiler pan. Place the fish in the wine, spoon the clarified butter over, and sprinkle with salt and pepper. Broil for 5 to 7 minutes, depending on the thickness of the fillet(s). Grouper takes a little longer than the other fish. Remove to a serving platter. Refrigerate, covered with plastic wrap, if not eating right away. Be sure to take the fish and the sauce out of the refrigerator 20 minutes or so before serving.

I suggest serving this dish with a potato and vinaigrette salad and cold steamed green beans.

Cold Broiled Fish Fillet with Coronation Curry Mayonnaise

This is a good dish to serve in the summer for a dinner party or buffet. To make a handsome dish, broil a large fish fillet, such as bluefish, mackerel, weakfish, or tilefish, and serve it with the sauce and garnish. You can also broil smaller individual fillets such as sole or flounder.
SERVES 8

1 4-pound skin-on fillet of bluefish, mackerel, weakfish, or tilefish, or 4 pounds small skinned fillets of sole, flounder, etc., small bones removed with pin nose pliers

CURRY SAUCE
1 medium onion, finely chopped (1 cup)
3 tablespoons vegetable oil
2 tablespoons curry powder or paste
1 teaspoon ground cumin
1 teaspoon ground coriander
1 cup red wine
1 tablespoon dark brown sugar
1 tablespoon tomato paste
salt to taste
freshly ground black pepper to taste
2 pinches cayenne
1 tablespoon soy sauce
1 cup Mayonnaise (page 286)
½ cup apricot preserves
juice of ½ lemon

dry white wine
4 tablespoons Clarified Butter, melted (page 304)
salt to taste
freshly ground black pepper to taste

1 bunch watercress
8 lemon curls (Thinly slice a lemon, then make a cut from the center outward; twist slice into a curl.)

In a small saucepan, sauté the chopped onion in the oil until soft over medium low heat. Add the curry, cumin, and coriander and cook over very low heat for 10 minutes, to allow the curry flavor to develop. Add the wine, brown sugar, tomato paste, salt, pepper, cayenne, and soy sauce and simmer uncovered for 30 minutes. The sauce will reduce and become quite thick. Let cool.

When the curry sauce is cool, mix it with the mayonnaise, apricot preserves, and lemon juice. Set aside at room temperature.

Preheat the broiler. Pour wine into the broiler pan to a depth of ⅛ inch. Place the fillet or fillets (if using sole or flounder fillets, fold them in half) in the wine, spoon the melted butter over, and sprinkle with salt and pepper. Broil the fish for 7 minutes or so, depending on the thickness of the fillet(s).

Arrange the fish on a large serving platter and let cool. If preparing beforehand, cover with plastic wrap and refrigerate until 20 minutes before serving time.

Before serving, spoon the sauce around the fish, decorated with watercress sprigs and lemon curls.

Shellfish

Abalone with Marsala

Dungeness Crab with Braised Leeks, Ginger and White Wine

Crab Cakes with Salsa

Crab and Dill Strudel with Leek Purée

Sautéed Soft-Shell Crabs with Lime Butter

Broiled Soft-Shell Crabs in Puff Pastry Shells

Stone Crab Claws with Assorted Cold Cooked and Raw Shellfish

Lobster Steamed with Beer

Lobster Wrapped in Cabbage Leaves

Sautéed Lobster with Champagne and Tarragon Sauce

Lobster Stew

Poached Sea Scallops with Ginger Béarnaise

Broiled Scallops with Fennel Sauce

Scallops en Brochette with Avgolemono Sauce

Bay Scallops with Garlic Butter, Garnished with Shrimp

Bay Scallops with Jalapeño Peppers, Garlic, and Parsley

Poached Scallops with Their Roe, with Shallot and Wine Sauce

Broiled Skewered Shrimp and Scallops with Sweet Red Pepper Glaze

Sautéed Shrimp with Snow Peas and Scallions, Deglazed with Vodka

Poached Shrimp with Sweet Red Pepper Sauce

Broiled Shrimp with Green Peppercorn Sauce

Barbecue Shrimp—New Orleans Style

Squid and Spinach Gratin

Stuffed Squid

Broiled Squid with Chives and Sesame Seeds

Ragout of Fish and Shellfish

Abalone with Marsala Sauce

I encourage you to try to find abalone; they have a delicious flavor and come in a beautiful shell you can save. Japanese fish stores often carry abalone.
SERVES 4

2 abalone (page 22)
1¼ sticks (5 ounces) unsalted butter
1 cup all-purpose flour
salt to taste
freshly ground white pepper to taste
3 large eggs, beaten
¾ cup Marsala
¼ cup dry white wine
1 tablespoon finely chopped fresh parsley

Push a wide wooden spatula under the abalone to detach it from the shell. Using a sharp knife, cut off the dark fringe that surrounds the flesh and scrape off the dark skin. Cut away the dark intestinal vein and finally cut off the lid (operculum), which will leave a nice piece of white flesh. Cut the flesh downward into ½-inch slices.

Using a smooth-headed mallet, gently pound each piece of abalone. The flesh tenderizes quickly, so be careful not to pound too hard and tear the flesh.

Preheat oven to 200 degrees.

Melt 1 stick (4 ounces) butter in a large frying pan over medium high heat. Dip the pieces of abalone in flour mixed with salt and pepper and then in the beaten eggs. Fry these pieces for 15 seconds on each side, browning them slightly. As soon as they are cooked, place the abalone on paper towels on a serving dish in the warm oven.

Deglaze the pan with the Marsala and wine, swirling the mixture around the pan. Raise the heat and when the liquid comes to the boil, cook for 4 more minutes. Add the remaining butter and whisk until melted. Remove the paper towels from the dish and pour the sauce over the abalone. Sprinkle with chopped parsley.

Dungeness Crab with Braised Leeks, Ginger and White Wine

Dungeness crabs are so often cooked and then served on ice—even though the flavor of the sweet meat is nearly obliterated by the cold. In my opinion, the best time to eat them is right after they have been steamed. Remove the apron, take off the top shell, remove the feathery gills, sand bag, and mouth, and they are ready to enjoy.

The juice (soup) and soft buttery substance inside the top shell can be eaten with a spoon or mopped up with bread; then it's time to get into the sweet meat contained in the body where the legs join, and the claw and leg meat. As Dungeness crabs are heavy (1 to 3 pounds) and have a larger percentage of meat content than most other crabs (25 percent), the pieces of meat garnered are substantial and delicious.

The claws and legs are easily cracked with a knife or nutcracker, and a small fork is useful for extracting the meat. You can break the softer shells with your teeth and suck the meat out.

Try Dungeness simply steamed or as in this recipe, where they are first partially cooked by steaming, the top shell, gills, and sandbag removed for the convenience of your guests, then reassembled and tied with string (this can be done beforehand). The crabs are then deep-fried in flavored oil. The colorful shells are served glistening on a bed of braised leeks, flavored with ginger, tarragon, soy sauce, and white wine.

SERVES 4

4 1-pound or 2 2½-pound Dungeness crabs, alive and kicking
16 thin leeks or 8 larger ones
¼ cup olive oil
salt to taste
freshly ground black pepper to taste
1 tablespoon finely chopped fresh tarragon, or 1 teaspoon dried tarragon
1½ cups dry white wine
2 tablespoons soy sauce
6 cups oil (Crisco preferred)
½ cup Szechuan-style hot and spicy oil (available in Oriental grocery stores)
3 tablespoons freshly grated ginger

Trim off the roots from the leeks and cut off most of the green part, reserving this part for the steaming liquid, and rinse thoroughly. To get the leeks thoroughly clean and free of sand, put them, green end down, in a bowl full of cold salted water for 15 minutes.

Preheat the oven to 400 degrees.

Heat the olive oil in a large sauté or frying pan over medium heat. Dry the leeks with paper towels. Sear the leeks in the hot oil (in batches if necessary), turning them to brown on all sides. Place them in an oven dish; sprinkle with salt and pepper and tarragon. Pour away any oil left in the sauté pan and deglaze the pan with the wine. Pour the wine over the leeks and bake them until tender, 20 to 30 minutes, depending on their size. When they are cooked, halve or quarter them if large, strew them on a large ovenproof serving dish, and keep warm in a 200-degree oven. Set the liquid from the leeks aside and add the soy sauce to it.

In the meantime, fill a large pot with 3 quarts water and bring to the boil with the green part of the leeks. Put a rack in the water and when the water has come to the boil put the crabs into the pot and cover. Be careful when handling Dungeness crabs; they have vicious claws and should be handled with heavy garden gloves, snappers, or tongs. Steam the 1-pound crabs for 8 minutes and the 2½-pound crabs for 12 minutes. Remove from the water and rinse with cold water. Remove the apron, then the top shell, the feathery gills, the sand bag, and the mouth. If using the larger crabs, cut them in half. Replace the top shell and tie with string, making a long loop with which to drop the crab (later) into hot oil.

While the leeks are braising in the oven, heat the frying oil with the hot and spicy oil in an electric deep-fryer, large heavy saucepan, or wok to 375 degrees. If you do not own a thermometer, throw in a 1-inch cube of bread and if it browns and crisps in 30 seconds you are ready to deep-fry. Fry the crabs one at a time for 3 minutes each, turning them after a minute and a half. Remember that the oil must return to 375 degrees before frying the next crab. Pat them lightly with paper towels and keep them warm on top of the leeks in the low oven. Remove the string before serving and drizzle the leek sauce over the crab claws and legs, so you can savor it with the crab meat when getting it out of the shells. Have plenty of napkins, little forks, and knives or nutcrackers on hand to enjoy the crabs.

Crab Cakes with Salsa

SERVES 6

> 2 pounds lump or back-fin crab meat, picked over and any cartilage
>   removed
> 6 large eggs, separated
> 3 tablespoons Dijon mustard
> salt to taste
> freshly ground white pepper to taste
> pinch cayenne
> 6 tablespoons Clarified Butter (page 304)
> 1 recipe Salsa or Mint Tartar sauce (page 295 or 288)

Beat the egg yolks, mustard, salt, pepper, and cayenne in a large bowl with a wire whisk until pale yellow and thick. Mix the crab meat into the yolks. In another bowl, using an electric beater or Kitchen Aid mixer, beat the egg whites until stiff. Fold into the crab meat mixture just before cooking.

Shape the crab meat into 18 cakes about 3 inches in diameter. Melt the clarified butter in 2 large frying pans over medium high heat. Fry the crab cakes until nicely browned, about 3 minutes on each side. Drain on paper towels.

Serve 3 crab cakes per person, accompanied with salsa or mint tartar sauce.

Crab and Dill Strudel with Leek Purée

SERVES 6

> 2 pounds lump or back-fin crab meat, picked over and any cartilage
>   removed
> 14 leaves (¾ pound) strudel or phyllo pastry (page 74)
> 1¾ sticks (7 ounces) unsalted butter
> 3 tablespoons all-purpose flour
> ⅓ cup dry white wine
> ½ cup heavy cream
> ½ cup milk

salt to taste
freshly ground white pepper to taste
¼ cup chopped fresh dill weed
juice of 1 lemon
pinch cayenne
1 recipe Leek Purée (page 293)

Defrost the frozen pastry for 4 hours or overnight in the refrigerator. It is preferable not to defrost at room temperature because
the inside sheets tend to stick to each other while the outside
thaws.

Make a white sauce. Melt 6 tablespoons butter in a large frying
or sauté pan over medium heat, add the flour, and beat with a
wire whisk. Pour in the wine, cream, and milk, and continue to
whisk. Lower the heat and keep stirring until the sauce thickens.
Simmer over very low heat for 5 minutes. Add salt and pepper.

Crumble the crab meat into a large bowl; add the white sauce,
dill, lemon juice, and cayenne and stir with a large spoon to blend
well. Set aside.

Melt remaining stick (4 ounces) butter in a saucepan over low
heat. Remove the pastry from the package and unroll the leaves
on a clean surface. Carefully place a sheet of phyllo with the
longer (15-inch) side facing you on another clean surface. Keep
the rest of the pastry leaves covered with a slightly damp cloth.
Lightly brush the pastry all over with melted butter, using a wide
pastry brush. Lay another sheet on top and brush with butter;
repeat until you have 7 buttered layers, one on top of the other.

Place half the crab meat mixture along the short (12-inch) end
of the pastry and roll it up. Put the strudel on a buttered baking
sheet. Repeat this operation with the rest of the crab meat, making 2 strudels. Brush more melted butter on the tops and sides
and refrigerate for 15 minutes.

Preheat the oven to 400 degrees. To facilitate serving, with a
sharp knife cut halfway through the strudel, producing 6 slices
from each strudel. (These slices are quite large; you may want to
cut each strudel into 7 slices to allow for a couple of second
helpings).

Bake until golden brown, 20 to 25 minutes. In the meantime,
gently heat the leek purée in a small saucepan and serve alongside the strudels.

Sautéed Soft-Shell Crabs with Lime Butter

These delicious creatures, available fresh from April through September, delight many. They must be alive when you ask for them; the fish store will prepare them for cooking. Or see page 32 to do it yourself.

Serve four, three, or two per person, according to size and appetites.

SERVES 4

> *8 to 16 soft-shell crabs, cleaned (page 32)*
> *1½ cups all-purpose flour*
> *1 tablespoon sweet paprika*
> *1 teaspoon salt*
> *1 teaspoon freshly ground white pepper*
> *6 tablespoons Clarified Butter (page 304)*
> *1 cup fresh lime juice*
> *⅓ slice lime per crab*

Sift together the flour, paprika, salt, and pepper into a shallow pan.

In 2 large frying pans over medium high heat, melt the clarified butter. Lightly coat the crabs with the flour and shake off the excess. Place them upside down in the butter and sauté for 2 to 3 minutes, depending on their size, then turn to cook through—another 2 to 3 minutes.

Place the crabs on a warmed serving platter. Add lime juice and a pinch of salt to the remaining butter in the pans. Over medium heat swirl the lime and butter mixture around the pan for 30 seconds and pour over the crabs.

Garnish each crab with lime.

Broiled Soft-Shell Crabs in Puff Pastry Shells

Intead of serving broiled soft-shell crabs on toast, which they do in Maryland, I suggest making a more elegant meal by inserting the cooked crabs in puff pastry shells.
SERVES 6

12 soft-shell crabs, cleaned (page 32)
2 pounds Puff Pastry (page 307) or frozen prepared puff pastry
   (Saucier makes a good one)
1 large egg yolk
1½ sticks (6 ounces) unsalted butter
finely grated zest of 1½ lemons
6 tablespoons fresh lemon juice
salt to taste
12 parsley sprigs

Thaw the puff pastry, if using frozen, in the refrigerator for 4 hours.

Preheat the oven to 350 degrees.

Roll out half the pastry ¼ inch thick on a floured surface. Saucier puff pastry is the right thickness and does not need to be rolled out any further. Using a 4-inch fluted oval pastry cutter (if you have only a round cutter, bend it into an oval), cut out 6 ovals of pastry. Roll each oval out to measure 5½ inches long by 4½ inches wide. With a sharp thin knife, cut halfway through the pastry 5/16 inch from the edge. This will create a lid for the pastry case. Beat together the egg yolk and 1 tablespoon cold water and brush the middle of each oval and then around the edge. Avoid getting the beaten egg yolk into the cut or on the outside edge of the pastry, because this will prevent the pastry from rising properly. Make 3 or 4 light crisscross incisions in the center of the pastry with the sharp knife. Place the pastry ovals 1 inch apart on a baking sheet and lightly brush with water.

Make 6 more oval pastry cases just like the first with the remaining pastry. Bake until well risen (about 1 inch) and golden in color, about 15 minutes. Let cool on a wire rack. When cool enough to handle, cut the lid away from the case with a sharp thin knife. Pull out and discard the partially cooked pastry underneath. Reserve the lids.

Lower oven heat to 200 degrees and preheat the broiler.

Melt the butter in a small frying pan. Lightly brush the broiler pan with some butter. Lay the crabs, bottom side up, on the butter and brush with more melted butter. Broil the crabs for 3 minutes; then turn, brush with butter, and broil 3 to 4 minutes more.

At the same time, warm the pastry cases in the 200-degree oven for 2 minutes. Place the cases on a warmed serving platter or individual serving plates. When the crabs are cooked, put one in each case.

Add the lemon zest, lemon juice, and salt to the butter left in the pan and boil hard over high heat for 1 minute. Pour the sauce over the crabs, cover with the lids, place parsley sprigs at side of pastry cases, and serve immediately.

Stone Crab Claws with Assorted Cold Cooked and Raw Shellfish

Because stone crab claws are always sold precooked, it is a good idea to include them in a large assortment of cold cooked and raw shellfish. Lay the table with little forks to pick with, lobster crackers or nutcrackers, napkins, and bowls to put the empty shells in.

I suggest serving some or all of the following. Choose what is available in your fish market. You will have to be the judge of how much to buy; it depends on the number of guests and their appetites.

cooked stone crab claws
steamed lobsters, halved
steamed blue or Dungeness crabs
boiled shrimp—any size, heads on or off
boiled periwinkles
steamed crawfish
raw shucked clams
raw shucked oysters
seaweed (optional)
lemon wedges
lime wedges
1 recipe Mayonnaise (page 286) flavored with lime or lemon juice

Steam the shellfish just a few hours before serving. Refrigerate them when cool but remove them from the refrigerator 15 minutes before serving time so their flavors can develop.

Choose a beautiful large serving platter to put the shellfish on. Drape it with seaweed if available and intersperse with lime and lemon wedges. Spoon the mayonnaise into individual serving bowls.

Lobster Steamed with Beer

This method of cooking lobster was suggested to me by a man who sold lobsters in Stonington, Connecticut.

It is a thrilling experience to select a lobster from a huge tank filled with running seawater. The next decision is who is going to put the live lobster in the pot. Even those with nerves of steel have to brace themselves, but inevitably the desire to eat the cooked lobster prevails over the fear of killing it. If you are very squeamish, use a pot holder, snappers, or tongs to pick up the lobster by its back. Head and claws in first!

Cooking the lobsters in beer cheers them up (I think), improves the flavor, and sweetens the meat. Steamers (soft-shell clams) and shrimp cooked in beer are also delicious.

A 1- to 1¼-pound lobster serves one person. Sometimes I buy a 2½-pound lobster to divide between two people. I prefer the meat of the larger lobsters and do not find the meat tough if properly cooked (that is, not overcooked). However, everyone has his own preference.
SERVES 2

> 2 1¼-pound lobsters or 1 2½-pound lobster
> 3 cans (4½ cups) light (not dark) beer
> 1 stick (4 ounces) unsalted butter
> juice of ½ lemon

Pour the beer into an 18-quart lobster pot with enough water to cover the lobsters—about 8 quarts.

Bring the beer and water to a boil and put the live lobster(s), head(s) and claws in first, into the boiling liquid. Cover with a lid. Cook the smaller lobsters for precisely 10 minutes from the time the liquid returns to the boil. Boil the larger lobster for 15 minutes.

In the meantime, melt the butter and to it add the lemon juice.

When the lobsters are cooked, remove them from the liquid and let drain in the sink for a few minutes. Turn the lobster onto its back and with a sharp heavy knife or chopper cut down the middle from the head to the tail; cut completely in half if sharing the larger lobster. Remove the little brain sac from the head. Crack the claws with nutcrackers, or with a hammer if they are large. Serve the lobster with nutcrackers, lobster forks, spoons for the delicious red coral and tomalley, and bowls of melted butter to dip the lobster morsels in.

Lobster Wrapped in Cabbage Leaves

This is a fanciful idea of mine. Maybe it sounds foolish to wrap rich lobster meat with the humble cabbage, but I think the combination tastes wonderful.

This dish is best made when Savoy or other green cabbage is available.

SERVES 2

> 2 1¼-pound lobsters
> 1 small green cabbage (1½ to 2 pounds)
> ½ cup tomato juice
> 1½ cups chicken stock (homemade preferred)
> 1 tablespoon Pernod or Ricard
> salt to taste
> freshly ground white pepper to taste
> 2 heaping tablespoons crème fraîche or sour cream

Follow the instructions in the next recipe on how to kill the lobsters and extract nearly raw meat. Save the green tomalley and red coral. Cover and refrigerate the pieces of lobster meat.

Trim any spoiled leaves from the outside of the cabbage. Bring a medium saucepan of lightly salted water to a boil. Drop the cabbage, bottom end down, into the boiling water and boil for 3 minutes. Remove 4 outer leaves and return the cabbage to the boiling water for another 3 minutes, after which you will remove 4 more leaves. Repeat until you have 16 leaves. If the leaves are not tender, cook them some more in the boiling water until they are tender and soft. You do not want to overcook the lobster when it is wrapped in the cabbage, so the leaves must be tender before wrapping.

Cut the thick membrane in the center of each leaf and reconstitute the leaf by slightly overlapping the 2 halves.

You should have 16 pieces of raw lobster meat: 8 pieces of tail; 4 claws; and the meat from the knuckle joints, attached to the claw, collected into 4 bundles.

Place some tomalley and coral (if any) and a piece of lobster meat on the top edge of a leaf, fold over the sides onto the meat, and roll up. Fasten with a toothpick and put, open end down, into a saucepan just large enough to house all 16 cabbage rolls in 1 layer. Continue to wrap the rest of the lobster in the cabbage leaves and add to the saucepan.

Pour the tomato juice, chicken stock, Pernod, salt, and pepper on top of the stuffed cabbage rolls and bring to the boil. Simmer for 6 minutes.

Remove the stuffed cabbage leaves, picking out the toothpicks, and keep warm on a serving platter. Reduce the sauce by hard boiling to ¾ cup and pour over the cabbage leaves.

Serve with crème fraîche or sour cream on the side.

Sautéed Lobster with Champagne and Tarragon Sauce

This is a dish for a special occasion.
SERVES 4

> 4 1¼-pound lobsters
> 2 cups dry champagne
> 3 cans (4½ cups) light (not dark) beer
> 4 tablespoons Clarified Butter (page 304)
> ¼ cup chopped fresh tarragon
> salt to taste
> freshly ground white pepper to taste
> 1 cup Beurre Blanc (page 289)

Boil the champagne in a medium saucepan over high heat until reduced to ¾ cup. Reserve.

Thirty minutes before serving, prepare the beurre blanc.

Pour the beer and enough water to cover the lobsters (about 12 quarts) into an 18-quart lobster pot. Bring the beer and water to a boil and add the live lobsters, heads and claws first. When the water returns to the boil, the lobster shells should be red. You don't want to cook the lobsters, just kill them, so that you can remove the raw meat from the shells. Remove the lobsters from the water, drain, and let cool in your kitchen sink. Let the liquid continue to boil.

Turn the lobsters onto their backs and pull off the tails and claws. Return the lobster bodies and legs to the liquid and boil for 10 minutes; serve them cold on another occasion.

With kitchen scissors, cut through the middle of the underside of the tail shell and remove the tail meat intact. Turn the tail meat over and remove the vein after making a shallow incision down the back. Gently break the shells of the claws and knuckles with a nutcracker or hammer and remove the meat intact. Cut each piece of tail meat crosswise into 4 slices.

You can prepare the lobsters before your dinner, but be sure to refrigerate the meat, covered with plastic wrap.

Just before serving, heat the clarified butter in a sauté pan over medium high heat. Add the lobster meat, tarragon, and a sprinkle of salt and pepper. Cook, turning the meat over, until cooked through, about 3 minutes.

Pour the reduced champagne over the lobster meat and swirl it around the pan. Remove the lobster meat to a warmed serving platter and keep warm. Cook the champagne until it is syrupy and barely covers the bottom of the pan. Remove from the heat and stir in the beurre blanc. Pour the sauce over the lobster and serve immediately.

The lobster looks attractive served in the middle of a ring of wild rice with steamed green beans around the outside edge.

Lobster Stew

Using leftover cooked lobster meat, this dish is quickly and easily made. However, if you do not have leftover cooked lobster, simply steam some lobster and pick out the flesh from the shells.

This dish is a meal in itself and needs very little to accompany it.

SERVES 4

*1½ pounds cooked lobster meat (page 259), from 2 1½-pound
    lobsters or 1 3-pound lobster*
2 ears cooked corn (if not in season, use ¾ cup canned or frozen corn)
3 tablespoons unsalted butter
4 shallots or 1 small onion, finely chopped
1 teaspoon sweet paprika
1 cup dry white wine
2 cups light cream
2 large egg yolks, lightly beaten
*1 large tomato, skinned, seeded, and cut into ¼-inch cubes (page
    305)*
1 teaspoon finely chopped chives
1 tablespoon finely chopped basil (do at the last moment)

Cut the cooked lobster meat into 1-inch pieces. Cut the corn kernels off the corncobs, if using fresh.

Melt the butter in a medium saucepan over medium heat and sauté the chopped shallots or onion until translucent. Stir in the paprika and cook, stirring, for 1 minute. Add the wine and simmer until the wine has reduced to ½ cup. Reduce heat to low, add the lobster pieces, and turn to warm through. Still over low heat, add the cream and heat through. Take out ¾ cup hot cream and beat into the egg yolks. Add the rest of the ingredients and, when hot, stir in the cream and egg yolk mixture. As soon as the stew begins to bubble, give a last swirl and serve immediately.

You could serve the stew with hot bread, followed by a green salad.

Poached Sea Scallops with Ginger Béarnaise

Large fat sea scallops are the ones to use for this dish. They have a fine sweet flavor that is rich and luscious.
SERVES 4

> 2 pounds sea scallops
> 1 recipe Poaching Liquid (page 304)
> 2 tablespoons finely grated ginger
> 1 recipe Béarnaise Sauce (page 284) omitting tarragon

Prepare the poaching liquid in a saucepan into which you will later lower a sieve or strainer containing the scallops. Stir the grated ginger into the béarnaise sauce. Set aside uncovered at room temperature.

Cut off the small tough muscle from the side of each scallop. Bring the poaching liquid to the simmering point and into it lower the scallops in the sieve or strainer. Cook for 3 to 4 minutes, depending on the size of the scallops. They must be cooked through, but don't let them toughen. I check by picking one out of the liquid and cutting it in half to see if it is opaque all the way through.

Drain the scallops. Place on a warmed serving platter and pour the ginger béarnaise over.

Broiled Scallops with Fennel Sauce

The fennel sauce can also be served with shrimp, halibut, lobster, and any non-oily white fish.
SERVES 6

> 2½ pounds sea scallops
> 2 pounds fennel bulbs
> 6 tablespoons (¾ stick) unsalted butter
> 1 medium onion, chopped (1 cup)
> ½ cup dry white wine
> 1 cup heavy cream
> 1 tablespoon fresh lemon juice
> salt to taste
> freshly ground white pepper to taste
> 1 teaspoon Pernod or Ricard

Trim and slice the fennel, using some of the top stalks containing most of the flavor. Discard the hard core at the bottom; reserve some of the leafy fronds from the top of the bulbs for garnish.

In a medium saucepan, melt 3 tablespoons butter and sauté the onion until translucent. Add the sliced fennel and swirl around in the butter. Add the wine with ½ cup water and cover. Simmer over low heat for 20 minutes. Uncover, add the cream, and simmer for 15 minutes. Pour into blender, adding the lemon juice, and liquidize until smooth. Add salt and pepper to taste. Then push the sauce through a chinois to obtain a smooth and velvety texture. Stir in the Pernod or Ricard.

Preheat the broiler.

Cut off the small muscle from the side of each scallop.

Melt the rest of the butter and coat the scallops with it. Sprinkle the scallops with a little salt and pepper and lay them in the broiler pan. Broil the scallops, turning once, and warm the sauce at the same time. The scallops will take 2 to 3 minutes on each side to cook, depending on their size. They tend to toughen if overcooked.

Serve with fennel sauce and garnish with fennel fronds.

Scallops en Brochette with Avgolemono Sauce

The scallops are coated with sesame seeds before broiling, which gives a fascinating crunch to the sweet scallops.
SERVES 6

> 2½ pounds sea scallops
> 1 stick (4 ounces) unsalted butter
> 2 tablespoons soy sauce
> 2 tablespoons fresh lime juice
> freshly ground white pepper to taste
> ¾ cup sesame seeds
> 3 limes, very thinly sliced
> 1 recipe Avgolemono Sauce (page 299)

Cut off the small muscle from the side of each scallop and discard.

Melt the butter in a small saucepan and add the soy sauce, lime juice, and some pepper. Pour this mixture into a shallow platter. Coat the scallops all over in the butter-soy mixture and marinate for 10 minutes, turning occasionally.

Cut the lime slices into halves.

Preheat the broiler. Push wooden or metal skewers through the scallops, alternating them with halved lime slices. Put the sesame seeds in a flat dish and roll the skewered scallops in the seeds, coating well. Broil for 2 to 3 minutes on each side; longer cooking will only toughen them.

Serve the broiled scallops with the sauce on the side.

Bay Scallops with Garlic Butter, Garnished with Shrimp

The bay scallop season begins on September 15 on the East Coast and many people look forward to enjoying these sweet and delectable shellfish. Because the "calicos" from Florida are steamed open (and therefore partly cooked before you buy them), they lack the flavor of the northern bays, which I urge you to find for this recipe.

I suggest serving the shrimp and scallops with wild rice.➤
SERVES 4

2 pounds bay scallops
4 ounces small shrimp, shelled and deveined only if necessary
3 cloves garlic
4 tablespoons (½ stick) unsalted butter, softened
1 tablespoon fresh lemon juice
½ teaspoon salt
freshly ground white pepper to taste
1 tablespoon finely chopped fresh parsley

To make the garlic butter, put the garlic cloves in a food processor or blender and process until finely chopped. Add the butter and process. When the mixture is light and airy, add the lemon juice with a pinch of salt and process to mix. Set aside.

Transfer the garlic butter to a frying or sauté pan large enough to later hold the bay scallops in a single layer (use 2 pans if necessary). Over medium high heat melt the butter. When the butter is hot, add the shrimp, turning once. Then add the scallops, sprinkle with salt and pepper, and toss, cooking for just a minute or 2. Cooked too long, scallops will lose their liquid and toughen.

On individual plates or a serving platter, put the scallops in the center of a ring of wild rice, draping the shrimp over the rice. Sprinkle the scallops with a little chopped parsley.

Bay Scallops with Jalapeño Peppers, Garlic, and Parsley

SERVES 4

2 pounds bay scallops
½ fresh, canned, or bottled jalapeño pepper
4 tablespoons (½ stick) unsalted butter
2 cloves garlic, finely minced
pinch salt
freshly ground white pepper to taste
1 tablespoon fresh lime juice
3 tablespoons finely chopped parsley

To avoid the consequences of the fiery hotness of jalapeño peppers, use rubber gloves and a small chopping board reserved solely for hot peppers if you cook with them often; otherwise use a plate and wash immediately. Cut the pepper in half, remove the seeds and pink ribs, and finely chop. You should have 1½ teaspoons chopped pepper.

Heat the butter in a frying or sauté pan (large enough to later hold all the scallops in a single layer, or use 2 pans) over medium high heat. Add the scallops, jalapeño pepper, garlic, salt, and pepper. Turn and toss the scallops until they are just cooked through, 1 to 2 minutes. Add the lime juice and chopped parsley at the last moment and swirl around before serving.

Poached Scallops with Their Roe, with Shallot and Wine Sauce

At the time of this writing, scallops with roe (coral) are not generally available in the United States. The roe is a colorful orange, tastes good, and enhances the look of the dish. They are imported from the Isle of Man, Holland, and New Zealand but are becoming available from Cape Cod, now that the fishermen know there is a growing market for them.

This is a particularly good-looking dish when the scallops are served on a bed of sautéed spinach with, if you like, a spoonful or two of wild rice in the middle. The sauce coats the scallops.

Sea Scallops can be substituted.

SERVES 4

2 pounds scallops with their roe (coral) or sea scallops
½ cup wild rice (optional)
salt to taste
2 tablespoons (¼ stick) unsalted butter (for rice)

SHALLOT AND WINE SAUCE
6 shallots, very finely chopped (½ cup)
2 cups dry white wine
2 cups heavy cream
freshly ground white pepper to taste
1 recipe Poaching Liquid (page 304)

4 tablespoons Clarified Butter (page 304)
2 pounds spinach, stemmed, rinsed twice, and dried (10½ cups
*   lightly packed)*
2 slices lemon, cut into thirds

Rinse rice under cold water, put in a saucepan with 3 cups cold water and 2 teaspoons salt, cover, and simmer until tender and fluffy, about 40 minutes. Don't overcook—it can turn to mush! Drain and stir in butter before serving.

Cut off the small tough muscle from the side of each scallop.

To make the sauce, gently simmer the shallots and white wine together in a small sauté or frying pan on medium high heat until the wine has reduced to ½ cup. Reserve.

At the same time, reduce the cream, by gently simmering in a small heavy saucepan, to 1 cup. Whisk the shallot and wine mixture into the reduced cream and season with salt and white pepper. Keep warm over low heat.

Bring the poaching liquid to a steady simmer. Put the scallops into a sieve or strainer, lower the scallops into the liquid, and poach for 3 to 5 minutes, depending on how large they are. At the same time, heat the clarified butter in a large frying pan over high heat. When the butter is hot, discard it, immediately throw in the spinach leaves, and still over high heat toss the spinach in the pan just until it has wilted.

Portion the spinach onto individual serving plates, and, if desired, place a spoonful of wild rice in the middle. Drain the scallops and arrange them around the wild rice in a circle. Pour the sauce on top of the scallops and put a lemon third in the center of the rice.

Broiled Skewered Shrimp and Scallops with Sweet Red Pepper Glaze

The idea of skewering each shrimp around a scallop came from Chef Wayne Ludvigsen, of Ray's Boathouse in Seattle, Washington.

You will need six wooden or steel skewers, ten inches long.
SERVES 6

> 30 medium to large shrimp (16 to 20 per pound), shell on
> 30 sea scallops (about 2 pounds)

SWEET RED PEPPER GLAZE

> 4 sweet red peppers, stems, seeds, and ribs removed, cut into 2-inch
>   squares
> 5 shallots
> 4 cloves garlic
> 3 tablespoons olive oil
> 2 tablespoons raspberry vinegar
> 2 tablespoons fresh lemon juice
> salt to taste
> freshly ground white pepper to taste

> 6 tablespoons (¾ stick) unsalted butter, melted

Put the red pepper squares, shallots, garlic, and oil in a medium saucepan and cook covered over low heat for 1 hour, stirring occasionally. There is no need to add a liquid because the peppers will make their own.

Process the red pepper mixture in a food processor or blender until very smooth, about 1 minute. Add the vinegar, lemon juice, salt, and pepper; process for another 5 seconds. Set aside.

Shell and devein the shrimp, leaving on the tails. Cut the small muscle from the side of each scallop.

Push a skewer through the tail end of one shrimp, then through a scallop, and then through the head end of the shrimp, so that the shrimp encircles the scallop. Repeat until you have 5 shrimp and scallops on each skewer.

Preheat the broiler. Lay the skewers on a broiler pan and broil for 2 minutes. Turn the skewers and pour the melted butter over the seafood. Broil for 3 more minutes.

At the same time, warm the red pepper glaze in a small saucepan over low heat. Pour the glaze onto warmed individual plates or a warmed serving platter and place the skewers on top.

Serve with wild rice and snow peas.

Sautéed Shrimp with Snow Peas and Scallions, Deglazed with Vodka

SERVES 4

> 28 medium to large shrimp (16 to 20 per pound), shell on
> 4 ounces snow peas
> 2 scallions, trimmed of their roots and some of the green leaves
> 4 tablespoons Clarified Butter (page 304)
> ⅔ cup vodka
> salt to taste
> freshly ground white pepper to taste

Peel and devein the shrimp, leaving on the tails.

Strip the snow peas of the string along the top. Cut the scallions lengthwise in half and slice into 2-inch lengths.

Melt the clarified butter in a large frying or sauté pan over medium heat. Add the shrimp and cook for 2 minutes on each side. Add the snow peas and scallions and toss with the shrimp. Pour in the vodka and swirl around the pan, coating the shrimp and vegetables, for 30 seconds. Transfer the shrimp, snow peas, and scallions to a warmed platter and reduce the vodka by hard boiling until syrupy. Season with salt and pepper and pour over the shrimp.

Poached Shrimp with Sweet Red Pepper Sauce

SERVES 6

> 48 medium to large shrimp (16 to 20 per pound), shell on
> 4 large sweet red peppers (about 1½ pounds), stems, seeds, and ribs
>   removed, cut into 2-inch squares
> 6 shallots, halved
> 4 cloves garlic
> ½ cup olive oil
> 1 cup red wine
> 2 teaspoons whole cloves
> salt to taste
> freshly ground black pepper
> 1 recipe Poaching Liquid (page 304)
> ¼ cup dry white wine
> ¾ cup Beurre Blanc (page 289)

Preheat the oven to 375 degrees.

Put the red pepper squares in a roasting pan with the shallots, garlic, olive oil, red wine, cloves, salt, and pepper. Roast in the oven, stirring occasionally, until the red peppers are tender and a little browned, about 1¼ hours.

Remove the red peppers from the oven, and when cool enough to handle pull any burned pieces off and discard with the cloves. Put all into the bowl of a food processor or blender and purée. Push this mixture through the fine mesh of a food mill. This may be done in advance.

Bring the poaching liquid to a gentle boil for poaching the shrimp.

Put the wine in a frying or sauté pan over medium heat and reduce it to one third its original volume. Add the red pepper purée and stir. Place the shrimp in a sieve and lower into poaching liquid. Cook for 3 minutes.

Finish the sauce by stirring in the beurre blanc. Pour the sauce onto warmed individual plates or a warmed serving platter and place the shrimp on top.

Broiled Shrimp with Green Peppercorn Sauce

This marvelous aromatic sauce goes well with shrimp. It is also excellent with grilled breast of duck.

It is best to use canned green peppercorns preserved in liquid rather than the dried ones for this recipe.

SERVES 4

28 medium to large shrimp (16 to 20 per pound), shell on
2 tablespoons drained green peppercorns
½ cup cognac
¾ cup dry white wine
2 cups heavy cream
salt to taste
6 sprigs fresh thyme
4 tablespoons (½ stick) unsalted butter, melted

Prepare the sauce. Put the peppercorns into a medium heavy saucepan, over medium high heat. Add the cognac and cook for 1 minute. Flame it, and when the flames have died down and the cognac has nearly evaporated, add the wine. Cook until the wine has reduced and you are left with only a little liquid in the saucepan, about 2 tablespoons. Add the cream and simmer over medium heat until thick, about 25 minutes.

Push the sauce through the fine mesh of a food mill, turning the handle forward and backward. Occasionally scrape the green peppercorns off the underside of the fine mesh into the cream. Stir with a wire whisk and taste the sauce. Some green peppercorns are stronger-tasting than others, so it is advisable to taste this sauce often, before you push all the peppercorns through the food mill. The sauce should taste peppery, so that it hits the back of the throat in a delicious way. Also add a little salt if you think the sauce needs it. This sauce may be prepared beforehand.

Shell and devein the shrimp, leaving on the tails.

Pick the thyme leaves from their stalks; 2 tablespoons will be enough. The easiest way to do this is to pull the index finger and thumb nails downward from the top of the sprigs.

Preheat the broiler.

Pour half the melted butter into a broiler pan and place the shrimp side by side in the butter. Warm the sauce in a small saucepan while you cook the shrimp. Broil the shrimp for 2 to 3 minutes. Then turn them over with a spatula, sprinkle a few leaves of thyme on each, and finish broiling. The shrimp will take no longer than a total of 5 minutes to cook. If cooked too long, they will become tough.

Pour the sauce on a heated serving platter with the shrimp arranged decoratively on top.

Barbecue Shrimp—New Orleans Style

SERVES 6

>2 pounds small or medium shrimp (36 to 40 per pound), shell on
>6 tablespoons (¾ stick) unsalted butter
>3 cloves garlic, finely minced
>¾ cup (6-ounce can) tomato paste
>4 tablespoons Dijon mustard
>½ teaspoon dried thyme
>1 teaspoon dried oregano
>1 teaspoon salt
>1 teaspoon freshly ground black pepper
>½ teaspoon cayenne
>2 tablespoons Worcestershire sauce
>2 tablespoons fresh lemon juice
>10 basil leaves, rinsed if necessary and dried, finely shredded at the
>   last moment

I prefer to serve small shrimp in their shells, because of the added flavor. However, if this is not your preference, shell and devein the shrimp. Deveining may not be necessary because the veins are usually negligible in small shrimp.

Melt the butter in a large frying pan over medium heat. (The pan should be large enough to hold all the shrimp and sauce later.) When the butter is hot, add the garlic and cook for barely a minute. Lower the heat and add the tomato paste, the mustard, and 1¼ cups water, stirring with a wire whisk. It takes a little time to mix these particular ingredients together, but persevere! Add all the remaining ingredients except the basil. Cook for 10 minutes over low heat, stirring occasionally.

Preheat the broiler. Add the shrimp to the sauce, raise the heat a little, and cook for only 3 minutes, turning the shrimp in the sauce.

Transfer the shrimp with whatever sauce clings to them to a broiler pan. Broil the shrimp until slightly browned, 1 or 2 minutes. Place the barbecued shrimp on a warm serving platter and sprinkle the finely shredded basil leaves on top.

These shrimp are typically served with steamed white rice.

Squid and Spinach Gratin

This dish could also be made with small skinned fish fillets such as flounder, petrale sole, or smelt.
SERVES 6

> 3 pounds squid, cleaned (page 53)
> 1 medium onion, finely chopped (1 cup)
> 3 cloves garlic, finely minced
> 3 tablespoons olive oil
> 1 pound spinach, stemmed, rinsed twice, and dried (5 cups lightly packed)
> salt to taste
> freshly ground white pepper to taste
> ¼ cup sesame seeds, bread crumbs, or coarse cornmeal

Cut the cleaned squid lengthwise in half. Put the tentacles aside. Lightly score both sides of each squid half with a sharp knife to help prevent them from curling up while they bake.

Preheat the oven to 400 degrees.

Sauté the onion and garlic in the oil in a frying pan over medium heat until translucent.

Lightly oil a round or oval gratin dish, a shallow casserole, or a pie plate 8 to 10 inches in diameter.

Alternate halves of squid with spinach leaves, overlapping them in rows starting around the edge of the dish and ending in smaller circles in the center. If you like the tentacles, place them between the rows of squid and spinach. Sprinkle all with salt and pepper. Pour the cooked onions, garlic, and oil over, and scatter sesame seeds, bread crumbs, or cornmeal on top. Bake in the oven until the squid is opaque, 15 to 20 minutes.

Stuffed Squid

Stuffed squid look a little like white mice, but don't let this put you off!
SERVES 4

> 8 squid at least 4 inches long (heads and tentacles included), cleaned
> (page 53)

STUFFING
> 6 1-inch slices good white bread, crusts removed, and crumbed in a
> food processor (2 cups)
> 2 tablespoons finely chopped fresh parsley
> 4 canned flat-filleted anchovies, chopped
> 2 tablespoons finely grated Parmesan cheese
> 2 tablespoons coarsely grated fennel bulb, plus ¾ cup sliced fennel
> 1 clove garlic, finely chopped
> 2 tablespoons cooked, strained, and chopped spinach
> 1 teaspoon dried oregano
> salt to taste
> freshly ground black pepper to taste
> ¼ cup olive oil, plus some for sprinkling on squid
> grated zest of ½ lemon
>
> dry white wine
> ¼ cup Pernod or Ricard

Finely chop the tentacles and mix with all the ingredients for the stuffing in a medium bowl. Loosely stuff the squid and close the openings with toothpicks.

Preheat the oven to 400 degrees. Pour wine to a depth of ⅛ inch into a shallow baking pan and lay the stuffed squid in the wine. Sprinkle a little oil, salt, and pepper on the squid and bake for 20 minutes.

Remove the squid to a warm serving platter. Mix the Pernod or Ricard with ½ cup water in a small saucepan, add the juices from the baking pan, and cook over high heat until somewhat reduced, about 2 minutes. Add sliced fennel after 1 minute and pour sauce and fennel over the squid. Serve immediately.

Broiled Squid with Chives and Sesame Seeds

For this recipe try to purchase the squid bodies cleaned and without tentacles and heads.
SERVES 4

> 1½ pounds large squid bodies (about 6 inches long), cleaned (page 53)
> ½ cup sesame oil
> ¼ cup fresh lime juice
> ½ teaspoon salt
> freshly ground black pepper to taste
> 2 teaspoons finely chopped fresh chives
> ½ cup sesame seeds

Mix the sesame oil, lime juice, salt, and pepper in a small bowl and then pour into a shallow dish.

Halve the squid bodies lengthwise. Marinate in the oil and lime juice for 30 minutes.

Use 2 wooden or steel skewers 8 to 10 inches long for each 3 squid. With a skewer pierce one side of each squid half lengthwise in 2 or 3 places; use a second skewer to pierce the other side of the squid half in the same way. Repeat this operation with the rest of the squid halves, 3 per pair of skewers. This will keep the squid flat during cooking.

Prepare a charcoal fire or preheat the broiler. The heat must be very hot, as the squid must be seared quickly before they toughen.

Mix the chives and sesame seeds together in a shallow dish and coat the skewered squid on both sides.

Broil for about 1 minute on each side. Heat the marinade in a small saucepan and pour it over the broiled squid.

Ragout of Fish and Shellfish

Nearly any mixture of fish and shellfish cooked with a little oil, wine, and garlic is a very easy dish to make and a treat for your guests. I have suggested an assortment of fish and shellfish below that can easily be changed to suit the availability of fish the day you plan to serve this dish.

Once the fish is prepared for the ragout, the actual cooking time is barely 10 minutes.

Serve with hot bread, prefaced or followed by a salad.
SERVES 8

> 1 pound skinned fillet of monkfish (page 41), cut into 1-inch slices
> 1 pound mussels (cultivated preferred), cleaned (page 42)
> 1½ pounds squid (tentacles and heads included), cleaned (page 53)
> 1 pound medium shrimp (16 to 20 per pound), shelled and deveined
> 1 pound skinned fillet of cod, scrod, or other white fish
> 3 tablespoons fresh parsley
> 3 tablespoons finely chopped scallions
> 4 tablespoons olive oil
> 5 cloves garlic, finely chopped
> 1 cup red wine
> 1 tablespoon fresh thyme, or 1 teaspoon dried thyme
> 4 medium tomatoes, skinned, seeded, and finely chopped

Slice the squid into ⅛-inch rounds. Cut the tentacles away from the heads and pop out the little transparent balls. Also trim the longer tentacles.

Remove any small bones from the scrod or cod fillet and cut into 1½-inch cubes.

Mix the parsley and scallions together in a small bowl.

Heat the oil in a large frying or sauté pan or shallow casserole over medium heat. Add the garlic and the monkfish pieces and cook, turning in the oil, for 4 minutes. (Monkfish will take the longest of the seafood to cook.)

Add the mussels, wine, thyme, and tomatoes. When the mussels have opened, add the squid, the shrimp, and the scrod or cod. Stir all together.

A fair amount of juice will exude from the fish, and if you think the ragout has too much liquid, remove the fish to a heated serving platter or bowl and boil the liquid until somewhat reduced, about 2 minutes. Pour the sauce over the fish and shellfish and sprinkle with the mixture of chopped parsley and scallions.

Sauces

Leek Purée

Mint Dressing

Pesto

Salsa

Sorrel Cream Sauce

Sorrel Purée

Spinach Sauce

Tomato Coulis

Watercress Sauce

Avgolemono Sauce

Sauce Gribiche

Sea Urchin Roe Sauce

A Word About Sauce Making

Sauces that are emulsions of oil and egg yolks, or butter and egg yolks, or butter and a wine reduction, are liable to curdle or separate. (In restaurant kitchens we use the terms "broken," "split," "cracked"—or worse, depending on the circumstances!)

In the cases of Mayonnaise, Aïoli, or Sauce Gribiche, where oil is added to beaten egg yolks, the curdled mixture may be rescued by adding a tablespoon of cold water or an ice cube and stirring briskly to regain the emulsion. Failing that, break another egg yolk into a clean bowl, beat for 1 minute, and add the curdled mixture very slowly, thereby rebuilding the emulsion.

Curdling of this sort is caused by (1) adding the oil in too great a quantity at first, before the emulsion has begun to take place; (2) adding too much oil; or (3) the bowl of a machine such as a food processor becoming too hot.

In the cases of Fish Hollandaise, Blender Hollandaise Sauce, and Mint Béarnaise, where butter is added to hot beaten egg yolks and a wine reduction, the sauce may curdle or break because (1) the egg yolks have been overheated and have scrambled or (2) you have added the butter too quickly. The remedy for the second of these ills is the same as the above instructions for mayonnaise; if the egg yolks have scrambled, however, you will have to start again.

In the case of the Sabayon, where a juice or flavoring is added to hot beaten egg yolks, the sauce may curdle or separate because the egg yolks scramble. In this event, again I think the only remedy is to start over.

Beurre blanc, too, may separate, as it is an emulsion of cold butter added to a hot wine and cream reduction. It is essential that the butter be cold, that it be added in small pieces, over low heat, and that you whisk continually while adding it to obtain the desired velvety smooth sauce. Even so, it may crack before being served if it is kept in too cold or hot a spot; then there is nothing to do but start again.

Béarnaise Sauce

This sauce is made much like a hollandaise, except that the yolks are flavored with a reduction of wine, vinegar, shallots, and tarragon before adding the butter.
1½ CUPS

>   1 cup dry white wine
>   2 tablespoons white wine vinegar
>   ¼ cup finely chopped shallots
>   1 tablespoon chopped fresh tarragon, or 2 teaspoons dried tarragon
>   2 large egg yolks
>   1 cup (2 sticks) unsalted butter, melted
>   pinch salt
>   pinch freshly ground white pepper

Put the white wine, vinegar, shallots, and tarragon in a small saucepan. Reduce over medium heat until nearly dry (that is, until about 2 tablespoons of liquid are left in the pan). Strain this into a small bowl that will fit over a saucepan of simmering water. Add the egg yolks to the wine reduction and beat with a wire whisk until pale and thick. Pour in the melted butter in a steady stream, whisking all the time, until the sauce thickens and coats the back of a wooden spoon. Add the salt and pepper and set aside. (See the notes starting on page 283 if the sauce breaks or curdles.)

Blender Hollandaise Sauce (and Mousseline Sauce)

This delicious sauce, served with flatfish, like sole, flounder, turbot, brill, and John Dory, greatly enhances their flavor. It can be
altered in many ways. Here are some suggestions: mustard, ginger, cayenne, basil, tarragon, dill weed, and, best of all, caviar.

The sauce is also wonderful with steamed broccoli, asparagus,
or new potatoes.

With a blender, preparing the sauce takes minutes. It should
be made just before serving, as the sauce cannot be reheated
without it "breaking." Freshly made hollandaise is thick and can
be served directly on top of a piece of hot fish, without fear of its
breaking. If you do not have a blender, make the hollandaise as
instructed in the Fish Hollandaise recipe on the next page.
1 CUP

2 sticks (8 ounces) unsalted butter
2 large egg yolks
pinch salt
1 tablespoon fresh lemon juice

Find a medium bowl that will fit over a saucepan. Fill the saucepan one third full of water and bring to a simmer. Turn the heat
to low. Melt the butter in a small frying pan or saucepan over
medium heat. Take off the heat.

Put the egg yolks, 1 teaspoon cold water, salt, and lemon juice
into the bowl and place on top of the barely simmering water.
Beat with a hand whisk until pale, thick, and hot.

Fill the blender container with hot water to heat it through,
discard the water, and put the egg yolk mixture in it. Fit the
container back onto its base and blend for 3 seconds. Add the
melted butter in a thin stream, pulsing or turning the machine on
and off a few times, until all the butter is absorbed. Pour immediately into a sauceboat and serve right away.

Note: A mousseline sauce can be made by folding ½ cup
whipped heavy cream into the hollandaise. Serve right away.

Fish Hollandaise

This sauce is good with fish. Although it is made along the same lines as the hollandaise on the previous page, it has a base of reduced fish stock and white wine, which is thickened with egg yolks and butter.

This hollandaise is light and fluffy and should be served as soon as it is ready.

1½ CUPS

⅓ cup reduced Fish Stock (page 305)
2 tablespoons dry white wine
½ teaspoon salt
4 large egg yolks, lightly beaten with a fork
2 sticks (8 ounces) unsalted butter
a few drops fresh lemon juice

Find a medium bowl that will fit over a saucepan. Mix the fish stock, wine, and salt in the bowl. Fill the saucepan one third full of water and bring to a simmer. Turn the heat to low. Melt the butter in a small frying pan or saucepan over medium heat. Take off the heat.

Put the bowl of fish stock, wine, and salt on top of the barely simmering water and, when warm, add the egg yolks, beating with a hand whisk or an electric beater all the while. Be careful not to overheat, for the eggs may scramble. When the mixture has doubled in volume, add the melted butter in a fine stream. Beat until the mixture thickens and coats the back of a wooden spoon. Add the lemon juice. Put immediately in a warm (not hot) pitcher or bowl. See notes on curdling and breaking on pages 283–84.

Serve right away.

Mayonnaise

Homemade mayonnaise, easily made, is a delight to eat compared with most bought mayonnaise.

1 CUP	5 CUPS
2 large egg yolks	5 large egg yolks
1½ teaspoons Dijon mustard	2 tablespoons Dijon mustard
1 scant cup mild olive oil (see Note)	4 cups mild olive oil (see Note)
salt to taste	1½ teaspoons salt
1 tablespoon fresh lemon juice	5 tablespoons fresh lemon juice

Using a hand whisk, electric beater, food processor, blender, or Kitchen Aid mixer, beat the egg yolks and mustard together until the mixture starts to turn a pale yellow. Gradually beat in the oil, pouring in a steady trickle of drops to begin with, until the yolks and oil begin to emulsify. It is then possible to add the oil in a thin stream, but with care. (See notes on curdling on pages 283–84.) When the mayonnaise is thick and all the oil is absorbed, add the salt and lemon juice.

Fold in a tablespoon or 2 of hot (not boiling) water if the mayonnaise needs further thinning. Taste for seasoning, adding more lemon juice and salt if necessary.

Note: Vegetable, sunflower, or peanut oil may be substituted for all or part of the olive oil.

Aïoli

This garlic mayonnaise, here flavored with saffron, is very popular in the south of France. It is a wonderful dip for crudités, a perfect accompaniment to fish dishes, and essential to a fish soup called bourride.

2 CUPS

> 4 cloves garlic, crushed with the flat of a heavy knife
> ½ teaspoon coarse salt
> 3 large egg yolks
> 2 cups olive oil
> juice of ½ lemon
> 1 teaspoon saffron steeped in 2 tablespoons dry white wine for 1 hour
> salt to taste
> freshly ground white pepper to taste

Place the garlic with the coarse salt in a mortar. Pound and work with the pestle to a paste. (If you do not have a mortar and pestle, use a medium bowl and a heavy spoon.) Transfer the garlic paste to a bowl and add the egg yolks. With a wire whisk or electric beater, beat the egg yolks with the garlic until slightly thickened. Gradually beat in the oil in a very thin stream until an emulsion is formed. Then pour in the oil more quickly. If the mixture separates and curdles, start with another yolk in a clean bowl and gradually introduce the curdled mixture until it emulsifies again. When the sauce thickens, stop beating and add the lemon juice with the saffron and wine. Beat again, taste for seasoning, and add salt and pepper if necessary. Cover with plastic wrap and reserve. Refrigerate if it must be held more than 2 hours.

Basil Mayonnaise

This basil-flavored mayonnaise is good with broiled or baked weakfish (sea trout), tilefish, and swordfish.

When counting basil leaves, count two small leaves as one leaf.
1 CUP

25 basil leaves (about 1 cup), rinsed if necessary and dried
1 cup Mayonnaise (page 286)
1 tablespoon fresh lemon juice

Coarsely chop the basil leaves and put in a food processor or blender. Process until finely chopped. Add the mayonnaise and lemon juice and, when all is blended, transfer with a rubber spatula to a serving bowl and refrigerate until needed.

Mint Tartar Sauce

Much as I abhor serving the ubiquitous tartar sauce, I do think this one is suitable with crab cakes. The mint gives it a pleasant sharpness.
2 CUPS

2 small shallots
1 clove garlic
1½ cups Mayonnaise (page 286)
6 tablespoons nonpareil (small) capers

6 small sour gherkins (cornichons)
juice of 1 lemon
1 teaspoon Dijon mustard
pinch cayenne
¼ cup finely chopped fresh parsley
3 tablespoons finely chopped fresh mint

Process the shallots and garlic in a food processor or blender until very finely chopped. Add the mayonnaise, capers, gherkins, lemon juice, mustard, and cayenne and process until finely chopped, about 20 seconds. The capers and gherkins should not be reduced to mush. Transfer the mixture to a bowl and fold in the parsley and mint.

Beurre Blanc

This creamy, silky sauce—essentially an amalgamation of cold butter to a reduction of white wine, shallots, and cream—is a perfect accompaniment to many fish dishes. It can be flavored differently by adding ingredients such as lemon juice, dill, ginger, horseradish, basil, tarragon, orange juice, and raspberry vinegar.

It is advisable to make this sauce just before it is needed as it is impossible to reheat it successfully.

Leftover beurre blanc may be clarified following instructions on page 304.

You may halve or double the recipe according to your needs. One stick (4 ounces) of butter will yield a half cup of sauce. Adjust the other ingredients accordingly.
1½ CUPS

6 shallots, finely chopped (½ cup)
1½ cups dry white wine
½ cup heavy cream
3 sticks (12 ounces) cold unsalted butter, cut into 1-inch cubes
salt to taste
freshly ground white pepper to taste

Place the shallots and wine in a heavy medium saucepan and boil over medium high heat until the wine has all but evaporated.

Add the cream and continue to cook over low heat until all that is left are the shallots and a very small amount of the reduction of wine and cream.

Still over low heat with a wire whisk stir in 4 cubes of butter at a time, adding more as the butter blends into the sauce. When all the butter is blended in, remove the saucepan from the heat and strain through a chinois or strainer into a bowl. Add a small pinch of salt and white pepper. Keep in a warm place until needed. Do not reheat over direct heat—it will "break" (separate). (See notes on curdling and breaking on pages 283–84.)

Basil Butter

This butter can be melted on top of various broiled fish with delicious results and a tantalizing aroma. It is particularly good with broiled swordfish and provides a simple alternative to the pesto sauce used in the recipe on page 294.

When counting basil leaves, count two little leaves as one leaf.
1 CUP

> 30 basil leaves (about 1¼ cups), rinsed if necessary and dried
> 2 sticks (8 ounces) unsalted butter, softened
> ½ teaspoon salt
> 1 tablespoon fresh lemon juice

Coarsely chop the basil leaves and put in a food processor or blender. Process until finely chopped, 30 seconds. Add the softened butter and when all is blended, add the salt and lemon juice. Process for another 20 seconds.

Cut a piece of plastic wrap or aluminum foil 1 foot long. Remove the butter from the bowl of the food processor with a rubber spatula, placing the butter 2 inches from one end of the plastic wrap. Pull the plastic wrap up around the butter to form a log shape about 2½ inches in diameter. Roll the rest of the wrap around the butter and refrigerate for 2 hours.

To use, cut ¼-inch slices of the butter to lay on top of the fish halfway through broiling.

Anchovy Butter

8 1½-ounce portions

   2 ounces canned flat-filleted anchovies
   3 sticks (12 ounces) unsalted butter, cut into pieces and softened
   1 tablespoon fresh lemon juice
   freshly ground black pepper

Drain the anchovy fillets and put in a food processor or blender. Process until finely chopped. Add the softened butter and process until light and airy. Add the lemon juice and black pepper and process for just 5 seconds more.

Turn the butter out onto a sheet of plastic wrap in a long, log shape. Wrap the plastic wrap around the butter and refrigerate until ready to serve.

Asparagus Sauce

Vegetable-based sauces go well with fish. I recommend serving this dish with salmon—either broiled escalopes, poached fillets, or cooked whole fish. To obtain a smooth velvety sauce, you will need a fine strainer or chinois.
2½ cups

   1 pound green asparagus
   4 tablespoons (½ stick) unsalted butter
   1 medium onion, coarsely chopped (1¼ cups)
   ½ cup dry white wine
   salt to taste
   freshly ground white pepper to taste
   1½ cups heavy cream

Break off the tough ends of the asparagus stalks and discard. Remove the pointed leaves up to 1½ inches from the tips and peel or scrape the lower half of the stalks. Cut the stalks into 1-inch lengths.

Melt the butter in a medium saucepan over medium heat and sauté the onion slowly until translucent. Add the asparagus, wine, and ½ cup water. Cover and cook over low heat until the asparagus is tender, about 45 minutes. Uncover and add the salt, pepper, and heavy cream. Cook for 20 minutes longer. Let cool a little.

Liquidize the mixture in batches in a blender until you get a smooth consistency, about 2 minutes. Push this mixture through a fine strainer or chinois with a wooden spoon or small ladle. Reheat when needed.

Celeriac Sauce

This sauce is nice with the broiled salmon escalopes on page 208, or with the poached sea scallops on page 264.
2 CUPS

  1 pound celeriac bulb (celery root)
  1 lemon
  4 tablespoons (½ stick) unsalted butter
  1 medium onion
  1 cup dry white wine
  salt to taste
  freshly ground white pepper to taste
  1 cup heavy cream
  ¼ teaspoon ground mace

Peel the celeriac bulb and cut it into 1-inch chunks. Put the celeriac in a bowl of cold water with the juice of half the lemon.

Melt the butter in a medium saucepan over medium heat and sauté the onion slowly until translucent. Add the drained celeriac, the wine, and the juice of the remaining half lemon. Cover and cook over low heat until the celeriac is tender, about 45 minutes. Uncover and add salt, pepper, cream, and mace. Raise the heat and, when the liquid begins to simmer, cook for 10 minutes longer on low heat. Let cool a little.

Liquidize the mixture in a blender for 1 to 2 minutes, until you achieve a smooth consistency. Push this mixture though a fine strainer or chinois. Reheat when needed.

Leek Purée

2 CUPS

> 4 medium leeks (about 1¾ pounds), trimmed of their roots and some green leaves
> 4 tablespoons (½ stick) unsalted butter
> 1 medium onion, coarsely chopped (1¼ cups)
> 1 cup dry white wine
> 1 tablespoon finely chopped fresh tarragon, or 2 teaspoons dried tarragon
> 1 cup heavy cream
> salt to taste
> freshly ground white pepper to taste

Quarter each leek lengthwise. Rinse thoroughly and chop into ½-inch lengths.

Melt the butter in a medium saucepan over medium high heat and sauté the onion slowly until translucent. Stir in the leeks and continue to cook over medium heat, stirring occasionally, for 5 minutes. Add the wine and tarragon. Cover the saucepan and cook for 15 minutes. Then uncover and cook until the wine has reduced by half. Add the cream and cook for another 10 minutes, adding salt and pepper to taste.

Let cool for 5 minutes.

Liquidize in batches in a blender until it reaches a fairly smooth consistency, about 3 minutes.

To serve, reheat gently.

Mint Dressing

This sauce goes well with broiled red mullet, striped bass, or
pollock.

2 CUPS

> ¾ cup fresh mint leaves, finely chopped
> ¾ cup parsley leaves, finely chopped
> 2 tablespoons white wine vinegar
> 4 cups white Fresh Bread Crumbs (page 308)
> 1 tablespoon nonpareil (small) capers
> 2 teaspoons sugar
> 1 large egg
> 5 canned flat-filleted anchovies, chopped
> 1 tablespoon fresh lemon juice
> ½ cup light olive oil

Put 1 cup water and the vinegar in a medium bowl and add the
bread crumbs. Soak for 5 minutes, then squeeze the bread and
put in a food processor or blender. Add the mint, parsley, capers,
sugar, egg, anchovies, and lemon juice. Process until well
blended.

Through the feed tube and with the motor running add the oil
in a fine stream and process until the mixture has thickened.

Pesto

This is a favorite summer sauce with pasta, but it also tastes fine
with swordfish or weakfish (sea trout).

The sauce is available in little (3½-ounce) jars from Italy, where
the sauce originated, and many specialty shops sell containers of
fresh or frozen pesto, so you may savor this sauce all through the
year. However, there is nothing so satisfying as making your own
pesto.

If you are going to freeze your own, leave out the cheeses and
butter and add them just before serving.

When counting basil leaves, count two small leaves as one leaf.

1¾ CUPS

75 basil leaves (3 cups lightly packed) rinsed if necessary, dried, and
   coarsely chopped
4 cloves garlic
3 tablespoons pine nuts (pignoli)
3 tablespoons finely chopped parsley
¼ teaspoon salt
freshly ground black pepper to taste
½ cup olive oil
4 tablespoons (½ stick) unsalted butter, melted
3 tablespoons finely grated Parmesan cheese
1 tablespoon finely grated Romano cheese (Pecorino)

Put the garlic and the pine nuts in a food processor or blender
and process until finely ground. Add the basil leaves, parsley,
salt, and pepper. Process, scraping down the sides of the bowl
occasionally, until all is finely chopped. With the processor or
blender running, pour in the oil in a fine stream. Remove the
mixture to a bowl and stir in the melted butter and cheeses.

Salsa

Serve this sauce with the crab cakes on page 254, or as a dip for
Crab Critters (page 80), or Conch Fritters (page 81).
2 cups

4 ripe medium large tomatoes, skinned, seeded, and cut into ¼-inch
   cubes (page 305), drained
1½ fresh, canned, or bottled jalapeño peppers, stems and seeds
   removed, finely chopped (1 tablespoon)
1 medium red onion, finely chopped (1 cup)
1 clove garlic, finely minced
2 tablespoons fresh flat-leaf (Italian) parsley or coriander leaves
2 tablespoons olive oil
2 tablespoons fresh lemon juice
4 drops Tabasco
¼ teaspoon salt
⅛ teaspoon freshly ground black pepper

Mix all the ingredients well in a medium bowl and refrigerate,
covered with plastic wrap, for 30 minutes.

Sorrel Cream Sauce

Try this sauce with poached salmon or halibut. It also can accompany Hot Crab Timbales (page 110).

The sauce is made by reducing wine and cream separately, then combining them and adding sorrel and spinach.

3½ CUPS

> ¾ pound sorrel (72 leaves), stemmed, rinsed if necessary, and dried
> ¾ pound spinach, stemmed, rinsed twice, and dried (4 cups lightly packed)
> 3 cups heavy cream
> 1½ cups dry white wine
> salt to taste
> freshly ground white pepper to taste
> 2 teaspoons fresh lemon juice

In a medium frying pan over medium low heat, reduce the cream to 2 cups. Reduce the wine in a small frying pan to ½ cup.

When the cream and wine are reduced, put the cream in a large saucepan and add the wine, whisking well. Add the sorrel and spinach leaves and cook for 3 minutes over medium heat, turning the leaves in the wine-cream mixture until they are wilted. Add the salt, pepper, and lemon juice, stir, and let stand for 5 minutes to cool.

Liquidize in a blender until the sorrel and spinach leaves are finely chopped, about 20 seconds. There should be little specks of green in the sauce. (Actually the sorrel turns a grayish green, but the spinach should retain its green color.)

If serving cold, pour the sauce into a bowl and let cool a little before putting in the refrigerator until serving time.

If serving hot, reheat gently before serving.

Sorrel Purée

1¾ CUPS

> 8 ounces sorrel (about 45 leaves), stemmed, rinsed, and dried
> 4 tablespoons (½ stick) unsalted butter

5 tablespoons finely chopped shallots
1 cup dry white wine
1 tablespoon all-purpose flour
salt to taste
freshly ground white pepper to taste
1 teaspoon fresh lemon juice

Melt the butter in a medium saucepan and sauté the shallots over medium heat for 5 minutes. Add the wine and cook for 10 more minutes. Add the sorrel leaves and cook for 1 minute, turning the leaves over until they wilt.

Mix the flour with ¼ cup cold water; stir this mixture with the salt and pepper into the sorrel. Simmer over low heat for 3 minutes, then stir in the lemon juice.

Liquidize the mixture in a blender until completely smooth, about 30 seconds.

To serve hot, reheat gently.

To serve cold, add the cooled purée to a mixture of ½ cup Mayonnaise (page 286) and ¼ cup heavy cream.

Spinach Sauce

This beautiful green sauce is used in the Panache of Fish and Shellfish, on page 240.
1½ CUPS

1½ pounds spinach, stemmed, rinsed twice, and dried (8 cups lightly
  packed)
¼ teaspoon freshly grated nutmeg
salt to taste
freshly ground white pepper to taste
a squeeze of fresh lemon juice
1 cup heavy cream

Cook, drain, and chop the spinach as directed on page 121 for the spinach roulade. When the spinach is squeezed dry, put it in the bowl of a food processor or blender. Add the nutmeg, salt, pepper, and lemon juice. Process until very finely chopped. Add the cream and process until well blended.

To serve, reheat the sauce gently.

Tomato Coulis

In summer, when tomatoes are fully ripened in hot sunshine and have good flavor, this sauce should be made with fresh tomatoes and fresh herbs. In winter canned tomatoes and dried herbs can be used.

2½ TO 3 CUPS

> 1¾ or 2¼ pounds fresh tomatoes, or 1-pound, 12-ounce or 2-pound,
>   3-ounce can of tomatoes—see specific recipe for amount
> ¼ cup olive oil
> 3 cloves garlic, finely chopped
> 2 medium onions, finely chopped (1½ to 2 cups)
> 1 teaspoon fresh thyme leaves, or pinch dried thyme
> 1 teaspoon chopped fresh oregano leaves, or pinch dried oregano
> 1 tablespoon chopped fresh basil, or pinch dried basil
> salt to taste
> freshly ground black pepper to taste

If using fresh tomatoes, bring a saucepan of water to the boil and immerse the tomatoes for 1 minute. Lift them out of the water and peel. With a small sharp knife cut the flesh from the outside of the tomato from top to bottom in a curve, as if you were cutting off the outer layer of the moon. You will have 4 or 5 curved pieces of flesh and the inside flesh of the tomato. Scrape the seeds from these pieces. Roughly chop with a knife, then process in a food processor or blender until evenly chopped, about 10 seconds.

If using canned tomatoes, put a sieve or strainer over a bowl. Open the tomatoes with your fingers over the sieve, and scrape out the seeds and juice, transferring the flesh to another bowl. Reserve the strained juice. Process the tomatoes, as above, until evenly chopped.

Heat the oil in a medium saucepan over medium high heat and sauté the chopped garlic and onions until translucent and slightly browned.

When the garlic and onion have browned, add the tomatoes with the herbs, salt, and pepper. Turn the heat to low and simmer uncovered for 15 minutes. If using canned tomatoes and the sauce seems to be drying out, add ½ cup reserved juice.

Watercress Sauce

This sauce goes with the salmon terrine on page 105, as well as with poached salmon, halibut, or weakfish (sea trout).
3 CUPS

> 3 large bunches watercress
> 3/4 pound spinach, stemmed, rinsed twice, and dried (4 cups)
> 3 canned flat-filleted anchovies finely chopped (optional)
> 5 tablespoons fresh lemon juice
> 2 cups Mayonnaise (page 286)

Pick the watercress leaves off their stalks.

Bring a large saucepan of water to a boil. Blanch the watercress and spinach for 30 seconds and drain. Put on a chopping board and finely chop. When cool enough to handle squeeze handfuls of the watercress and spinach dry and put in the bowl of a food processor or blender.

Add the anchovies (if using) and the lemon juice to the food processor with the watercress and spinach and process until all is finely chopped. Add the mayonnaise and process until well blended.

If necessary, add some lukewarm water to thin the mayonnaise —it should be just pourable.

Avgolemono Sauce

This recipe is adapted from Claudia Roden's wonderful *Book of Middle Eastern Food*.
2½ CUPS

> 2 cups Fish Stock (page 305, using 3 cups water)
> 1 tablespoon cornstarch
> 3 large egg yolks
> 1/4 cup fresh lemon juice
> 1/2 teaspoon salt

Heat the fish stock in the top of a double boiler or in a heavy saucepan over medium heat until hot. Mix the cornstarch with 2 tablespoons cold water and gradually stir the paste into the stock, whisking vigorously to avoid lumps. Cook gently, whisking fairly often, until the sauce thickens, about 15 to 20 minutes.

Beat the egg yolks in a bowl. Add the lemon juice and salt and whisk well. Add a little of the hot sauce, beat well, and then gradually stir the mixture into the remaining sauce. Cook over low heat, stirring with a wooden spoon, until the sauce has thickened to a smooth, custardlike consistency. Do not let it come to the boil or it will curdle.

Serve hot or cold. It can be poured over the fish or served in a separate bowl.

Sauce Gribiche

3½ CUPS

> 3 large eggs
> 1 large egg yolk
> 1 teaspoon salt
> freshly ground white pepper to taste
> 1 tablespoon Dijon mustard
> 2 cups vegetable oil
> 1 tablespoon chopped fresh tarragon leaves
> 2 tablespoons finely chopped fresh parsley
> ½ cup sour gherkins (cornichons), finely chopped
> ½ cup nonpareil (small) capers (3½-ounce jar)
> 3 tablespoons fresh lemon juice
> 1 tablespoon white wine vinegar

Boil the eggs for 10 minutes, drain, and cover with cold water. When they are cold, shell them. Cut in half and sieve the yolks into a medium bowl. Chop the whites fine.

Add the raw egg yolk, salt, pepper, and mustard to the cooked yolks. Using an electric beater at medium speed or a Kitchen Aid mixer, add the oil in a fine trickle. This mixture may curdle; see pages 283–84 for remedy.

When all the oil has been absorbed, stir in the chopped egg whites, tarragon, parsley, gherkins, capers, lemon juice, and vinegar.

Sea Urchin Roe Sauce

This sauce can be served with the broiled salmon escalopes on page 208 or with the poached sea scallops on page 264.

The sauce is rich and just a little is enough to accompany the fish. Instead of the sea urchin roe, you can use the roe from mullet, Dover sole, or herring.

1½ CUPS

> *4 ounces roe from about 12 sea urchins (page 48)*
> *3 shallots, finely chopped*
> *2 cups dry white wine*
> *1½ cups heavy cream*
> *freshly ground white pepper to taste*
> *1 teaspoon fresh lemon juice*

Cook the shallots and wine in a medium frying or sauté pan over medium low heat until reduced to about ½ cup. Add the cream and cook until the liquid thickens and is reduced to 1¼ cups. Strain the liquid through a fine strainer and discard the shallots. Put the liquid into a blender and add the sea urchin roe. Blend until smooth and transfer to a saucepan. Season with a little pepper and stir in the lemon juice. Gently heat the sauce until almost boiling.

Miscellaneous

Clarified Butter

Poaching Liquid

Fish Stock

Tomato Concassé

Pastry

Puff Pastry

Fresh and Dry Bread Crumbs

Clarified Butter

2 STICKS (8 OUNCES) UNSALTED BUTTER PRODUCES ¾ CUP CLARIFIED
BUTTER
4 STICKS (1 POUND) UNSALTED BUTTER PRODUCES 1½ CUPS CLARI-
FIED BUTTER

Clarified butter is used in many of my recipes. Restaurants usually have a large amount at hand, and I would advise you to do
the same, scaling down the amount for household use. It keeps
well in the refrigerator. It is best to use an unsalted butter with
minimum water content and milk solids. Land o' Lakes unsalted
butter is my favorite.

To clarify butter, take 2 sticks (8 ounces) or 4 sticks (1 pound),
according to your needs, and cut each stick into 5 pieces. Put the
butter in a bowl placed over a saucepan of simmering water.
When the butter has melted, take the bowl off the saucepan and
let cool at room temperature for 10 minutes. Using a large spoon,
spoon off the milk solids from the top. Pour the clear (clarified)
butter into a bowl until you see the water at the bottom, then
carefully spoon off the rest of the clarified butter. Store in the
refrigerator. It will keep well for 1 to 2 weeks. It can be frozen
successfully for a month.

Poaching Liquid

This recipe can be multiplied.
4 CUPS

  1 large carrot, peeled and thinly sliced
  1 large onion, coarsely chopped
  2 leeks, roots and some green leaves removed, halved lengthwise,
    rinsed, and coarsely chopped
  3 stalks celery, root and leaves removed, coarsely chopped
  1 cup dry white wine

Put all the above ingredients in a medium saucepan with 4 cups
water and bring to the boil. Lower the heat a little and boil gently
for 20 minutes.

Fish Stock

Fish stock, for the purposes of this book, is made with available fish bones, heads, and skin added to water. Fish merchants will give you these bones if they fillet their own fish. Flounder, cod, haddock, hake, whiting, halibut, red snapper, rockfish, bass, monkfish, and all other lean fish make good stock. Salmon, mackerel, and herring bones are not suitable for a stock because they contain too much fat. All gills should be removed from the heads for they may impart a bad flavor to the stock. Also do not include any skin that has not been scaled.

The amount of water and fish bones you need depends on how much stock you want. If you have any stock left over, cool it and then freeze it for use at another time.

QUANTITIES
Six cups of water and 2 pounds of fish bones will make 4½ cups strained stock. Divide or multiply this amount to give the amount needed.

METHOD
Rinse the bones and put them in a large saucepan. Add the water and bring slowly to a boil, skimming if you want a very clear stock. When the stock begins to boil, turn down the heat and simmer for 20 minutes. Sniff the stock; if it has a good fish aroma, you've made a tasty stock. Strain the stock through a fine chinois, sieve, or cheesecloth.

Note: If I am in a jam and find that bones are not easy to come by, I buy a small amount of very cheap whiting to make a stock. Twelve ounces of whiting, cut into 1-inch steaks, and 6 cups of water make a good stock.

Tomato Concassé

This is a method of skinning and seeding tomatoes for use in sauces and as garnish. The tomato flesh is either coarsely chopped or cut into ¼-inch cubes.

It is essential to use ripe tomatoes, preferably sun-ripened.

These instructions are for one tomato; multiply as needed.

Bring a medium saucepan of water to a boil. Immerse the tomato in the water for 30 seconds. Remove the tomato and quickly rinse under cold water. Peel off the skin and cut out the core from the stem end. Lay the tomato, stem end down, on a cutting board. As if you were cutting off the outer layer of the moon, start with your knife at the top of the tomato and slice downward, following the curve of the tomato to remove its outer shell. You should end up with 4 to 5 pieces.

Remove all seeds with your fingers from the center of the tomato and the slices. Depending on whether you are asked to coarsely chop the flesh or cut it into ¼-inch cubes, slice the center flesh into ½-inch or ¼-inch slices. Lay all the pieces flat and slice them lengthwise ½ inch or ¼ inch wide. Then cut again crosswise so you end up with little cubes.

Pastry

In hot weather pastry should be made as quickly as possible, so that it won't get sticky. It is wonderfully easy to make in a food processor.

1 BOTTOM SHELL (10-INCH PIE PAN)
  scant 1½ cups unsifted all-purpose flour
  ¼ teaspoon salt
  1 stick (4 ounces) cold unsalted butter, cut into ¼-inch slices
  ¼ cup cold water

1 TOP AND 1 BOTTOM SHELL (10-INCH PIE PAN)
  2 cups unsifted all-purpose flour
  ½ teaspoon salt
  1½ sticks (6 ounces) cold unsalted butter, cut into ¼-inch slices
  ⅓ cup plus 1 tablespoon (3 fluid ounces) cold water

Put the flour and salt into the bowl of a food processor. Process for 2 seconds. Add the butter and process until the flour and butter become crumbly, 5 seconds. With the motor running, gradually add the cold water and process until the dough amalgamates and becomes a rough ball, 10 seconds.

Remove the dough from the container and form into a flat disk 5 to 6 inches in diameter. Wrap with plastic wrap and refrigerate for 1 hour before rolling.

Puff Pastry

Although frozen puff pastry can be bought (there is a very good product made by Saucier in New York), you might like to make your own. It is perfectly simple and not time-consuming (except on hot days, when the dough must rest in the refrigerator between "turns").

The dough—all the flour, salt, and water with only a small portion of the total butter—is made in the food processor. Then the dough rests in the refrigerator while you soften the butter and shape it into a square. The trick is to have both the *détrempe* (the preliminary mixture of flour, salt, butter, and water) and the block of butter at the same consistency and roughly the same temperature before working them together.

1 POUND, 2 OUNCES PASTRY

> *1¾ sticks (7 ounces) unsalted butter*
> *1½ cups unbleached unsifted all-purpose flour*
> *1 teaspoon salt*
> *½ cup cold water*

Let 1¼ sticks (5 ounces) of butter warm to room temperature.

Make the *détrempe.* Put the flour and salt in the bowl of a food processor and process for 2 seconds. Cut the remaining (cold) butter into ¼-inch slices and add to food processor. Process until you can't see the butter anymore, about 5 seconds. With the machine on, pour the water through the feed tube and process until the mixture gathers into a rough ball. Take it out of the food processor disk, and shape it into a smooth ball. Press it into a round disk, cut a cross in the top of it with a sharp knife, wrap it in plastic wrap, and refrigerate for 1 hour.

With wet hands, work the room-temperature butter until soft and then, on a lightly floured surface, roll it with a rolling pin into a 5-inch square.

When the *détrempe* has chilled in the refrigerator for 1 hour, roll it out on a lightly floured surface to a 10-inch square. At this point try to ascertain if the *détrempe* and the 5-inch square of butter are of the same consistency and nearly the same temperature. It does not matter if the *détrempe* is somewhat cooler than the butter but they must be equally pliable. Place the 5-inch square of butter in the middle of the dough at an angle and fold the corners *diagonally* over the butter, pressing them firmly together.

Roll the square into a rectangle, about 12 inches long and 6 inches wide. Fold into thirds and with the edge of the fold facing you, roll the pastry again into a rectangle 12 inches long and 6 inches wide. Fold into thirds and make an impression with your forefinger in the dough to indicate that you have made one turn. With the edge of the fold facing you, repeat this operation up to 4 or 5 turns, depending on the heat of the day. Mark the number of turns with your fingers, cover the dough with plastic wrap, and let the dough rest in the refrigerator. Don't forget to mark the number of times you have turned. It may be necessary to refrigerate the dough for 20 minutes between turns. Make 7 turns in all and refrigerate, wrapped, for 1 hour before using. If carefully wrapped with heavy plastic wrap, it can be kept up to 2 days in the refrigerator or kept frozen for 1 month.

When ready to use, let the pastry warm at room temperature for 20 minutes, or, if it is frozen, defrost in the refrigerator for 4 hours. Use as directed.

Fresh and Dry Bread Crumbs

I find that good Italian white bread is suitable for making fresh bread crumbs. At any rate, use a bread that does not have sugar or honey in it.

To make 2 cups fresh bread crumbs you will need 6 ounces or 6 1-inch slices of white bread with crust. Cut the crusts off the bread and pull the bread into 1-inch pieces. Put the pieces in the bowl of a food processor or blender and process to fine crumbs, 30 seconds to 1 minute.

To make dry bread crumbs, you can either take fresh bread crumbs and bake them for a few minutes in a 350-degree oven, or you can coarsely chop stale bread and process it in a food processor or blender. Sift the dry bread crumbs in a fine strainer to remove the larger crumbs.

Bibliography

The Audubon Society Field Guide to North American Fishes, Whales, and Dolphins. Alfred A. Knopf, New York.

The California Seafood Cookbook, by Isaac Cronin, Jay Harlow, and Paul Johnson. Aris Books, Berkeley and Los Angeles.

North Atlantic Seafood, by Alan Davidson. The Viking Press, New York.

The Frank Davis Seafood Notebook. Pelican Publishing Company, Gretna, Louisiana.

The Encyclopedia of Fish Cookery, by A. J. McClane. Holt, Rinehart and Winston, New York.

McClane's New Standard Fishing Encyclopedia, edited by A. J. McClane. Holt, Rinehart and Winston, New York.

Retail Training Guide for Seafood, New England Fisheries Development Foundation, Inc. Boston, Massachusetts.

Seafood Leader, 1985 Seafood Buyer's Guide. John Pappenheimer, Seattle, Washington.

Fish and Shellfish, by Charlotte Walker. HP Books, Fisher Publishing, Inc., Tucson, Arizona.

Index